Reassessing Gender and Achievement

The debate around 'boys' underachievement' shows no sign of diminishing. Concerns with standards and performance data has ensured the continued focus on gender and educational achievement. But, within the furore, key questions tend to go unasked such as: Why focus on boys at this time? How is achievement being conceived? What are the various explanations for the underperformance of some boys and can these be justified? And, crucially, is the diverse array of strategies suggested to improve boys' performance effective?

Reassessing Gender and Achievement sets out to ask and answer the practical and philosophical questions at the heart of the debates around gender and achievement. The book:

- Reviews the work on gender and educational performance, and outlines the various theories and viewpoints on which this work has been based.
- Critically assesses evidence supporting explanations for gender differences in educational achievement, and the strategies intending to tackle such differences.
- Examines the ideas implicit in current education policy about the kinds of boys and girls that schools should be aiming to develop. The authors analyse the policy drives around gender and achievement, and the ways in which they produce education, teachers and pupils.

Avoiding 'quick-fix' solutions for raising boys' achievement, the authors also highlight the continuing problems experienced by girls in terms of achievement and classroom interaction. Teachers, education professionals and students will welcome the authors' critical expertise on this vital issue in schools today.

Dr Becky Francis is Reader in Education and Deputy Director of the Institute for Policy Studies in Education, London Metropolitan University. **Professor Christine Skelton** is Professor of Education at Roehampton University.

Reassessing Gender and Achievement

Questioning contemporary key debates

Becky Francis and
Christine Skelton

 Routledge
Taylor & Francis Group

LONDON AND NEW YORK

First published 2005
by Routledge
2 Park Square, Milton Park, Abingdon, Oxon OX14 4RN

Simultaneously published in the USA and Canada
by Routledge
270 Madison Avenue, New York, NY 10016

Routledge is an imprint of the Taylor & Francis Group

© 2005 Becky Francis and Christine Skelton

Typeset in Galliard and Gill sans by
Graphicraft Limited, Hong Kong
Printed and bound in Great Britain by
MPG Books Ltd, Bodmin, Cornwall

British Library Cataloguing in Publication Data
A catalogue record for this book is available
from the British Library.

Library of Congress Cataloging in Publication Data
A catalog record for this book has been applied for.

ISBN 0-415-33324-5 (hb)
ISBN 0-415-33325-3 (pb)

Contents

Acknowledgements

We wish to thank all those who have helped and advised us in the production of this book. Sumi Weldon-Hollingworth has provided invaluable support in identifying sources and information, and we greatly appreciate her assistance. Thanks also to colleagues who read and commented on draft chapters – Louise Archer and Vanda Corrigan for their insightful thoughts and responses to our ideas about a reconstruction of gender identities, and Paul Connolly for his constructive and supportive feedback on our interpretation of the statistics.

Various organisations have given us permission to use their data: we thank the DfES, HESA and OECD for allowing us to reproduce their tables. Some of the discussion on the 'feminisation' of schooling in Chapter 5 is drawn from Christine's article in the *International Studies in Sociology of Education* journal, and we thank Triangle publishers for allowing us to reproduce this material. We appreciate the ongoing support for our work by the Routledge team. And finally thanks to our friends and family for their patience and encouragement during the book's production.

Chapter 1

Introduction

Writing on gender and achievement has swamped the British education media in recent years, yet concerns around issues of 'gender gap' appear to be growing rather than receding. And the issue of boys' apparent educational underachievement in comparison to girls is increasingly identified as an international issue. So, given the proliferation of books and articles on this subject in recent years, is there really a need for another one? We can provide a positive answer to that question, on two counts. First, there is a need to draw together the diverse research and arguments concerning the 'gender gap', and to analyse the various different claims, counter-claims and assumptions underlying these debates, in order to provide a thorough, critical, contemporary guide to the debates and work in the area. Second, we believe that the majority of contributions to this field (including some of our own works) have been locked into micro issues. Either they concentrate on the nuances of the arguments (For example, to what extent are boys really 'underachieving'? What effect is the focus on boys having on girls? Why are generalisations being made that are not representative of particular groups of boys and girls?); or they focus on possible pedagogic and institutional approaches which seek to narrow the gender gap in achievement. There is far less attention to the broader philosophical or political questions upon which these debates might be seen to be predicated, but which usually remain unarticulated.

At this point we can hear readers who are teachers asking 'what do these matter when we are constantly told that we need to "do something" about boys' attitudes, behaviour, self-esteem and performance in tests?' The reply to this is that the political and philosophical contexts provide answers that point the way to how we might realistically tackle inequities through schooling. These broader questions include: Is the gender gap actually important? Why is it? If it is, to what extent can/should we do anything about it? Is equity in achievement either desirable or attainable? And if, in light of these discussions, we decide we do need to address some boys' achievement, to what extent do we actually want boys to change their behaviours? We would also point out that the various theories utilised to explain the 'gender gap' have not been taken to their (often radical) logical conclusions, or the implications of such conclusions been explored.

The nature of 'achievement'

'Achievement' is extraordinarily narrowly conceived within the debates around 'gender gap', which position achievement as exclusively reflected by credentials from performance in examinations. Broader views of educational aims and 'achievements', such as increased understanding, social competence, citizenship, extension and diversification of abilities and so on, are marginalised and effectively invalidated by the hegemony of the credentialist terminology and focus. Mahony (1998) relates what she refers to as the 'obsession with academic achievement' to the rise of the 'competition state' (p. 39); the neo-liberal implication of education as ensuring vital human capital in a competitive global economic climate. This book is concerned with the debates around 'gender gap' and the origins of the discourses which produce them; and, as such, engages with this conception of 'achievement'. But we also hope to show that other issues such as the social life of the school, the extent of pupils' engagement with each other and with school culture and so on are important in their own right, as well as in relation to the attainment of education credentials.

Our own position

We shall in this book be examining ideological perspectives and policy preoccupations that underlie different standpoints in the debate on gender and achievement. It is therefore appropriate that we pause for a moment to elucidate our own positions in relation to the subject.

We are both white, feminist academics, middle-class in terms of our current professional positioning, although one of us (Christine) is of working-class origin. One of us (Becky) is a mother of young boys.

Feminists have been extremely sceptical of, and often hostile to, concerns about boys' educational attainment. Some of the reasons are discussed more fully later on in this chapter. Indeed, in Britain, the feminist response to the media and policy furore on 'boys' underachievement' can be characterised as initial hostility followed by scornful silence. When the claims about boys' underperformance first hit the headlines in the mid-1990s, feminist academics engaged closely with the debate, producing key works in the area (such as Epstein *et al.*'s *Failing Boys*, 1998). These works expressed concerns with a lack of accuracy in the analysis of gender and achievement reflected in the debate, and an unjustified skewing of interest and resources away from girls. But as the debate continued unabated, and often apparently impervious to feminist critiques, feminists disengaged from the discussions. Talk of boys' achievement is now often met with disdainful sarcasm in these circles, and feminist writing in the area has dried to a trickle (certainly in the UK at least). Indeed, due to the validity of many feminist concerns about the perpetuation of the 'boys' underachievement' debate, we have both experienced periodic anxiety during the writing of this book as to whether our project is a legitimate one, and the implications of our analyses from a feminist perspective. However, we maintain that feminist engagement with the achievements of both boys and girls remains vital for the following reasons:

1   Boys' underachievement at literacy and languages *is* a valid cause for concern.
2   Unless we engage with the debate, the arena is free to be dominated by conservatives and/or propagators of 'short-term solutions', who *are* engaging with it.
3   The policy concern does at least focus on equity, hence ensuring the legitimacy of attention to different sorts of equity (gender, social class, 'race' etc.). (This is in contrast to current policy drives which seem to be moving away from equity altogether.)

These issues will be elucidated further throughout the book.

So, to summarise, this book attempts to outline both the micro and the macro issues around gender and achievement. Some of the key issues are briefly touched on below, and developed more fully in the following chapters.

So *is* there a 'gender gap' that favours girls?

Basically, yes. Certainly at schooling level, in the vast majority of countries where education is equally open to girls and boys (by this we mean in terms of access, rather than in terms of non-discriminatory practices within institutions). On the other hand, female out-performance of boys is strongly connected to their overwhelmingly higher achievement at language and literacy subjects, which somewhat skews the achievement figures overall. For example, the OECD PISA study (2003) showed that boys were doing slightly better than girls at maths in almost all the participating countries, and that girls and boys were performing to relatively equal standards at science (although where there were gender gaps these favoured boys). However, in all 43 countries involved in the PISA research, girls demonstrated greater proficiency than boys in the combined reading scale, with an average difference of 32 points across countries (this gap was somewhat slimmer in Britain, but still stood at 26 points). In Britain girls do better than boys at GCSE (the exams taken at the end of formal schooling, age 16) in almost every subject (DfES, 2004b). In 2002–3 58.2 per cent of girls gained five or more A–C grades, compared to 47.9 per cent of boys. This picture is replicated or exceeded in most OECD countries: although there are grave concerns among British policy-makers and journalists about 'boys' underachievement', Britain is actually one of the five countries where the OECD PISA study (2003) identifies the gender gap as narrowest.

Hence, the comparative underachievement of boys at school is an international phenomenon. Why then is it so contested? Generally, it has been feminists (such as ourselves) who have resisted the notion of 'boys' underachievement' and challenged the assumptions behind the claims and concerns about boys' underperformance. The challenges have been made on several counts, and for a variety of reasons. Some reflect a concern with *accuracy*. For example, in Britain it is not the case that boys are significantly underachieving in comparison with girls at all subjects. Quite apart from the fact that boys' overall performance has been improving on a yearly basis, boys almost match girls at science and maths: in 2003 52 per cent of 15-year-old boys in England, and 53 per cent of girls, attained GCSE grades A*–C for any science; and 50 per cent of boys attained these grades in maths compared to 52 per cent of girls. (And in both cases, more boys than girls were actually entered as candidates, DfES, 2004b.) The significant difference is at English and modern languages (for instance, in 2003 68 per cent of girls and only 52 per cent of boys in England gained a GCSE A*–C grade at English). So their poor performance at language subjects drags boys' overall achievement figures down. There are also concerns at the way in which data is recorded and analysed (such research will be examined further in Chapter 4).

These concerns about accuracy reflect an anxiety on the part of some researchers that the issue of boys' ('under') achievement is being inflated and over-hyped (Epstein *et al.*, 1998; Lucey, 2001; Skelton and Francis, 2003). Take a look at the following quote from a broadsheet newspaper:

> The male backlash is here, and it has nothing to do with Robert Bly men discovering the wild man within by banging the bongos in American forests. We are talking about boys. They cannot read, write their own names or speak properly. They are physically and socially clumsy. Increasingly they cannot even do the boys' stuff, the maths and the science. As a result, they . . . are outnumbered in the workforce, and left to their own often criminal devices.
>
> (*The Observer* newspaper, 5 January 1998: 12)

This quote is not from an ironic 'tongue in cheek' piece or opinion column, but from the leader comment in a 'serious' broadsheet newspaper, and is not unrepresentative of what Griffin (1998) has referred to as the 'moral panic' among British journalists and policy-makers concerning boys' educational achievement. Hence the main reason for feminist apprehension is that an over-estimate and consequent over-concern with boys' achievement will (a) mask the continuing problems faced by girls in schools, (b) justify a greater focus and expenditure on meeting boys' needs (at the expense of girls), and (c) deflect attention from the larger achievement gaps according to 'race' and social class. Certainly, in Britain and elsewhere a great deal of money is being channelled into research, policy strategies and institutional and teaching practices geared at 'raising boys' achievement'. For example, the British government has invested in 'Playing for success', a country-wide scheme ostensibly aimed at both sexes to encourage after school homework but, given its links to football, was most evidently targeted at boys. In Australia the Minister for Education, Science and Training trumpeted a

$4 million budget for identifying 'lighthouse' schools in boys' education in 2002, also heralding a review of the existing gender equity policy framework which had previously focused on girls.[1] In Canada, pilot projects to engage boys with reading and encouraging their educational aspirations have been set up across the country (TES, 2004). Meanwhile in the USA, $1.2 million is being spent on a 36 month study of single-sex settings to counter boys' apparent disaffection and underachievement; and the single-sex strategy is being actively pursued by the government (TES, 2004). Even some key policy makers in Britain are beginning to acknowledge that such work and the general focus on boys can lead to the marginalisation of problems facing girls.[2]

Moreover, as we discuss fully in Chapter 4, the gender gaps in achievement according to 'race' and (particularly) social class remain more significant in Britain in comparison with gender, and hence the focus on gender in government education policy has led some to suspect that gender is the 'easy option' for government, as tackling the gender gap (unlike the gap according to social class) does not raise social justice issues around the distribution of wealth, and any *re*distribution which might be required to raise the achievement of those underperforming (Regan, 1998; Griffin, 1998). The point that other variables are more significant predictors of achievement than are gender also has implications within the gender and achievement debate, as clearly some groups of boys and girls are doing better than others (we discuss these trends in detail in Chapter 4). Yet this is not recognised in the general debate that positions (all) girls as outperforming (all) boys. To suggest that all girls are now achieving, or all boys underachieving, and proceeding on that basis, clearly risks ignoring (and hence potentially exacerbating) the continuing underachievement of particular groups of girls.

The gender and achievement picture becomes particularly complex at post-16. In Britain girls are increasingly outstripping boys at A level (59.8 per cent of girls gained A–C A level in 2002–3 compared to 51.7 per cent of boys), although particular issues remain (such as the fact that three times as many boys as girls are entered for physics A level). It is at this level in British education that the element of subject-choice is reintroduced (as the National Curriculum for compulsory schooling involves the same core subjects for all pupils). The extent to which young men and women immediately revert to gender-stereotypical subjects is striking, and clearly has an important bearing on their futures, as we discuss further in Chapters 4 and 6. These stark differences in subject choices along gender lines are perpetuated at undergraduate degree-level, although this level of education is also beginning to reflect clearly the general out-performance of young men by young women. In Britain it has been the case for over a decade now that more women than men enter higher education, and more women have been gaining 'good' degree awards than have men for some time.

All this complexity impacts even on the use of terminology when writing on gender and achievement. For example, many of us put inverted commas around 'boys' underachievement' in order to reflect either the authors' scepticism about the notion/extent of boys' underachievement, or (as in our case) to flag up the concept as a generalisation within which many complexities and contradictions are subsumed.

All this being said, it is clear that *generally* boys are doing less well than are girls in terms of exam performance, and that in spite of much effort on the part of policy-makers and many teachers, this gap remains evident (particularly in relation to language and literary subjects). This is not because boys' performance is getting worse (in Britain their exam performance is improving), but rather because girls are continuing to do better. We want to turn now to consider the broader political and philosophical questions raised earlier, beginning with whether the gender gap is important. The very asking of this question introduces a national/international dimension. For example, while boys' underachievement is seen as 'the' important issue in the UK and the USA, in Australia and Canada debates on gender and education often centre more around masculinities, particularly in relation to boys' behaviour and attitudes (Mills, 2001; Martino and Berrill, 2003).

Does the gender gap matter?

The underachievement of boys is not actually a new phenomenon. Michelle Cohen (1998) demonstrates this point by citing John Locke's concern at boys' lack of language skills back in 1693, and how boys have historically been seen to demonstrate 'a habit of healthy idleness' (Board of Education, 1923, cited in Cohen, 1998). As Arnot *et al.* (1999) point out, although it tends to be assumed that in Britain girls were underachieving in comparison with boys until the late 1980s and that they then began gradually to 'overtake' boys, this was not, in fact, the case. More girls than boys actually gained five or more exam passes at age 16 in the 1970s and 1980s. It was simply that, prior to the introduction of the National Curriculum, girls' success tended to be in the 'wrong' subjects (e.g. arts, domestic science, etc.), meaning that their achievements were rarely noticed or valued. (Indeed, even in feminist research at the time the onus tended to be on raising girls' achievement at maths and science, rather than on highlighting their out-performance of boys at English and languages.[3]) Girls' performance at maths and science has certainly improved since then: in the case of science the introduction of the National Curriculum made this subject compulsory for the first time in 1988, so the sudden increase in girls' science qualifications mainly reflects the fact that considerably more girls were forced to pursue it. This illustrates how social policy and expectations can have a strong effect on gender and achievement (girls' former underachievement at science and maths had often been explained away as the result of biological predilections for the sexes to do better at different subjects).

Likewise, in the days of the tripartite system of schooling in Britain (1940s–1960s), the level of '11 plus' exam result required for entry to grammar schools was actually set lower for boys than for girls, to ensure that sufficient boys gained entrance. This was in recognition that girls do better than boys at exams at age 11, and was seen at the time as due to natural developmental differences (boys catch up in secondary school). More recent developments in gender and achievement have thrown a new light on such arguments, as the general trend is for young women to continue out-performing their male counterparts right up to degree level.

So, some boys have always tended to educational underachievement. As Reay (2003) observes wryly when tracing the history of boys' disaffection back to the institution of compulsory state education in the 1870s, 'This "new" phenomenon is very old indeed' (p. 153). Is this underachievement and/or disaffection important?

It would be important if it were shown to be having a negative impact on boys' and men's quality of life. And is it? There are various ways in which to assess this. There is the key point about boys' futures in the adult workplace, earning capacity and so on in relation to their educational qualifications. Related to this are the skills which education can provide. Then there are the more intrinsic issues of self-perception and social skills and knowledge which can also be provided by education. How are boys generally doing in these regards?

It tends to be assumed that boys' underperformance at GCSE exams in Britain in comparison with girls is having a detrimental impact on their employment on leaving school, and on their subsequent life-chances. But actually research shows that young men continue to be better-paid than girls on leaving school (Stafford et al., 1999). Stafford and colleagues found that there is slightly higher unemployment among young men, but this can be explained by the fact that far more young women than men are working part-time. This male advantage continues and grows throughout working trajectories. As Rees (1999) observes, across Europe the majority of powerful jobs continue to be held by men (gender differences in occupation may be more or less pronounced in different European countries, but men continue to dominate top positions in all locations). Male domination of business and of policy and decision-making is reflected in the resistance to family-friendly working practices in many countries (including Britain), illustrating in turn how it is still widely expected that women will bear the main responsibility for childcare. We have already touched on the way in which subject choice at post-16 continues to be highly gender segregated: this of course has a bearing on future employment. Those subjects disproportionately pursued by young men at A and degree level (i.e. sciences) tend to be higher status than 'feminine' subjects (arts and humanities), leading to jobs which are more highly remunerated. Clearly there are complexities here as with gender and achievement: for example, unemployment among young British-Caribbean men remains particularly high, and social class and ethnicity have a profound bearing both on career aspirations and employment practices, and on consequent occupational location (Mirza, 1992; Pang, 1999; Archer and Yamashita, 2003). However, these gendered, classed and 'raced' processes all contribute to the contemporary patterns in gender and employment in which the highest status, most powerful and best paid jobs continue to be overwhelmingly dominated by (white, middle-class) men.

So 'boys' underachievement' does not appear to be impacting significantly on their future positions and/or remuneration in the adult workplace. And while it might have been expected to impact on their self-esteem around their educational abilities and general confidence levels, studies by the AAUW (1992), Barber (1994) and Chaplin (2000) show that boys' confidence about their ability remains generally higher than girls'. This may be because in relational constructions of gender femininity is constructed as modest, self-effacing, hesitant and lacking in confidence in relation to masculinity as brash, assertive, and confident. Boys and girls pursue these different ways of behaving as they seek to construct and delineate their gender identities (Davies, 1989). Research has shown that some schoolboys are aware of the discussion in the media and among teachers about 'boys' underachievement' (Francis, 2000a; Younger and Warrington, 1999), and that some feel resentful or defensive about this (Warrington et al., 2000). There are also suggestions that some boys adopt 'laddish' classroom behaviours in order to maintain their self-worth in the light of their underachievement (Jackson, 2002b). However, there is little evidence to suggest that underachievement is generally denting boys' self confidence. Kelly (1988) and Jones and Jones (1989) describe how boys tend to explain their underachievement as being the fault of external factors such as the inadequacy of their teachers or the format of the exam, rather than blaming themselves. Conversely, even girls who were achieving well saw themselves as inadequate, and blamed any failings on themselves rather than on external factors (see also Walkerdine et al., 2001).

So far, then, it would seem arguable that their tendency to underachieve in comparison with girls is not harming boys, and hence is not an important issue. Indeed, given that girls are still not competing with boys evenly in the post-16 employment market, and tend to lower levels of self confidence than boys, it might be argued that any raising of boys' achievement will only exacerbate these problems for females. Yet, there are clear costs to being a boy, too. And we maintain that the area of the provision of skills (including social skills) is one where 'boys' underachievement' does have strong implications for boys' (and girls') futures.

Our key issue here is that boys have always underperformed significantly in comparison with girls at literacy, English and modern languages. Written English (or relevant first language in other countries) and communication are arguably more valued now in our service-led economy than was previously the case, but actually men continue to do better at ICT and the new technologies of communication than do women (and pursue these subjects/interests in larger numbers). Modern languages continue to be low-status in the UK. So in these regards, perhaps boys' underperformance in these subject areas may not be considered very important. However, boys' lesser skills in communications subjects may place them at real inconvenience and disadvantage in many aspects of life, let alone signifying an early stultification of an aspect of creativity for many boys. We are considering here not just the reading and writing tasks that are involved in almost all jobs, but also communication more generally, in terms of 'emotional literacy' (being able to articulate yourself clearly, and particularly your feelings and emotions). For example, a key thesis of John Gray's (1992) *Men are from Mars, Women are from Venus* is that men cannot communicate their feelings as women can. While we reject his inference that all men (and all women) are the same, and that these differences are natural and inevitable, his vast book sales attest that his basic thesis has rung true to millions of readers. We want to argue simply that boys' underachievement at English and languages is extremely important: it may be seen to have grave implications both for boys' quality of life and for their ability to form effective relationships with others.

Moreover, for us as social constructionist feminists, boys' clear underachievement at these communication subjects is a product of relational gender constructions which produce communication and emotion as 'feminine', and hence as inappropriate subject areas for boys to pursue/enjoy/do well at. These ideas have recently been recognised even at policy level, particularly around boys' (lack of) reading. Hence suggested strategies to counter boys' perceptions of reading as feminine and thus to be avoided include fathers reading to sons (Ofsted, 2003a; 2003b) and the introduction of boy-oriented reading materials in the classroom (Swan, 1998). Such strategies intend to make reading 'safe territory' for boys in the knowledge that it is 'okay' for boys and men to read.[4] We maintain that the construction of relational gender difference which steers girls and boys into different subject areas is highly pejorative, leading to restrictions and stultification in particular areas of learning and expression for both boys and girls.

This also raises the issue of boys' disaffection from schooling, which is increasingly recognised as a result of a construction of masculinity that is in opposition to schooling. Studies have found that the highest status versions of masculinity among boys are 'laddish' constructions which value rebelliousness, risk, 'having a laugh', sporting prowess and heterosexual activity above academic study and achievement, and which position behaviours required by the school for classroom-based learning (such as diligence and obedience) as feminine. The disruptive behaviour of many boys in school has been shown to have negative impacts both for their own learning and for those of their male and female classmates (Francis, 2000a; Warrington *et al.*, 2000; Skelton, 2001a). Reay's discussion of 'Sean's story' (2002) illustrates the psychic costs for boys who want to achieve at school in attempting to do so while remaining 'proper boys' (or even avoiding being ostracised or bullied). As well as this, our previous work has highlighted the general brutalising effects involved in boys' collective productions of, and struggle for, masculinity (Francis, 2000a; Skelton, 2001a; see also Salisbury and Jackson, 1996; Martino, 1999; Mills, 2001; Martino and Pallotta-Chiarolli, 2003). We believe that in order for boys *and* girls to fully develop their potential they must be encouraged to deconstruct the gender boundaries which delineate certain types of behaviour and expression as only appropriate for one gender or the other.

Is equity in achievement possible, or desirable?

Of course, in spite of our conclusion that boys' underachievement at language and literacy is important, it might be argued that nothing can be done about it. Some argue that differences between boys and girls in subject ability (and indeed, the behavioural differences we allude to above), are based on inevitable, natural sex differences – and as such, that little can be done about them. For example, it has been argued that boys' poorer performance at English is due to innate differences: boys are better at spatial skills (orienting them toward subjects such as maths and science), girls at communication (orienting them toward English and languages). Later in this book we investigate differing explanations for gender differences such as boys'/men's apparently under-developed communication skills, including the notion that these are caused by inherent, biological differences. But arguably the fact that British girls are now equalling (largely) boys at maths and science, at least at GCSE level, demon-strates how social factors have played a part. We have already highlighted the role that social policy and assumptions or expectations can play in gender and achievement. Michelle Cohen (1993) shows how, when French was a highly valued, prestigious subject in Britain in the eighteenth century, boys were thought better at French than girls. This changed: as the French language lost its social status so it came to acquire more feminine associations.

In relation to notions of biological difference explaining different perform-ances at different subjects according to gender, it is interesting to reflect that this 'biological difference' thesis is not applied to other variables besides gender. It is (thankfully) rarely suggested that working-class children do not achieve as well as middle-class children because they are more stupid.[5] Similarly, although eugenicists regularly used to suggest that differences in achievement according to 'race' are due to biological differences, these works were roundly discredited, and modern works relating achievement, 'race' and biological difference are met with dismay and scorn.[6] But with regard to gender there is an increasing, rather than receding, movement to link innate sex difference to ability. And yet, this explanation is never extended to its logical conclusion, which is that men are less intellectually able than women. Given that girls seem to be outperforming boys in most countries where there is a level educational playing field, and increasingly at all levels (i.e. right up to degree level), the ultimate conclusion of the biological difference thesis might simply be that females are more intelli-gent. We, however, do not subscribe to such an essentialist thesis. As we have illustrated, causes of differences in achievement according to gender clearly include a social component (the extent to which we will debate in this book).

On the other hand, it seems that the thinking of British policy-makers is moving from concerns with equity to notions of individualism and 'individual potentials'. In this view, we are all different, and come from different educational 'starting points'. Hence, inevitably, we will not all be able to achieve the same educational outcomes. In this view, the role of education becomes one which aims to meet the particular learning needs and (different) potentials of each individual, rather than to expect equality of achievement across social groups. Indeed, this very argument was put by David Hopkins, then Head of the Standards and Effectiveness Unit at the Department for Education and Skills, in a recent speech at a seminar on 'the gender gap'[7] concerning gender and achievement. He argued that he no longer saw the debate in terms of concerns about 'the boys' and 'the girls', but rather advocated a system of 'personalised learning', in which the aim is to 'add value' according to the different starting points and consequent needs of each individual child. This sounds, initially, benevolent, in its nurturing of each individual rather than seeing pupils as faceless homogeneous groups. Yet it also conveniently jettisons the equality agenda altogether. As we discuss further in Chapter 3, this change in policy discourse may be more than a coincidence as it occurs just as a large body of research is demonstrating that the reasons for boys' underachievement are profound and will not be affected by short-term strategies, rendering government targets on raising boys' achievement unpolitic. The focus on the individual at the expense of structural issues also ties in with other neo-liberal individualist policy drives which, as many commentators have pointed out, place responsibility for any 'failure' squarely on the shoulders of individuals, seeing each as disparate, rather than acknowledging the social factors which make achievement far more difficult for some than for others (e.g. Sampson, 1989; Rose, 1999; and in relation to education, Ball, 1999; Walkerdine *et al.*, 2001; Reay and Lucey, 2003).

We would argue then, that although complete equality in achievement may never be possible it is worth maintaining it as an ideal (particularly regarding equity in terms of provision of opportunities and resources); and, with this in mind, monitoring achievement data according to factors such as social class, ethnicity and gender (we are not here advocating school-based league tables!).

The structure of the book

In the proceeding chapters we seek to tease out and evaluate the various explanations, claims and counter-claims around gender and achievement.

Chapter 2 provides an overview of the theoretical and ideological perspectives underlying the debates on gender and achievement, from feminist to anti-feminist; and from evolutionary-biological to social constructionist. We attempt to set out the various different positions and their relation to one another, as well as the ways in which they have been drawn on and influenced the debates. In Chapter 3 we analyse the policy movements in relation to gender and achievement, comparing concerns and strategies in different countries and the explanations for these differences in approach. We examine the way in which girls and boys have been positioned by these policies, particularly focusing on notions of 'self-esteem' and the medicalisation of the debates which position boys as in need of rescue and remedy. Resulting emergent discourses on 'boys' underachievement' are identified and discussed.

The contemporary figures for achievement in various subjects, at various levels, are examined in Chapter 4 (focusing on the national picture). Here we discuss the trends that the figures represent, and consider their implications in the light of international findings on gender and achievement. And having set out the figures on gender and achievement in Chapter 4, in Chapter 5 we turn to the explanations provided for these patterns. Here we see in action the theories discussed in Chapter 2 in terms of the explanations for, and suggested strategies to alter, the 'gender gap'. Focusing on explanations of biological difference, gendered learning styles, 'feminisation' of schooling and assessment practices, and social construction of masculinity, we seek to evaluate the evidence presented in support of these explanations, and the critiques made of them. Our conclusion is that evidence in support of any of the explanations is relatively scant, but that those maintaining that dominant constructions of masculinity are detrimental to learning have built the most convincing body of evidence.

Girls' experiences of schooling, and the continuing problems many girls face concerning both their achievement and other aspects of education, have often been overlooked in the rush to address the needs of boys. So Chapter 6 is devoted exclusively to the experiences of girls and the relationship with gender and achievement, charting the various issues they face around achievement, and their implications. Particularly, it is argued that girls remain problematised and marginalised in educational discourses.

The various themes and emerging questions raised by the book thus far are drawn together and discussed in Chapter 7. We explore the newly emergent discursive problematisation of boys, and examine how boys present themselves in relation to their schooling and achievement. These reflections lead us to a discussion of what the 'ideal pupil' appears to look like as produced by educational policy. We maintain that the archetype is not a girl, but that as 'boyhood' is now problematised too, this infers a proscribed reconstruction of gender identities in relation to gender and achievement. Discussing such trends in popular culture, we maintain that what is required to enable the achievement of boys and girls is not a *re*construction but a *de*construction of gender identities.

Teachers will of course wish to know what contemporary research has said is most effective in meeting the educational needs of both girls and boys, and we review findings in this area in the final chapter. As we have identified language and literacy as those in which boys as a group are underachieving, we attend to pedagogic practices in this area. But as our analysis suggests that a deconstruction of gender identity will remove gendered impediments to achievement, we particularly focus on approaches which can help to challenge oppositional gendered cultures in schools and support greater flexibility in productions of gender identity.

While analysing these various theoretical explanations, statistics and discursive constructions around gender and achievement we hope to provide elucidation and evaluation of the key issues at stake; to chart how the changing representations of gender and achievement are tied to wider socio-economic developments; and always to keep in mind how other factors aside from gender – notably ethnicity and social class – continue to have a major bearing in this area.

Chapter 2

Perspectives on gender and achievement

Whether articulating concerns that girls are being marginalised, or expressing anxiety about the extent to which boys underachieve at languages, the various concerns and debates around gender and achievement reflect identifiable theoretical perspectives and discourses. This chapter sets out the different theories which are drawn on in discussion of, and often to explain, 'the gender gap'. We seek to tease out the different ideological and/or theoretical approaches that have been drawn from wider understandings about gender, behaviour, and ability, and applied to debates concerning gender and achievement. While the claims and justifications forwarded from different ideological/theoretical view points are examined and evaluated in other sections of the book, this chapter seeks rather to explore the relationships between the ideas that are reflected in discussions of gender and achievement, whether in academic writing, policy documents, teaching aids or newspaper articles.

The chapter is organised into discussion of each of these theoretical perspectives in turn, as follows:

- Functionalism
- Sex role theory
- Evolutionary psychology
- 'Brain difference'
- Psychoanalytic theory
- Social constructionism
- Post-structuralism
- Human capital theory
- Neo-liberal individualism.

Separation of theories from ideological positions is impossible. Theoretical perspectives are often adopted due to the 'fit' with an individual's ideological stance, and in this way particular theories sometimes come to be associated with particular ideological views. Conversely, on occasion a particular theory may be drawn on by opposing groups in order to pursue different arguments. We hope to elucidate some of these trajectories. So we begin by examining the role of political ideology in these debates, and then progress to a discussion of the various theoretical tools with which the debates are built. We see discourses[1] as constituting the *materials* for this construction, and so in the next chapter we analyse the various discourses which underlie and produce the concerns and arguments about gender and achievement. Finally, the last section of this chapter examines the impact of these theoretical perspectives on changing notions of teaching and learning.

Ideological perspectives: the durability of the nature versus nurture debate

Thanks to the contribution of second-wave feminist theory (and later post-modernist viewpoints) it is now commonly accepted that the researcher or writer can never be entirely free from their 'standpoint': their view of the world is inevitably affected by their social position and consequent experiences, ideology and so on. As such, research cannot be entirely objective: the researcher's particular concerns will impact on their selection of area for study; the types of questions that the research asks; the methods adopted to answer these questions; the aspects of data used in writing up the research; the direction of findings and conclusions, and the choice of methods and locations of dissemination. Of course, given such acknowledgements, debate continues about how far researchers can or ought to take measures to minimise 'bias' and subjectivity in their studies. But, generally, the recognition that the researcher cannot be removed from the research, and use of reflexive practices to recognise and explore such issues in one's research, are in the ascendancy (David, 2003).

As we have already seen, gender and achievement is an issue that arouses strong passions. Commentators hold differing views about the nature of the issues at stake, the extent to which 'boys' underachievement' is a concern, and what should be done to address any problems. The perspective analysts take, and the remedies they envisage, largely depend on their standpoint concerning 'the nature of gender'. By this we mean, their beliefs as to whether sex difference is inherent and 'natural', or socially constructed (or a mixture of the two). These two different views have been popularly referred to as 'the nature/nurture debate'. This debate is extremely long-running, and always hotly debated (Oakley, 1972; Halpern, 1992). Within the academy, the debate has been based on research findings which are seen to 'demonstrate' either that gender is socially constructed, or that gender differences are inherent. In this sense some might claim that such academic research and discussion is not ideological but driven by 'pure' scientific interest. However, it is certainly more than a coincidence that academic proponents of either side of the 'nature/nurture' argument tend to hold political beliefs which correspond with their support of either the 'nature' or the 'nurture' thesis. So, for example, many social constructionists and other proponents of the view that gender is socially produced are liberal, left-wing thinkers, and/or feminists. Whereas the proponents of 'brain sex' differences and socio-biologists writing in the field of education and arguing that the sexes are innately different tend to be conservative, and many believe that feminism has 'gone too far' in relation to education. Outside the academy such ideological approaches to the argument are often even less subtle.

Not that we are arguing for de-politicisation of the debate! Rather, what we are observing here is the link between politics and paradigm, which some still try to mask. For example, Hoff Sommers (2000) maintains that girl-centred equity programmes in US schooling are the consequence of poor quality, politically-biased research by liberal (and feminist) academics; whereas research demonstrating innate sex differences (the position she supports) are 'rigorous' and a-political studies – omitting to discuss the debate to the contrary. (In our opinion she then proceeds to over-extend some of the findings from this latter body of research, and routinely uses anecdotal evidence from the US and UK to support her own thesis.)

Although arguably a social constructionist position on gender has held sway in the social sciences in recent decades, the 'common-sense' view that gender differences are 'natural' and inevitable has always remained strong in society at large. Recently there has been a re-emergence of gender essentialist viewpoints in the academy thanks to the rise of 'brain difference' research, proponents of which have produced key popularist texts that appeal to 'common-sense' understandings of gender difference. We will examine the work in this area in relation to gender and achievement in detail in Chapter 5. For the moment it is sufficient to reiterate the point that people view the issues around gender and achievement differently, and formulate and articulate these viewpoints differently, depending on their views on 'the nature of gender'. Some commentators may approach this area directly because of their political interests – for example, feminists, and anti-feminists/conservative traditionalists. The interest of other parties may be driven by other concerns – those of teachers as professional practitioners, for example, or as concerned parents, or policy-makers. But all these individuals too tend to hold pre-conceived positions on 'the nature of gender', and 'read' the debate on achievement accordingly. So we pause here for a moment to explore feminist and anti-feminist positions.

Feminist (and 'pro-feminist'[2]) perspectives

There are many different versions of feminism. Feminist research in education has represented liberal feminism; radical feminism; black feminism; Marxist or socialist feminism; and poststructuralist feminism, to name a few. These various facets are united in the shared view that currently masculinity is privileged over femininity, and a focus on ending gender discrimination and inequalities. But within and beyond this, different perspectives result in different concerns regarding gender and education. For example, Marxist feminists might be concerned with the way in which schooling apparently reproduces gender roles that support capitalist systems. Liberal feminists, on the other hand, might be concerned with girls' equitable access to the self-same systems that Marxist feminists deplore. Facets of post-structuralist feminism deconstruct the very category 'girl' on which such debates are founded (see Poststructuralist discourse analytical perspectives, page 30, this chapter, for explanation of poststructuralism).

Feminist educationalists have traditionally been concerned with the position of girls and women in education, so their interest in achievement has focused on the position of girls and women in relation to this. Earlier manifestations of feminism during the nineteenth century campaigned for girls' rights to compulsory and higher education, and to be allowed to pursue the same subjects as boys and men. In the latter part of the twentieth century 'second-wave' feminists focused on girls' apparently negative and 'second class' experiences of schooling, and the ways in which they were systematically marginalised by the education system. In relation to achievement, feminists identified girls' underperformance at high-status, traditionally masculine subjects such as maths and science. Feminist responses to this identification reflected and illustrated different feminist positions. Liberal feminists were concerned to facilitate access and to enable girls to demonstrate their potential (i.e. achieve) in these prestigious subject areas. Hence in Britain interventions such as the Girls Into Science and Technology (GIST) and Women Into Science and Engineering (WISE) projects were set up by feminist educators to encourage girls into these subject areas. In contrast to this liberal 'equal opportunities' model, other feminists adopted more radical approaches in challenging the gendered assumptions underlying the teaching and curriculum of masculinised subject areas, or engaging the (often valid) reasons why girls may not want to pursue such subjects (e.g. Walkerdine, 1988; Walkerdine and Girls and Mathematics Unit, 1989; Henwood, 1996).

As we saw in Chapter 1, in relation to current debates around 'boys' underachievement', many feminists have been concerned that populist writings are misrepresenting gender and achievement patterns, and that the resulting focus on boys is hiding and sidelining (a) the continued problems of girls; and (b) the larger achievement gaps depending on social class and ethnicity.

Liberal feminists concerned with gender equity point out how boys continue to numerically dominate the most prestigious academic subjects, to (partly as a consequence) be more highly paid than girls on entering the adult workforce, and how men overwhelmingly continue to hold the most powerful positions in society. Radical feminists and those concerned with social class tend to focus more on the ways in which the attention to boys is concealing (and even reflecting) misogynist agendas in education, and social inequalities produced by inequities in the distribution of wealth and power. But increasingly such feminist stances cannot be easily separated, with individual feminists expressing concerns about all of these aspects. For example, some of the contributors to Epstein et al.'s collection Failing Boys? (1998) critique the continuing masculine bias in education policy discourses and in school organisation and curriculum, and catalogue the ways in which girls and women (as well as various groups of males) continue to be disadvantaged in spite of their apparent achievement.

Anti-feminist perspectives

The idea that we are witnessing a contemporary 'crisis of masculinity' emerged during the 1990s, and has become the accepted position of many commentators and journalists. As MacInnes (1998), Whitehead (2002) and many others have debated, rapid social change in the latter part of the twentieth century (continuing into the twenty-first) has had consequences for, and impacted on, the dominant versions of masculinity; just as it has for dominant versions of femininity. Hence constructions or productions of gender are to some extent evidently in flux and developing, as society changes. However, a dominant thesis has developed in which men are seen as particularly challenged by these social changes; positioning the changes as impacting negatively *on*, or provoking a negative reaction *in*, men. Hence men are said to be experiencing a 'crisis' in their masculinity. We are told by some that as the number of women engaging in paid work and careers increases, so men feel redundant as their role of 'breadwinner' is negated (White, 1989; Christian, 1994). This perspective is applied to many 'progressive' developments in gender equity, such as women's increased autonomy in sexual matters, and so on. As gender equity is progressed, men, and their masculine roles, are threatened.

This view positions men as in need of help in order to develop their emotional health and wellbeing; a medicalised perspective that we discuss further in Chapter 3. Increasingly women commentators have taken up the banner, with writers such as Fay Weldon and Susan Faludi maintaining respectively that in the new gender era men have been subjected to 'hatespeak' and 'Stiffed'. These views of men as threatened and damaged drive the 'men's movement' (sometimes called the mythopoetic movement), which sees men as having been emasculated and alienated by social changes precipitated by the women's movement. Hence the men's movement ('men's rights') advocates male bonding through which men can be healed by sharing their pain/anger and having their masculine values reaffirmed. Writers such as Bly (1990) prescribe archetypical rituals and myths that men may pursue in order to re-discover themselves.

Such movements have propagated the view that the women's movement has 'gone too far', and that it is now men rather than women who are under threat or in need of attention. One of the main characteristics of the 'men's rights' perspective is that it positions men as a homogenous group. Hence in 'men's rights' commentaries on education cognisance is not given to differences between boys/men because of social class, ethnicity, culture, sexuality, religion or age (Skelton, 2001b). Rather, boys are seen as sharing common experiences of schooling. In relation to education and achievement, these views manifest in arguments that education is alienating boys because of its 'feminisation' – there is an essential nature to men/boys and, because of the predominance of female teachers, schools are therefore, 'feminised' institutions which restrict or repress 'maleness'. This feminisation manifests, according to 'men's rights' proponents, in curriculum and (particularly) assessment models that favour girls, or in a focus on girls' needs at boys' expense.

Thus, the 'men's rights' perspective argues for a recognition of the way masculinity is curbed and advocates activities where 'boyness' can be exercised through, for instance, competitive sports, the inspiration of male role models, or by giving individual boys status for undertaking roles such as showing visitors round the school or pupil-leader responsibility. Furthermore, proponents of the 'men's rights' perspective argue that more evident school routines and practices are conducive to boys' styles of learning and support traditional forms of school organisation and the implementation of stricter discipline measures (Moir and Moir, 1999).

Theories used to explain gendered patterns in achievement

So, if we understand the ideological perspectives and interests underlying approaches to the gender and achievement debates, what theories are mobilised by individuals to frame their arguments and to analyse the issues at stake? We have noted eight key theories that are drawn on. Within these, various philosophical questions are played out – for example, the human self and its behaviour as biologically inherent or socially constructed, 'born or made'; and individual paths as determined or chosen. We try to show how these various perspectives produce and interpret 'gender and achievement' through their various different lenses. In each case we explain the basic premises of the theories concerned as well as critiques of each perspective, and outline the way in which each theory positions or relates to the gender and achievement debates.

Functionalism (meritocracy)

It seems logical to begin with functionalist perspectives, as these represent some of the first sociological accounts of education, but are still evident today in many of the forums discussing gender and achievement. The core of this perspective is that social institutions function, or ought to function, in ways that most benefit society as a whole. Social institutions, then, further the functioning of society. Examining the family, Talcott Parsons (1956) argued that the different roles of men and women (men as 'breadwinners'; women as homemakers) worked, and were perpetuated because they were the most effective way to ensure social and economic functioning of society. Education, another key social institution, is seen from a functionalist position as serving a myriad of purposes, including: teaching pupils about social norms and expectations; educating them for future roles both in the workforce and in the family; developing specific talents which will both benefit individual pupils and further their potential to contribute to society; and instilling behavioural patterns beneficial for society (such as discipline, time-keeping and so on). Talcott Parsons and his proponents believed that there is a limited pool of talent in existence. They maintained that the education system functions in a meritocratic way – the most able and hardest working pupils are facilitated and developed to reach their full potential, and are correspondingly rewarded with qualifications, enabling them to go on and take up appropriately skilled/powerful/responsible posts in the adult workplace.

This position was roundly critiqued in the 1960s and 1970s by Marxist and neo-Marxist sociologists who showed how, rather than producing meritocratic outcomes, the school functioned to systematically perpetuate social inequalities (and stymied the individual talents and potential of working-class pupils). This critique of a 'hidden curriculum' in reproducing inequalities was later drawn on by feminists in the 1970s and 1980s to illuminate the role played by the school in the reproduction of gender inequality. Women's lack of power in society and primary roles as housewives and carers were attributed to a process of socialisation reinforced by schools whereby girls and their experiences are systematically belittled and devalued in subtle ways through the school curriculum, ethos, and attitudes of teachers. In this way, Marxists and feminists challenged functionalist positions, arguing either that (a) education is *dys*functional in that it is not meritocratic, but rather reproduces inequalities hence wasting the potential talent of, for example, girls, and working-class boys. Or (b) that education functions for the benefit of privileged groups (the ruling class and/or men) to perpetuate inequalities and aid the smooth functioning of capitalist/patriarchal society. Following the influential contribution of Paul Willis (1977), many researchers have since shown how processes of interaction between pupils and school institution are more contradictory than the straightforward relations suggested both by functionalist and early 'hidden-curriculum' perspectives, and how inequalities are perpetuated in subtle, often unintentional and multiple ways, but also accommodated and resisted by pupils and teachers.

In relation to achievement, the functionalist perspective was used particularly in the latter part of the twentieth century to justify selective assessment models. These models are retained in some parts of the UK, and in these areas functionalist arguments are still deployed by some to support them (hence selectivity is seen as facilitating identification of the most able, and educating children of different abilities in ways that best meet their differing needs). Indeed, we may see an upsurge in such arguments to support current policy drives towards more 'specialisms' in English state schools. However, in recent years functionalist perspectives have been more commonly applied to issues around 'boys' under-achievement', maintaining that boys' apparent educational underperformance is resulting in their social disaffection and consequent dysfunctional behaviours (such as non-participation in further education, crime, drug-abuse, vandalism, unemployment, suicide). For example, Bennett (1996) argues that schoolboys who 'scorn homework, shun qualifications' are the root of 'increases in male crime and truanting' (p. 17).

Sex-role theory

Sex-role theories are an extension of role theories which say that children learn ways of relating to the world around them through observing how people act, and by being rewarded when they themselves demonstrate appropriate behaviour, or punished when they display inappropriate behaviour (Gregory, 1969). So in terms of children developing appropriate gender roles such theories suggest that young girls learn how to be a girl by receiving approval for feminine traits such as caring, gentleness and helpfulness, whilst young boys learn that they are expected to be boisterous, rough and energetic (Oakley, 1972; Byrne, 1978; Seidler, 1989). These messages are delivered to children through their interactions with their families, local communities, nursery workers and primary teachers, and the images transmitted through media (in relation to schooling, these sex-role perspectives underpinned much of the work on 'hidden curriculum' alluded to in the previous section).

Within this, there have been two key views on how children acquired their knowledge of gender. On the one hand there were the social-learning theorists who argued that gender identity was learnt by children modelling their behaviour on same-sex members of their family, peer group, local community as well as the gender stereotypes they saw in books and on the television (Sharpe, 1976). These studies also maintained that a self-fulfilling prophesy was in operation whereby girls' confidence was undermined by their schooling experience. Because their expectations were consequently lowered, girls did not prioritise exam success, seeing their futures primarily as wives and mothers, and hence perpetuating gender roles. An alternative stance was put forward by cognitive-development theorists who suggested that a child's understanding of its *gender identity* as opposed to its *biological sex* depended upon their stage of cognitive development; that is, their intellectual age. One such theorist was Lawrence Kohlberg (1966) who accounted for young children's avoidance of opposite sex behaviours, not in terms of punishment received for not conforming to gender stereotype, but by drawing on Piaget's theory of object constancy. Here the argument was that children at the concrete operational stage believed that a piece of plasticine changed weight when it changed shape – in the same way they would also believe that if a child dressed or played in a sex-inappropriate way its sex also changed (Emmerich *et al.*, 1977). It is such psychological theorising on gender constructions which has been used to support the idea that sexism is at its peak in children aged 5–6 years (Sayers, 1984).

As well as being developed by cognitive psychologists, sex-role theories were often drawn on by second-wave feminist sociologists and educationalists, because they show the ways in which gender differences are socially developed (rather than being due to innate biological differences). Feminist proponents of these views argued that in order to prevent children from developing along gender stereotyped lines, educationalists could encourage them to become involved in activities usually pursued by the opposite sex. For example, the booklet *Do you provide Equal Educational Opportunities?* (EOC, 1984) urges primary schools to ensure male and female dolls are available to boys and girls, and to encourage girls to engage with construction toys and the like. On the other hand, key criticisms of sex-role theories have been that they are unable to account for change and resistance, as they view roles as fixed and continually reproduced by the 'agents of socialisation'. Whereas more recently social constructionist and poststructuralist feminists have pointed out how people are not simply passive recipients of socialisation but instead actively construct and impact upon the world, thus shaping their own lives and those of others. The general increase in girls' and women's educational participation and success is one example of the kind of social change which is difficult to explain from a sex-role perspective. Many girls are now achieving relative educational success in spite of the continued[3] male domination of the co-educational classroom which sex-role theorists in the 1980s had previously postulated as explaining girls' apparent underachievement.

In this sense, then, it is no surprise that although sex-role theories comprised the dominant explanation for the apparent underachievement of girls in the 1970s and 1980s, they have not been drawn on so frequently to account for the (changed) contemporary patterns of gender and achievement. On the other hand, they are evident in some of the discussions of a 'crisis of masculinity', which position this as being one in which men and boys are no longer certain about what their masculine 'role' is (evoking a relatively unitary notion of masculinity which all men share). In this sense, it would be seen as 'natural' that boys and girls adopt different behaviours in schools as appropriate to their different sex roles (a very different view from that espoused by feminist sex-role theorists in the latter part of the twentieth century).

Evolutionary psychology perspectives

Evolutionary psychologists see gender differences in behaviour as reflecting innate sex differences which were configured during pre-historical times. Hence we are pre-destined to gendered expressions of behaviour, which are fixed and inevitable. There is sometimes a conflation between socio-biological, evolutionary psychology perspectives and 'brain difference' theory (which sees gendered behaviours as expressing innate differences in the brain according to a person's sex), particularly where scholars from either school subscribe to more than one explanation for gender differences – hormones, genes, the brain, and/or pre-historic attributes. But socio-biological and evolutionary psychology approaches tend to be broader in scope and argument than those around 'brain difference'. So we deal with these ideas here, while looking at theories of brain difference in the next section.

Evolutionary psychologists maintain that men's and women's 'natures' are essentially different. Building on Darwin's theory of natural selection and aspects of cognitive psychology, evolutionary psychologists maintain that human (sexed) capacities and behaviours were developed millions of years ago to best ensure the survival and propagation of the human race, and that contemporary gendered behavioural trends can be explained in these terms. Rose and Rose (2001) distinguish between socio-biological accounts and those of evolutionary psychologists by pointing out how socio-biology represents an older and less directly political movement; whereas evolutionary psychology largely represents cognitive and behavioural psychologists rather than biologists, and is more overtly political, with many protagonists maintaining that their arguments should inform the creation of social policy. These theories have been applied particularly commonly to aspects of sexuality, to argue that men and women have evolved different reproductive strategies. For example, Richard Dawkins (1976) and David Buss (1994) claim that men are more interested in casual sex due to the need to best ensure their genes are reproduced by spreading their 'seed' as widely as possible. Whereas women are more concerned about commitment due to the need to have a helpmate (other writers such as Tim Birkhead (2001) have argued that women too may be promiscuous as part of their 'mating strategy', though in different ways from men). Such arguments have been applied to provide 'evolutionary' explanations from everything from the phenomenon of rape to 'why men don't iron'.[4] As Whitehead (2002) observes, protagonists of the men's rights perspective often draw on evolutionary psychology perspectives as a means of understanding gender relations. They are often extremely appealing to the public because of their 'common-sense' explanation for observable trends of behavioural difference between men and women, which continue to have a vast bearing on our lives (hence the popularity of populist texts such as John Gray's (1992) *Men are from Mars, Women are from Venus*). They are appealing to anti-feminists because of their suggestion that gender behavioural differences are 'natural' and inevitable – hence attempts to challenge or change these natural behaviours are misguided and pernicious.

However, many biologists and neuroscientists (as well as feminist social scientists) have been extremely critical of the evolutionary psychology approach. Steven Rose, for example, maintains that 'very few biologists would accept that the mind is modular in the first place', and famously accuses evolutionary psychologists of having 'a Flintstones' view' of the human past based on 'endless speculation' (cited in Hill, 2000). Rose (2001) claims that evolutionary psychologists are preoccupied with their (political) project of trying to provide adaptionist explanations for all social phenomena, even when various local or social factors might easily account for the behaviour concerned. A further criticism which has been levelled at some evolutionary psychologists is their reliance on studies of other species, from which they extrapolate conclusions about human activities.[5] Hence the criticism that evolutionary psychology is based on inappropriate evidence. Of course, as many of the critics have observed, it is very difficult for evolutionary psychologists to provide any direct evidence for their theories (just as it is difficult for social constructionists to demonstrate that gender is entirely socially constructed – see below). Pro-feminist Stephen Whitehead (2002) reviews the criticisms of evolutionary biology positions from a variety of different disciplines, concluding that, 'the evidence for biologically grounded sex/gender differences is neither convincing nor conclusive, nor even coherent' (p. 11). He goes on to argue, though, that we cannot escape from the body due to our embodiment and the social consequences, so both biology and the social play a part in gendered behaviour.

In relation to gender and achievement, evolutionary psychology perspectives lend support to those arguing that the 'gender gap' is caused by essential differences between boys and girls. Where theories of brain difference are used to make specific arguments that boys and girls have different abilities and to explain these in relation to biological differences, evolutionary psychology perspectives are more rooted in the 'broader-brush' viewpoints that boys and girls are 'just naturally different', and, particularly in relation to boys' apparent educational underperformance, that 'boys will be boys' (see Epstein *et al.*, 1998). Where evolutionary psychology approaches have been articulated by 'men's rights' proponents they have tended to highlight the role of the father as providing a necessary role model to sons. 'Brain-difference' arguments tend to make a case for different sorts of educational methods to meet boys' specific needs (and *is* usually boys – specific methods for teaching girls do not tend to be expounded, presumably partly due to the assumption that their needs are being met by dominant models), and this approach might be supported by some developmental psychologists. But the 'boys will be boys' viewpoint tends to evoke a metaphorical shrugging of the shoulders, suggesting that boys will never be diligent and conscientious learners, but that they have other natural attributes that we ought to celebrate (such as their questioning approach to knowledge, competitiveness, etc.). In relation to the latter, Julia Dalton explains for example,

> I actually find boys more fun to teach! They are less concerned with doing the right thing and more with knowing what it is: less worried about getting the right answer and more interested in asking the right questions.
> (Julia Dalton, quoted in Pickering, 1997: 45)

Theories of 'brain difference'

Further to evolutionary psychology there are a number of other socio-biological perspectives which see gender differences in behaviour as reflecting the biological differences between men and women. For example, such approaches have variously explained male violence as due to hormones; to an 'aggressive gene' (Monaghan and Glickman, 1992); or to differences in the brain (Gurian, 2002). The term 'brain difference' theory is coined by commentators in allusion to the body of research that examines differences between the brains of males and females, and maintains that these differences manifest in different kinds of behaviour. Typically, it is observed that the bundle of nerves linking the two sides of the brain (the corpus callosum) tends to be thinner in boys, apparently limiting the communication between the two cerebral hemispheres (see also Chapter 5). This, brain difference theorists maintain, is why men often respond to certain problems by using only one side of their brain, while women tend to use both sides. This difference is seen to manifest in men taking a linear approach to problem solving, and women taking a more holistic approach; and also as expressed by developmental differences such as girls learning to talk sooner. These suppositions are then used to explain phenomena such as women predominating in the humanities and communications subjects, and men at maths.

'Brain sex' theories tend to be drawn on and developed by those who believe that feminism has 'gone too far' (as with those advocating a feminist position, for some the research findings lead to the political conclusions, and for others political predilections direct them to particular types of research evidence for support of political ideas; or a mixture of both aspects). Hence, Michael Gurian, a leading proponent of brain difference theory in education, accuses 1970s feminists of manufacturing findings of masculine 'bias' in the classroom: 'They found bias because it was there, and then they continued to find bias even when it wasn't' (p. 64). Proponents of brain difference perspectives set great store on the 'hard scientific' evidence of their studies, derived from the biological sciences, in relation to feminist studies which are usually based in the human sciences.

Yet it is openly recognised by many neuroscientists that studies of the brain are in their relative infancy, and that no-one can yet be sure what impact brain differences have, or the ways in which they manifest (this is also true of genes, which were previously seen by some as likely to reveal natural causes of gender differences in behaviour – but as the Human Genome project revealed, the approximately 30,000 genes that constitute human beings are insufficient to account for the diversity and complexity of human life). It is widely acknowledged, even by proponents of 'brain difference' as explaining gender differences, that in emphasising differences between male and female brains and relating them to behaviour a gulf of difference is evoked when, in fact, the discrepancies between the brains of men and women are slight. Raisman maintains that 'There are some differences between the brains of boys and girls, but most reflect the differences in their reproductive roles'. He continues,

> People think the brain is just a repository for personality and character. But it's not. Its prime job is to control our bodies, and if men and women have different anatomies, physiologies and behaviours, then this is bound to be reflected in different brain architectures.
>
> (Raisman, quoted in McKie, 1999)

Neuroscientific evidence showing that the brain develops through social interaction contests that of 'brain difference' theorists who see brain differences between the sexes as natural and unalterable. It has been suggested in some neuroscientific studies that neuronal connections are strengthened as a result of experience (see Paechter, 1998). Studies of victims of damage to the brain show how the parts of the brain still functioning develop to compensate for those parts which are damaged. Gerhardt (2004) draws on neuro-chemistry research to argue that who we are is *not* encoded at birth. Rather, daily interactions between a baby and its main carer have a direct impact on the development of the prefrontal cortex (said to enable social aspects such as empathy and self-control). As Paechter (1998) points out, it follows that different (gendered) experiences will lead to differences in neural connections. She maintains that sex differences in brain structure can be understood when taking into account that males and females 'do experience the world in different ways, both because of their different bodies and because they are differently positioned in society' (p. 48).

In relation to gender and achievement, it is argued by brain difference proponents that boys and girls inevitably have different learning skills and abilities (produced by the differences in their brains). Therefore, these differences need to be recognised, and teaching strategies designed to address the differences and meet the (differing) need of boys' and girls' approaches to learning. For example, Gurian (2002: 61–2) maintains,

> More impulsive and less mature than the female brain, the male brain gets a boy into far more trouble in class and in school. The kind of classroom discipline that works for girls . . . does not work for many boys in middle school and early high school. Male hormones are flooding, and many boys (especially at the high end of hormone composition) mature to a great extent through elder dominance systems – in which intense bonding and authority best manage them – until they learn to manage themselves.

Psychoanalytic perspectives

Psychoanalysis studies the 'inner self' and the unconscious. The 'founding father' of psychoanalysis, Sigmund Freud, rejected the idea of a unified, fixed individual self. Instead he saw the conscious and unconscious self as split, and a relationship between the psychic and the social. Psychoanalytic theory has had much to say on the nature of, and explanations for, gender difference. Freud maintained that as children mature they go through various stages of sexual development, the resolution or endurance of which signifies their 'successful' arrival in adulthood. In terms of gender identification, children come to understand the significance of their biological sex, and as a result their development of sexuality is influenced by their identification with their same-sex parent. For the boy child, progression from the 'oral' and 'anal' stages comes via his embarkation through the 'Oedipal stage', where he *learns* to be a male by suppressing his mother love and submitting to the authority of the father. In fear of 'castration' by the father, his desire for the (female) mother is transferred to other women, who are problematised by the fraught dualism of identification and rejection of the female in his subconscious. Girls, in this perspective, are relegated to desiring the phallus, a notion which has made Freudian theory unpalatable for many feminists.

This concept of 'Othering' of women by men was picked up and developed by de Beauviour (1960), who used this as an explanation for misogyny and male oppression of women. More recently, the theories of Lacan (1977) have influenced leading French feminists and been drawn on by post-structuralist feminists more broadly. Particularly, Lacan's conceptions of 'desire' and 'gaze' have been seen as helpful in explaining the perpetuation of gender positions. His prioritisation of the social in the development of the self has often been seen as able to contribute to social constructionist perspectives of gender, although as Hood Williams (1998) points out, Lacan's reliance on Freudian notions of the phallus ties his theories to a primary gender essentialism (it is only men who 'have' the phallus). Hood Williams points to Mitchell and Rose's (1982) development of Lacanian theory to illustrate how although gender identification is seen as a struggle in this perspective, gender identification is seen as inevitable, and tied to biological sex. As Mitchell and Rose (1982) assert, 'no human being can become a subject outside the division into two sexes. One must take up a position as either a man or a woman' (p. 6).

As Connell (1994) has documented, the work of Carl Jung has also been influential in gender theory, and has been particularly popular with writers from the mythopoetic men's movement. Jung shared Freud's belief that the inner self includes both masculine and feminine aspects, but was interested in why (apparently) masculinity outweighs femininity in men, and femininity outweighs masculinity in women. Jung's concept of a public self (persona) and a private self (anima) tied in with his thoughts about gender, as these selves come to be associated with gendered traits (see Connell, 1994). Jung saw this inner feminine side in men as requiring 'healing' through therapy, in order to ensure that the masculine prevails as the dominant aspect of male persona. These notions have been drawn on by the mythopoetic men's movement to argue that feminism has tipped the 'natural' balance in gender relations, and that as a consequence men's masculinity is under threat and in need of healing. Many social constructionists would however contest this view of gender as essentialist and unrepresentative of the ways in which gender is historically changing and played out in the lives of individuals (e.g. Whitehead, 2002).

In terms of gender and achievement, these notions of 'the Other' and psychic costs of both achievement and failure have mainly been drawn on by feminist researchers, in relation to girls' experiences of education. Particularly, Valerie Walkerdine (1990) has argued that in order to adopt the position of achieving female, girls must take up the position of the masculine other, a contradictory subject position that is psychically fraught. As well as drawing on Lacan in her work, Walkerdine also makes reference to the theories of Melanie Klein. Klein (1952) developed the 'object relations' psychoanalytical approach, wherein individual identity is formed through relations with objects (beginning with the mother/the mother's breast, but coming to include other objects, people, institutions, and so on). These objects are invested with our own unconscious emotions and energies and come to 'stand for' parts of our inner self (see Lucey, 2004). Klein believed anxiety (held at the unconscious level, rather than consciously articulated) to be central to the human condition, developed from the infant's precarious dependence in the first weeks of life. This unconscious anxiety leads to 'splitting' and 'projecting' as 'good' things are internalised and/or idealised, and 'bad' things are split off and projected on to other people or things. These 'bad objects' can then be 'demonised', as we construct them as other and separate to ourselves.

Helen Lucey (2001; 2004; Lucey and Reay, 2002b; 2002c) has applied Klein's ideas to issues around educational achievement and 'standards', drawing on theories of splitting and projection to analyse how individuals form identities around 'axes of social divisions' (Lucey, 2004). Like Hoggett (2003), Lucey maintains that usual human anxieties are heightened by Western culture which is 'in flight from dependency and the acceptance of human limits' (Hoggett, 2003: 11). Lucey argues that discourses of 'citizen-consumers' which position individuals as having free agency and rational choice within structural conditions which actually tightly constrain such behaviours heighten anxieties, hence exacerbating projected idealisations and demonisations around 'good' and 'bad' schools and the pupils who attend them (Lucey and Reay, 2002a). Arguably these ideas might be extended to the debate on gender and achievement – for example, working-class boys might now be seen as demonised repositories for fears around educational failure and/or lack of self-responsibility. And feminist educators may play a similar repository function for projected anxieties among commentators that we have apparently not been able to ensure 'our boys'' achievement.

Social constructionist theory

Social constructionist theory generally sees meaning, including identities, as socially situated and constructed through social interaction (e.g. Mead, 1934; Berger and Luckmann, 1966). Hence in this view gender is mutually constructed and developed due to the social expectations and perceptions perpetuated through interaction. Gendered behaviour is produced from social factors rather than biological programming. Consequently social constructionist approaches have appealed to and been utilised by many of those feminists who believe that gender relations can be altered and improved. Social constructionism differs from social learning theory because the latter is more rigid (and arguably determinist) in its evocation of a fixed self and direct reproduction of roles. In contrast the social constructionist view is not determinist as it is concerned with difference, contradiction and change – social constructionists attend to nuance, and micro aspects of local interactions. So, for example, many feminist researchers have observed how particular constructions of gender and gender relations are produced in individual classroom environments, and the differences which aspects such as school culture, teacher approach and expectations, peer group dynamics and so on can make to these productions. Many social constructionists see individuals as biologically sexed, with consequences flowing from this bodily difference in terms of the way others interact with them (for example, different expectations, talking to them in different ways or about different subjects, including or excluding them, etc.), hence perpetuating gender differences in behaviour and experience. In this view, men and women are physically (biologically) different, but gendered *behaviour* is socially produced. However, other social constructionists go further, seeing biological sex itself as socially constructed. This is particularly the case for those influenced by post-structuralism (see below).

Although there is overwhelming evidence to demonstrate that gendered behaviour is to *some extent* socially constructed (as, for example, forms of behaviour and activity associated with either sex differ between societies and cultures), proponents of inherent gender difference would argue that social constructionist positions cannot adequately account for why gender differences in behaviour are so deeply entrenched, and a feature of all societies (see MacInnes, 1998, for discussion). Hence just as social constructionists commonly accuse evolutionary psychologists and other gender essentialists of over-zealously attributing any manifestation of gendered behaviours to 'nature', this argument is applied to social constructionists in their eagerness to provide social explanations for such differences (e.g. Hoff Sommers, 2000).

Social constructionists are also commonly concerned with the ways in which different aspects of social identity (for example, 'race', gender, social class, age, sexuality and so on) impact in interaction and on individual constructions of identity, and the various consequences for individuals. In relation to educational achievement, researchers have explored the impact of group dynamics on classroom behaviours, and the relationship between such behaviours and educational outcomes. It is maintained that boys and girls endeavour to construct their gender identities in ways that are deemed most appropriate or desirable (and hence invested with status and power) to their peers and in the values of society at large. Connell (1995) terms the high status, socially accepted expression of masculinity 'hegemonic masculinity', identifying the way in which it excludes and subjugates other expressions of masculinity as well as femininity. Other researchers take different approaches,[6] but there is much agreement that the performance of masculinity most approbated by secondary school pupils is that typically incorporating characteristics such as humour, daring, resistance, competition, physical strength and prowess, assertive heterosexuality and active sexuality, homophobia, aggression and derision. These behaviours are seen as contrasting with the values of the school, which require obedience rather than resistance and diligence rather than distraction. Further, it has been argued that the dominant masculine values among schoolboys are antithetical to academic learning and application, and that such application is constructed as feminine. As gender is relationally constructed (there can be no conception of masculinity without a femininity to compare and contrast it to), there is then an onus on boys to avoid appearing to enjoy academic work or to be seen to work hard. It is argued that this avoidance in turn has a detrimental impact on their educational achievement (e.g. Salisbury and Jackson, 1996; Pickering, 1997; Epstein, 1998; Martino, 1999; Francis, 2000a). Researchers have examined the ways in which other facets of identity such as social class (e.g. Martino, 1999; Reay, 2002), 'race' (e.g. Sewell, 1998; Connolly, 1998; 2004; Archer, 2003; Francis and Archer, 2005), dis/ability (e.g. Hey *et al.*, 1998; Benjamin, 2003) mediate with gender in these constructions, producing varied behaviours and outcomes.

Poststructuralist discourse analytical perspectives

As we have seen, many contemporary social constructionists draw on aspects of poststructuralist thought. Poststructuralism is a particular strand of post-modernism, with its roots in literary criticism. It emerged in reaction to the structuralist movement in literary theory, which built on the work of Sassure to maintain that a universal structure of language exists and determines human thought (as we cannot think or speak outside the 'prison house of language'), and which can be scientifically analysed. Poststructuralists such as Barthes and Derrida set out to *deconstruct* these patterns of language, delighting in illustrating how the text can 'play' and be interpreted in multifarious ways, hence revealing that there are no fixed 'truths' of meaning. This work sat within a wider movement in reaction to modernism's belief in the 'reason of science' and Enlightenment rationalism and universalism. Postmodernism, as this movement came to be called, rejected claims to reason and 'truth', maintaining the relativist position that there is no transcendent position from which 'the real' can be identified and tested – rather, 'truth' and 'reality' depend on perspective, and no perspective can claim to be more valid or 'true' than another.

Of all the best-known thinkers identified with poststructuralist perspectives, the work of Michel Foucault has been particularly influential in the human sciences. Drawing on Freud and Nietzsche among other influences, Foucault developed a critique of the subject and an analysis of power as operating through discourses rather than held by particular groups of people and lacked by others. He also developed the application of genealogical and discourse analytic methods.

Poststructuralism has appealed to many feminists for a number of reasons, as we discuss elsewhere (Francis, 1999b; 2001). Foucault's explanation of power as operating through discourses was able to explain the phenomena of resistance and contradiction which had proved so problematic for sex-role theory (Foucault sees the self as passively positioned by certain discourses while simultaneously active in *positioning* in discourses). It was also able to explain some of the theoretical complexities that had challenged feminism in the 1980s: for example, the way in which power is constituted between women (and between men), as well as between women and men. This view of people as positioned in and produced by discourse can also explain the gendered nature of society as produced by gender discourses that position all selves as men or women, and present these categories as relational (Davies, 1989). This ties in with the third reason that poststructuralist theory has appealed to many feminists – gender itself is deconstructed. Rather than reflecting biological givens, 'maleness' and 'femaleness' is simply produced by discourse. Following from this, some feminists argue that the terms 'women' and 'girl' are misleading and redundant, implying a fixity and homogeneity that do not exist. Judith Butler (1990) and others have been at pains to argue that rather than just the behavioural aspects of gender being discursively produced, the apparent biological givens of sex differ- ence are also discursively (socially) constructed, being actually far less consistent and immutable than we are lead to believe.

The main critiques of poststructuralism have been from positivists and from emancipatory theorists such as feminists and Marxists. Positivists have pointed to the unscientific and eclectic approaches of postmodern theorists, who have sometimes felt free to appropriate the language of science in random ways (Sokal and Bricmont, 1998). Postmodern theories, in this positivist perspective, amount to nothing more radical than the relativist view of life adopted by the ancient 'sceptic' philosophical school, and as having no more substance than story- telling. Indeed, this is a position that some postmodernists/poststructuralists would unabashedly ascribe to. The critiques from emancipatory theorists have been more seriously engaged by poststructuralists and those influenced by poststructuralism. The key accusation here is that postmodernist perspectives advocate an a-political agenda. Basically, emancipatory movements such as feminism are argued by many to be grounded in Enlightenment principles of equality, justice, and 'rights' of the individual, and in notions of human progress and claims to truth (e.g. that women ought to be allowed the same rights as men; or black people given the same opportunities as white, etc.) (see Balbus, 1987; Soper, 1990; Assiter, 1996 for discussion). For many poststructuralists, all truth discourses or 'grand narratives' exercise a power relationship and need to be deconstructed. Moreover, as Jones (1997) and McNay (2000) discuss, poststructuralist theory revokes the agency required to further emancipatory projects due to its refutation of the coherent self which can make (rational or consistent) choices. Hence poststructuralism deconstructs 'principled positions' (Squires, 1990), leading some to see it as an androcentric and/or reactionary position that upholds the status quo (e.g. Hartsock, 1990; Soper, 1990). As a result of these debates, the emphasis in some feminist research has shifted towards the possibility of redirecting rather than completely breaking with en- lightenment principles in order to retain the feminist project of emancipation (see Assiter, 1996; Mouffe, 1996; McNay, 2000).

In relation to gender and achievement, some feminist researchers in education have applied discourse analysis to the debate in the academic and popular press, and to pupils' discussion of the issues. Hence rather than being concerned with the 'truth' or otherwise regarding the extent of 'gender gap' in achievement, they have identified and examined the discourses producing these arguments. For example, Francis (1999c; Francis and Archer forthcoming) identifies the various discourses drawn on by pupils to explain the apparent 'laddish' behaviour of boys and what most pupils believed to be their resulting educational underperformance. She shows how pupils tend to support the views of policy- makers concerning boys' behaviour and apparent underachievement, and how boys' behaviours are seen by pupils to be socially produced. She and her colleagues have also analysed the discourses emerging from lecturers' talk about undergraduate essay writing abilities in relation to gender, showing how a dichotomy manifests whereby 'natural' academic brilliance, rationality and incisiveness is located in the male (females were positioned as better communicators, but also as achieving through 'plodding' diligence rather than innate ability) (Francis *et al.*, 2003). Hence men are seen as having more innate potential, but as not necessarily realising this potential.

Some researchers have applied discourse analysis to the policy and media writing on 'boys' underachievement', identifying and examining the discourses producing these arguments. For example, Epstein *et al.* (1998) observe three discourses in this regard – 'boys will be boys', 'poor boys' and 'blaming schools'. We discuss these in detail in Chapter 3. Griffin (1998) identifies a 'boys' as victims' discourse underlying the debate (which appears to be the same as that termed the 'poor boys' narrative by Epstein *et al.*) and a parallel narrative of girls as 'having it all' (hence supporting a view of feminist excess). Griffin maintains that rather than being a crisis of boys' underachievement, there is simply a 'discourse of crisis'.

Human capital theory

Human capital theory in some respects evokes functionalist perspectives, in that it applies itself to the efficient functioning of the economy (where functionalist theory is concerned with the functioning of society). It stresses the importance of education for economic development and growth in a global economy. In this sense, it also overlaps with the 'individualised society' perspective (see below), which draws on human capital theory to position the individual as requiring skills to equip them for the competitive global marketplace, and able and responsible for doing so and for their progress (or lack of it). Human capital theory maintains that a country can only remain competitive in a global market by providing the workforce with adequate skills, and with the knowledge to enable them to flexibly adapt to technological innovations. High levels of education across the workforce will, then, result in economic competitiveness and resulting prosperity and low unemployment. This theory, coupled with governmental concerns about global economic competition and about social exclusion, has in Britain resulted in the development of the model of the 'learning society', and the related concept of 'lifelong learning'. The latter term is a vague one, tending to reflect a particular discourse which, as Ball (1999) points out, collapses educational policy into economic policy. The term is normally used to allude to the continuing post-compulsory education of young people and adults in terms of formal education and qualifications, work-based learning, and the development of new skills or knowledge (OECD, 1996). Such 'up-skilling' is considered vital in the increasingly technological workplace.

This view of lifelong learning as concomitant with individual and national prosperity is not universally supported, as the direct relationship between education and output is not always evident. Indeed, some commentators have even argued that cynical policy-makers privately recognise and accept discrepancies between the theory and the practice (see Ainley, 1998; Ball, 1999). For example, Ainley (1998) argues that there is now a consensus amongst European policy-makers that a certain section of the workforce must remain unemployed in order to restrain national inflation, and to provide a reserve army of labour. However, the human capital theory-influenced notion of the learning society has been propagated by the British Labour government since they came to power in 1997, and indeed broadly represents the consensus approach of governments throughout the European Union (Ball, 1999). Mass participation in lifelong learning is seen by the government as having the potential not only to secure Britain's continuing competitiveness in a global market, but also to contribute to the erosion of social exclusion (Fryer, 1997; DfEE, 1998). Lifelong learning has been presented as a source of access to career development and mental stimulation for those who have, for one reason or another, been less successful in initial education.

This view has lead to a massive expansion in education and training in Britain at post-compulsory level. Participation in higher education has risen from around 6 per cent of young people in the 1980s, to around 35 per cent at the present time (DfES, 2004b). Again, there is debate about the effects of this 'massification of higher education', with some commentators concerned at what they see as a diluting of excellence and lowering of standards as access is prioritised (Furedi, 2004); and others maintaining that the expansion in university places has been detrimental to the undergraduates involved, due to resulting 'qualification inflation' (Ainley, 1998). (And as it has been pointed out, it is the working-class students from the poorer, less-prestigious universities who are shown to fair particularly badly in the increasingly competitive graduate market, Reay et al., 2001; Archer et al., 2003.)

In terms of achievement, then, we can see that a human capital perspective prioritises educational attainment as ensuring a competitive economy. From this point of view, the apparent under-performance of any section of society is a concern – all the more so when this represents a large group, such as working-class pupils, or boys. In relation to debates around gender and achievement we can see human capital theory manifesting in concerns that boys' apparent underachievement will result in their inability to find jobs or to meet the needs of an increasingly service-led economy. In her analysis of British educational policy, Mahony (1998: 40) argues that,

> The preoccupation with increasing the competitiveness of the nation state plc in the global economy is pervasive and although the precise contribution of schooling to such competitiveness is controversial, the belief that national prosperity depends on high levels of knowledge and skill . . . is clearly presumed in the major educational policy documents of governments as far apart as Australia or New Zealand and the United Kingdom.

This leads her to surmise that from this perspective, 'Today's underachieving boy stands at the brink of tomorrow's unemployed youth as public burden number one' (Mahony, 1998: 42).

Neo-liberal, individualised society

The most recent perspective evident in discussion of gender and education is that of neo-liberal 'individualisation' and, in particular, the 'individualised individual' (Hey, 2003; Reay, 2003; Skelton, 2005). The notion of individualisation stems from Third Way theorists (e.g. Beck, 1992; Giddens, 1998; Beck and Beck-Gernsheim, 2002). Third Way theorists argue that (Western) societies have moved away from the old 'left' versus 'right' political distinctions and are being replaced by globalisation and globalised citizenship. As such, they argue, the majority of theories used by sociologists are those of a first modernity ('modern', organised, nation states) and are no longer relevant to our understandings of contemporary social actors in the second modernity (the hallmark of which is globalisation). Beck, in particular, argues that sociological theory tends to confuse industrial society with the first modernity and, together with Giddens, have attempted to address the problems of these by providing alternative theories centred around reflexive modernisation where the 'self' and 'individualisation' are key concepts. In brief, Third Way ideology centres on the changes taking place from a post-industrial to a reflexive society, one where a new relationship emerges between the 'individual' and society. Thus, Third Way politics is about encouraging an active civil society through a recognition of, and emphasis on, the rights and obligations of both the 'individual' and society. The key characteristics of a Third Way perspective are:

1 A new politics for a new, globalised world society thus transcending the old political distinctions between left and right parties.
2 Globalisation is the way forward.
3 Progressing equality of opportunity; this involves the recognition that patterns of equality are/have changed (i.e. not the 'old' distinctions based on gender, ethnicity, social class but those which relate more broadly to exclusion and inclusion).
4 Mutual responsibility of state and individual.
5 Strengthening communities through emphasis on active welfare with labour market reform (i.e. recognising that existing state systems may contribute to, rather than resolve, social problems).

The notion of the 'individual' in Third Way theory is one where both the state and people learn to see themselves as 'the centre of action, the planning office . . . (of) his/her own biography' (Beck, 1992: 135).

The implication of Beck's thesis is that people are the authors of their own lives and are no longer constrained by the 'totalities' of twentieth-century modernity

– such as social class, ethnicity, sexual and gender differences and so forth. In the new (second) modernity inequalities will not disappear, but the individual will produce 'biographical solutions to systemic contradictions' and these will be 're-understood' as personal risks and opportunities (Beck and Beck Gersenheim, 2002: xxii).

What this means in terms of education can be seen by looking at New Labour policy which is informed by Third Way theories. In the UK the New Labour government puts a significant emphasis in its rhetoric and policy on what Fairclough (2000) calls a combined moral-contractual discourse. For example, Fairclough illustrates this 'something for something' pact by quoting Prime Minister Tony Blair saying:

> Our welfare system must provide help for those who need it but the deal that we are trying to create in Britain today is something for something. If we provide jobs we expect people to take them.
>
> (Blair, 1999, quoted in Fairclough, 2000: 39)

So what does this 'something for something' deal mean when it comes to education? Given that a central tenet of Third Way theory is that we are in a globalised society then the British government needs to provide an educated, competitive workforce (DTI, 1998; Blair, 2002; Clarke, 2004). At the same time, this has to be achieved within a 'respectful to the individual' manner. Thus, whilst education is seen as a means of producing the 'human capital' (see above) which is critical for economic success (Fairclough, 2000), schools and colleges are expected to achieve this whilst simultaneously encouraging social inclusion, personal fulfilment and democratic citizenship (Ecclestone, 2004a). So in relation to gender and achievement, the current efforts to fund research and strategies on raising boys' achievement may be seen as facilitating boys' achievement (and their inclusion, as we shall see in the next chapter). However, as the individualised society thesis sees the individual as responsible and mutually obliged, it is no surprise to see policy statements increasingly expressing frustration at the apparent lack of progress among some boys. We discuss these developments further in Chapter 3.

Having explored the theory in the field, we turn now to the specific issues around gender and achievement addressed in the rest of the book. Within the ensuing discussions the operation of these theories and approaches, and the way in which they position achievement, learners, teachers and educationalists will be illustrated further.

The construction of gender and achievement in education policy

Introduction

To say that successive governments in the United Kingdom (UK) have placed academic achievement at the heart of educational policy is almost stating the obvious. Ensuring that all children develop the knowledge and skills necessary for them to fit into and enhance the economy, society and culture of the world they live in is what state education has set out to do from its inception (see the Forster Act 1870). However, what those necessary educational knowledge and skills *are* has varied across time and in relation to perceptions of the 'ideal adult'. For example, if we look back to the end of the Victorian period in Britain we can see that the requisite knowledge and skills were determined by gender and social class. In the first place, state education was aimed specifically at the working-class as middle- and upper-class boys were educated in the public schools or at home by tutors or governesses. Middle-class girls were only expected to undertake a rudimentary education in terms of curriculum subjects but were educated in the 'arts' of painting, playing musical instruments and kinaesthetics. For working-class boys and girls state education provided a basis in literacy and numeracy but there was an emphasis on girls learning domestic subjects to fit them for their futures as mothers and domestic servants. During these early years of the state system in the UK what was taught was influenced by the Education Department – domestic economy was made a compulsory subject for girls in 1878 followed by grants provided for cookery in 1882 and laundry work in 1890 (Purvis, 1991). The point here is that by scrutinising educational policy it is possible to identify *what* skills are deemed important and *for whom* at any one point and that these are embedded within specific notions of gender, social class and, more recently, ethnicity and sexuality.

In this chapter we are going to look at recent educational policy to identify how different countries in the Western world are articulating differences in and concerns about achievement. From what we have said in earlier chapters it is evident that the main focus in terms of achievement is on the 'gender gap' and, in particular, boys' underachievement. Boys' underachievement is not just a 'problem' for the UK but is recognised and discussed in countries across the

Western world including Australia, Finland, Canada and the United States of America (Martino and Meyenn, 2001; Frank *et al.*, 2003; Weaver-Hightower, 2003; Van de Gaer, 2004). Policy in the UK will be considered in some depth as it is important to recognise the political context in which educational discourses are developed and implemented. Here we attempt to tease out and analyse some of the discourses evident in the policy and popular literature on boys, gender and achievement, and their implications.

Educational policy and achievement across the Western world

Policy on gender is not uniform in content or focus across countries in the Western world. In Australia and the UK the boys' underachievement debate takes a central role and, whilst not maintaining the centrality it has in these two countries, it is a phenomenon recognised in other countries. One conclusion that could be drawn by looking at the popular press is that boys' underachievement emerged in the mid-1990s and a brief look at the headlines of newspapers in three countries gives some indication of where the main anxieties lie:

> *UK*
> How exams are fixed in favour of girls
> > (*The Spectator*, Pirie, M., 2001)
>
> Boys Left Behind by Modern Teaching
> > (*Daily Telegraph*, Lightfoot, L., 1998)
>
> *USA*
> How Boys Lost Out to Girl Power
> > (*New York Times*, Lewin, T., 1998)
>
> Reexamining the Plight of Young Males
> > (*Washington Post*, Rosenfeld, M., 1998)
>
> *Australia*
> Turning boys into sissies
> > (*The Australian Women's Weekly*, Buttrose, I., 2000)
>
> 'Nobody loves us, everybody hates us . . .'. Why today's teenage boys have become pariahs
> > (*Sydney Morning Herald*, 1997)

Concerns about boys' motivations and attitudes to schooling appeared first in Australia in the late 1980s and early 1990s (Walker, 1988; Connell, 1989) although it should be emphasised this literature was not focused on underachievement as such. Rather the focus was on exploring how boys and young men construct their masculine identities in school settings. However, whilst researchers in other countries began to look more closely at how schooling contributed to boys' identities (Miedzian, 1992; Mac an Ghaill, 1994) it was not until schools began increasingly to be made to be accountable that the achievement of boys in relation to girls began to attract government and media attention. Since this time concerns and fears about boys' apparent falling behind girls in terms of examination success have spread to many European countries, Canada, North America and, more recently, South American countries such as Chile and Brazil.

What needs to be made clear from the outset is that the 'problems of boys' might be a feature of discussions about education in many Western societies but these problems are not seen as exactly the same nor are they prioritised in exactly the same order. Also, government involvement in tackling the 'problem of boys' at school varies from country to country. Whilst the Australian and UK governments directly initiate discussions and interventions on boys' achievement, the US Department of Education places greater emphasis on racial educational inequities. These differences and their implications will be considered in the following sections of the chapter. The focus will be on three countries in particular, Australia, the USA and the UK although reference will be made to European countries as appropriate.

Policy in Australia, USA and UK

It has been observed by writers on boys' schooling that, certainly at the beginning of the debates in Australia and the UK, the policy context in which the issue was discussed was markedly different (Mahony and Smedley, 1998; Foster et al., 2001). The Australian policy context was underpinned by a notion of social justice whereas in the UK the shifting of schools into the market-place means that the debates have been the result of economic rationalism rather than concerns over equity. As globalisation takes an increasing hold and countries measure themselves up against each other in terms of pupil achievement (OECD Report 2003) then it will increasingly be the case that the focus will be on those groups who are seen not to be 'performing' to the prescribed levels. For example, it has been pointed out that in Finland any demands by the ministry of education for greater numbers of male early years workers has been prompted by equal opportunities for men and women and gender equality for children (Cameron et al., 1999) rather than the argument that more men teachers are needed to act as positive role models for boys. And it has been observed that Finland is one country which has not exhibited concern over boys' under-achievement (West, 2002). However, the findings of the OECD Report that noted that Finland had the biggest gender gap in reading out of all the countries taking part (with more than three times as many boys reading at Level 1 or below) prompted an outburst of concern in the Finnish media. But what had not been made clear was that scores of pupils in Finland were well above the average for all countries and there was no other country where boys did better. The gender gap was because females scored exceptionally well. This tendency to misread or to undertake only a superficial reading of statistics on achievement is a general problem (see Chapter 4) and it prompted at least one Finnish female academic to speak out against the inordinate and inappropriate focus on boys' underachievement on national television (Vuorikoski, 2004).

Australia

Whilst Australian policy has been, to a large extent, concerned with boys and schooling as a matter of social justice (although how that is interpreted differs markedly as will be discussed later) since the mid-1990s the performance of boys in examinations has risen in, if not become *the*, priority. In an excellent collection of papers on gender agendas in school in Australia and the UK, Hayes and Lingard (2003) observe that 'the problems of boys' has been *the* dominant gender problem for the last ten years in Australia. Unlike the situation in the UK they note that:

> The panic that followed has endured but some of us have started to wade back into the waters of gender equity in education to rejoin those that had bravely refused to leave, whilst others continue to look on from safer ground.
>
> (Hayes and Lingard, 2003: 1)

What Hayes and Lingard are referring to here is the situation in Australia where concerns about the position of boys have almost subsumed those about girls. From 1975 the Australian government has actively intervened in the education of girls. The strategies that were devised and implemented were based on feminist approaches and brought together in 1987 by 'The National Policy for the Education of Girls in Australian Schools'. An important point to note here is that 'policies for girls' education at both the national and state levels in Australia have reflected Australian feminism's close relationship with the state since the early 1970s (Lingard, 2003: 34). As Lingard goes on to explain, this close relationship was the result of a fortunate set of circumstances where the rise of second wave feminism in Australia coincided with the election of a socially progressive Keynesian Labour government. This led to a set of policies on girls, schooling and education which manifested in the above national policy. Such was the strength of a feminist presence in Australian policy-making that the term 'femocrats' was coined to denote those workers employed because of their feminist politics. However, as Lingard points out, this is not to assume that femocrats' endeavours in developing feminist practices in schools were easily achieved, and since the early 1990s the backlash effect has seen their numbers and their influence minimised. For the most part their work today is about ensuring that the policies on girls' schooling already achieved are not sidelined or even removed by the emphasis on boys. Certainly in Australia, as in other countries, the popular message in the media is that feminists have 'won' and girls are now doing well but boys have paid the price for this progress.

The shift from educational policy with a definite feminist involvement to one which placed a greater emphasis on boys can be seen in the 1997 policy *Gender Equity: A Framework for Australia's Schools*. However, this policy indicates the tensions in trying to accommodate two differing views of gender identity – that is, feminist concerns with the marginalisation of and restrictions on what it means to be a girl, and the somewhat anti-feminist stance adopted by men's rights or recuperative masculinity idealists (see Chapter 2) who see 'boyness' as something which is an essential core of boys and strategies to restrain it as having negative results. For example, recuperative masculinity supporters point to boys' higher rates of suicide, their alienation and disaffection with schooling as well as their lower performance achievements in examinations. Thus, boys are perceived as the 'newly disadvantaged' group in education (Mills, 2003). These tensions between the competing views meant that the policy *Gender Equity: A Framework for Australia's Schools* (1997) did not satisfy either faction as inevitably previous strategies about girls were curtailed and the call by recuperative masculinity supporters for more emphasis on 'boy-centred' approaches were constrained (Ailwood and Lingard, 2001).

The focus on boys came to the fore in *Boys: Getting it Right. Report into the Inquiry of Education of Boys* (House of Representatives Standing Committee on Education and Training, 2002). Mills (2003) has argued that the brief of this inquiry was indicative of the current concerns about boys in that it reported on 'the social, cultural and educational factors affecting the education of boys in Australian schools, particularly in relation to their literacy needs and socialisation skills in the early and middle years of schooling' (terms of reference cited in *Boys: Getting it Right. Report into the Inquiry of Education of Boys*, 2002). As was indicated at the beginning of this section, the response to this report and the emphasis on boys in Australian policy has been mixed. And, as will be shown in Chapter 4, there are very real issues about some boys' underachievement in aspects of the curriculum and in their attitudes towards education. However, what is emerging from some policy documents is a conflation of academic underachievement with psychological illness. In the foreword of *Boys: Getting it Right. Report into the Inquiry of Education of Boys*, it is observed that:

> . . . many parents, teachers, academics and community workers have expressed concern that, particularly in the area of education, boys are not coping with the changes as well as girls.

At this point, we are drawing attention to this tendency as it is a key factor in recent policy and one that has important implications for what recommendations can be made and strategies adopted in enhancing the educational opportunities for all pupils. This will be discussed more fully at the end of this chapter.

USA and Canada

In American and Canadian educational policy there has been a focus on equity and this is particularly in relation to charting and addressing differences between ethnic groups. Neither the Federal or Provincial educational ministries in Canada nor the US Department of Education had, at the time of writing, policies that could be compared to those in place in Australia or the UK. However, interest in boys' underachievement is on the increase in Canada which has begun to fund various research projects investigating boys and schooling (Frank *et al.*, 2003).

In many ways the US is a late entry into the debates on the links between boys' underachievement and 'standards' although literature on boys as victims of the educational system has been attracting media attention from the mid-1990s onwards (for example, Gurian, 1996; Pollack, 1998; Hoff Sommers, 2000). Indeed the absence of national government intervention into boys' under-achievement has proved frustrating for at least one best selling American author:

> The widening education gap threatens the future of millions of American boys. We should be looking not to 'gender experts' and activists for guid-ance but to the example of other countries that are focusing on boys' problems and dealing with them constructively. Like American boys, boys in Great Britain and Australia are markedly behind girls academically, notably in reading and writing . . . The big difference is that British educators and politicians are ten years ahead of Americans in confronting and specifically addressing the problem of male underachievement.
>
> (Hoff Sommers, 2000: 15)

The arguments of Christina Hoff Sommers (2000) and Michael Gurian (2002) fall into that category identified earlier with 'men's rights'/recuperative mascu-linity theorists which has a particular anti-feminist stance. The implications of the writings of Gurian (2002), Hoff Sommers (2000) and Pollack (1998) is that schools have either deliberately or by default taken on board feminist thinking and strategies which themselves have undermined boys' abilities, denigrated their skills, and destroyed their self-concepts. However, the tension identified in Australian policy between earlier feminist policies on girls and the current trend towards recuperative masculinity (men's rights) strategies in boys' schooling has yet to become an issue in US education policy. This is not to say that achieve-ment *per se* has not been of central concern in US educational policy – quite the reverse. As Weiler (1993: 219–20) argued, the US has blamed its 'inadequate education' for its inability to compete in the wider market-place and pays great attention to the mass testing of school children in order to 'justify differences in achievement of both children and schools, by imposing ideals of competition and hierarchy while accepting and exacerbating a divided and unequal society'.

In January 2002, the 'No Child Left Behind Act' was passed. The US Depart-ment of Education sustains the focus on the significance of mass testing whilst drawing on social justice objectives stating on its website 'Our commitment to you, and to all Americans, is to see every child in America – regardless of ethnicity, income, or background – achieve high standards.' The way of achieving this is by implementing State tests in reading and maths for children in grades 3–8. For UK readers the arguments will sound very familiar:

> *No Child Left Behind* puts the focus on instruction and methods that have been proven to work. It makes a billion-dollar annual investment to ensure every child learns to read by third grade. And it provides the resources for reform and unprecedented flexibility so states and local communities can get the job done.
>
> (http://www.ed.gov/nclb/overview/welcome/index.html)

This Act is innovatory in that it is the first time in US policy-making that it has been advocated that all students have the capacity to successfully achieve and to have this measured, although critics observe that the standards movement does not take into consideration those structures that might contribute to pupils' failures (Deschenes *et al.*, 2001). The major point of concern in US educational policy has been, and for now continues to be, differences between the achievements of ethnic groups. Here the differences between genders are minimal compared to the differences in achievement between minority ethnic groups in relation to the white population. For example, in a report entitled *Educational Achievement and Black–White Inequality* (National Center For Education Statistics: Statistical Analysis Report July 2001) it was noted that in grades 1–12 black–white reading gaps did not differ consistently for boys and girls. Given this kind of information it may well be that the US will continue to prioritise differences between ethnic groups rather than gender inequities although there is growing emphasis on the achievements and behaviours of Black, Hispanic and Native American boys (US Department of Education website: www.ed.gov/index.jhtml) which might encourage closer attention to how boys construct their identities in school settings. On the other hand, concerns about the achievement of boys generally has lead to a surge of policy support for single-sex education (TES, 2004). Single-sex education is positioned as benefiting boys (Hoff Sommers, 2000), but actually there is very little evidence that single-sex schooling benefits boys' achievement (indeed, in the UK the finding until recently was that, while girls apparently perform better in single-sex schools, boys perform better in mixed-sex schools (Lavigeur, 1980; Leonard, 1996).[1]

United Kingdom

In common with Australia, the UK currently has very clear policies on gender equality. There are two points that need noting about this. First, as can be seen from the DfES 'Gender and achievement' website the emphasis is on reaching the prescribed standards in public examinations and, as boys are the ones seen to be failing in reaching those standards, then strategies and recommendations are aimed at this group. Thus, the concern about boys is foremost about standards rather than social justice objectives. Second, this apparent underperformance of boys has generated a number of direct policy interventions; for example, a declared objective of the Teacher Training Agency's (TTA) Corporate Plan for 2003–6 is to 'annually achieve an increase of a further 20 per cent of male trainees on top of the previous year's baseline'. This objective is driven by the belief that boys need 'positive male teacher role models' to encourage their educational engagement.[2] Also, a number of booklets have been produced for schools to enable them to directly target the attitudes, behaviours and learning styles of boys (e.g. *Using the National Healthy School Standard to Raise Boys' Achievement* (DfES, 2003); *Yes He Can – Schools Where Boys Write Well* (Ofsted, 2003a); *Boys' Achievement in Secondary Schools* (Ofsted, 2003b).

This targeting of boys began in the mid-1990s with the introduction and publication of league tables whereby the performance of a school's pupils in standard assessment tasks (SATs) were measured and compared between schools. These league tables were published for the first time in 1994 for secondary schools and 1996 for primary schools – which provides an explanation as to why 'boys' underachievement' began to hit the media headlines in 1995. Before moving on to consider the current policy on gender (boys) and achievement some acknowledgement of the political context is required. Here we need to note how the swing towards creating an 'individualised society' has effected the conceptualisation of both the purpose and administration of the education system.

A Conservative government, under the leadership of Margaret Thatcher, introduced the major shift in education that was later to be developed under New Labour. Following the Second World War education had a social and economic function that involved the development of economic growth, equality of opportunity and social justice, but a series of acts culminating in the Education Reform Act 1988 replaced this with a notion of education as a means of enabling individual aspirations through the rough justice of market forces (Haywood and Mac an Ghaill, 1996). Thus education as a means of social democracy in which the eradication of inequalities was perceived as necessary for the collective good, was replaced with one of social diversity through promoting ideas of individual entitlement and freedom of choice. When New Labour came to power in 1997 and 'education, education, education' was the mantra of the new Prime Minister, Tony Blair, schooling became of even greater significance in that it was a central plank of Third Way politics (see Chapter 2). With regard to school pupils then it is the 'duty', as well as the 'right' of each individual to achieve.

Whilst both Australia and the UK place 'boys and schooling' as an 'educational priority' there are significant differences between the two countries. It has already been commented that social justice objectives were evident at least in the early days of the debates in Australia, but that in the UK in recent years the official priority has been economic determinants followed by social objectives (e.g. doing something about the tendency of boys towards destructive behaviours).

As Pat Mahony (2003: 75) points out 'One obvious difference between Australia and the UK is that we have had no tradition of a "femocracy" working within the central State'. The accuracy of this statement can be clearly seen when contrasting government policy intervention over boys' underachievement and the lack of willingness on the part of government to become involved in strategies to tackle girls' underachievement in an earlier period (Arnot and Weiner, 1987). Also, whilst changes in government in Australia have marked a swing to and then away from incorporating a feminist voice in educational policy (Lingard, 2003), Mahony comments on how a change in UK government (i.e. the winning of power by New Labour in 1997 marking the end of 18 years of Conservative rule) has not altered the general drift in policy. As she says:

> Policy continuity best describes the gender equality debate in the UK to date, albeit in a softer, less aggressive and overtly threatening way within the politics of the 'Third Way'. While the Third Way has been subject to considerable criticism and counter-criticism from a variety of standpoints on the political spectrum, a particular source of disenchantment has been the way that 'inequality' has been redefined as 'social exclusion'.
>
> (Mahony, 2003: 76)

We would add to this by saying that from the outset boys, as a group, have been positioned as socially excluded in New Labour educational policy documents. In an early consultation paper *Boys Will Be Boys?* (1996) the main theme was the 'laddish' behaviour and culture of boys. A 'laddish culture' is seen to be one where boys' groups adopt common practices such as 'having a laugh', disruptive behaviours, having an interest in pastimes commonly associated with male groups like football and drinking (Francis, 1999c). As can be seen from the comments of this 1996 document, a consequence of boys behaving laddishly was that they were seen as somehow 'outside of society'.

> . . . increasing numbers of young people – mainly boys – who have effectively ceased to be part of mainstream society.
>
> (Morris, E. (1996) *Boys Will Be Boys?* 1996: 2
> (Labour Party Consultation Document))

There are two different manifestations of boys as 'outsiders' offered in the paper, first, boys' adoption of anti-social behaviours:

> Boys who are failing to reach their full potential often cause problems in the classroom through disruptive and anti-social behaviour . . . Every day people working in and with schools are spending valuable time and money picking up the pieces after routine acts of disruption and vandalism which are mostly carried out by boys.
>
> (*Boys Will Be Boys?* 1996: 2)

The second signifier of boys as 'outsiders' comes through in the New Labour language of social exclusion where they are constructed as vulnerable and in need of support:

> The very future of our society depends on reconnecting young men and boys – particularly in the most economically and socially disadvantaged areas – with a sense of belonging and identity which will provide both hope and self reliance.
>
> (*Boys Will Be Boys?* 1996: 10)

In the case of boys' anti-social behaviours they are constructed as 'tough' and 'violent' i.e. stereotypically male, and therefore 'problem boys'. In contrast to this is the understanding of boys as vulnerable and 'at risk' thus requiring the support of others (as in communities, responsible adults, schools and so forth).

At this point we pause to clarify what the various discourses on boys and education have been, and are, in the years since 'boys' underachievement' became a topic for debate in the UK.

Boys and schooling in educational discourses

In their book *Failing Boys* (1998), Debbie Epstein, Jannette Elwood, Valerie Hey and Janet Maw identified three dominant discourses which were evident in government policy, the media and populist literature: 'poor boys'; 'failing schools, failing boys'; and, 'boys will be boys'.

The 'poor boys' discourse is akin to that of Griffin's (1998) 'boys as victims' discourse whereby feminist agendas in education are seen to have 'gone too far' in empowering girls, and hence created an imbalance in schooling (that is in teaching, learning and assessment practices, as well as the day-to-day organisation and routines, all of which are seen to favour girls). In this sense boys are positioned as having 'lost out' to girls, and as consequently disadvantaged.[3] This construction of the position of boys in schools is a feature of, not just UK education discourses, but also those in Australia (Kenway, 1995) and the US (Pollock, 1998). 'Failing schools, failing boys' is one which is less prevalent today than when Epstein *et al.* (1998) wrote their book as it is located within the school improvement and school effectiveness movements, both of which have a much lower profile today than in 1998 when *Failing Boys* was written. In this understanding of the position of boys, a 'failing school' lets down its male pupils in not enabling them to achieve the requisite benchmarks in the SATS, GCSE and A levels. Finally, the 'boys will be boys' discourse is based upon assumed 'natural' differences between boys and girls whereby the former are seen in conventional masculine stereotypes; that is, 'naturally clever' but lazy and difficult to motivate, competitive, independent, and intolerant of inadequate teaching (for examples of strategies couched within this discourse see Browne and Fletcher, 1995 (Australia); Gurian, 2002 (USA); Neall, 2002 (UK)). Before

summarising the main problems shared by these three discourses it is worthwhile spending a few moments examining how popular authors have used two
of these discourses to make particular points.

Christina Hoff Sommers' (2000) book *The War Against Boys* describes how
boys in America are let down by society, and education in particular, ascribing
the reasons for this to 'misguided feminism (which) is harming our young men'
(description on book jacket). Hoff Sommers' work oscilates between 'poor
boys' and 'boys will be boys' discourses. In her chapter 'Save the male' she
attacks writers, including feminist and pro-feminist writers, who have seen boys
as 'in crisis'. She instead claims to celebrate boys' difference, her adherence to
the 'boys will be boys discourse' illustrated particularly vividly by the concluding
sentence of her book: 'If you are a mother of sons, as I am, you know that one
of the more agreeable facts of life is that boys will be boys' (2000: 213). She
criticises those who have pathologised boys as 'in crisis', expressing especial
scorn for the 'therapy' approach that suggests that boys need rescue and healing.
Faludi's (1999) thesis that men are burdened 'with dangerous prescriptions
of manhood' (from *Stiffed*, quoted in Hoff Sommers, p. 148) and are consequently 'in agony' is subject to particular disparagement. Hence Hoff Sommers
appears to take a stand against the problematisation of boys, as expressed by
both 'poor boys' and 'problem boys' discourses.

Yet in other parts of the book she seems to go further in pathologising boys
than many of the authors she critiques. For example, she claims that boys 'need
to be educated and civilised. They need to be turned into respectful human
beings' (2000: 64). More than a 'poor boys' narrative, Hoff Sommers is clearly
articulating a 'problem boys' discourse (see below), her words implying that boys
are currently uneducated and uncivilised, and even not functioning as (respectful)
human beings! She maintains that there are problems with boys' morals, as well
as with their educational development, both of which need addressing with 'firm
discipline'. Having attacked feminists for problematising boys, Hoff Sommers
approvingly quotes Janet Daley of the *Daily Telegraph* newspaper who says,

> boys need far more discipline, structure and authority in their lives than do
> girls . . . Boys must be actively constrained by a whole phalanx of adults
> who come into contact with them – parents, teachers, neighbours, police-
> men, passers-by in the streets – before they can be expected to control their
> asocial, egoistic impulses.
>
> (Quoted in Hoff Sommers, 2000: 180–1)

If this is not problematising boys, it is hard to imagine what is! Here *all* boys
are sweepingly dehumanised as anti-social brutes in need of civilising and taming
by society's officials – the analogy that springs to mind is of beasts threatened by
whips in a circus tent. There is no recognition here of the vast mass of successful, amiable, socially competent, even sensitive boys that we experience everyday
in classrooms. Such positionings illustrate the emergence of a 'problem boys'
discourse which presents boys as dangerous threats to civilised society.

The 'boys will be boys' discourse is as popular as the 'poor boys' discourse in educational literature, probably because of its 'common sense' notions of boys i.e. such texts assume that we 'know' that boys are more slap-dash, noisy, demanding, and take-up more physical space than girls. The edited collection *Raising Boys' Achievements in Schools* (Bleach, 1998a) is largely based on this 'taken for granted' (i.e. boys will be boys) approach. A telling point of the 'boys will be boys' discourse is that it is theoretically devoid of any recognition of feminist literature. For example, in the introduction to the book which details gender interventionist strategies there is no recognition in the first 156 pages of two decades of feminist gender reforms. Then there are the appeals to 'natural' biological differences which are a core feature of the 'boys will be boys' discourse. Colin Noble argues:

> The anti-swot culture is not born of the ether. It has roots in the range of experiences boys go through which interplay with a genetic pre-disposition, the importance of which we can only guess.
>
> (Noble, 1998: 28)

It is important to note too that Noble's (1998), Hoff Sommers' (2000) and Faludi's (1999) production of the 'poor boys' discourse illustrates how particular discourses relating to gender can be produced by individuals of different political persuasions (here anti-feminist and feminist) to support different arguments.

The important point about the three discourses identified by Epstein *et al.* (1998) ('poor boys', 'boys will be boys', 'failing schools, failing boys') is that all of them perpetuate conventional conceptions of masculinity and education. To begin with in all three discourses educational *lack* of progress is seen as something which is a consequence of something extrinsic to boys, for example, the fault of poor teaching, an uninteresting or 'feminised' curriculum, unstimulating and/or 'feminised' management structures, whilst educational progress is something internally generated through boys' natural cleverness (Cohen, 1998; Mahony, 1998). Second, all three discourses fail to consider the social, cultural and economic contexts of academic success and educational underachievement (Raphael Reed, 1998; Lingard and Douglas, 1999). As has been shown from case study research into the educational experiences of working and middle-class girls and boys (Ball *et al.*, 2000; Reay, 2001a, 2002; Walkerdine *et al.*, 2001), ethnic minority groups (Sewell, 1997; Francis and Archer, 2005) as well as the OECD PISA data (see Chapter 4), the consideration of these factors is crucial in gaining insights into 'achievement' and 'underachievement'.

The emergence of new discourses on 'boys' underachievement'

Since 1998 when Epstein and her colleagues first noted the presence of three discourses around boys and schooling in the UK, trends in education have changed although the debate on boys' underachievement has continued

Table 3.1 Discourses on boys and schooling

Discourse	Theoretical basis	Premise	Characteristics
'Poor boys'	Men's rights	Boys have been victimised through feminist agendas.	(i) Boys lose out to girls at school and university. (ii) Suppression and control of 'boyness' by women generally because they do not understand how 'maleness' develops.
'Boys will be boys'	Evolutionary psychology	Psychological, as well as physical, masculinity is something males are born with.	(i) Competitive sports and target setting are needed as these respond to boys' learning needs. (ii) Boys have to be given status and recognition of their individuality as these are fundamental to the healthy development of the male psyche.
'Problem boys'	Individualisation	The 'laddish' culture of boys' peer groups.	Boys voluntarily adopt and enact anti-social and self-abusive behaviours.
'"At risk" boys'	Individualisation	Social exclusion: boys are disconnected from society.	(i) Low self-esteem. (ii) Disaffection, alienation from schooling and subsequent underachievement.

unabated. Although the 'poor boys' and 'boys will be boys' discourses remain prevalent, that of 'failing schools, failing boys' has slid into the background (see Table 3.1). As we said earlier, in the years since 1998 two further discourses on boys have come to the fore – that of the 'problem boy' and the ' "at risk" boy'. The growing significance of these discourses can be seen by comparing headlines in the professional papers at the beginning of the stirrings of concern with more current day versions. In 1994 boys' underachievement was measured against girls' achievements (as they still are) but at this point there was no attempt to pull together different elements of the boys' debate (i.e. whether achievement was in part affected by attitudes and behaviour), thus the following were representative of the headlines in the *Times Educational Supplement* (*TES*): 'Lapped by girls' *TES*, 14 July 1995; 'Stop giving boys wrong messages' *TES* 20 October 1995. More recent headlines see an added emphasis on badly behaved boys and their educational abilities and achievements, for example: 'Teachers mark down bad boys' *TES*, 26 March 2004; 'Naughty boys will fail if we trust teachers' *TES* 28 May 2002; 'Keep the bad boys busy' *TES*, 30 July 2004.

The various discourses on boys and schooling each have a theoretical underpinning which shapes how the 'problem' is seen and what strategies are devised to tackle it (see Table 3.1). In the case of the 'poor boys' discourse the theoretical basis stems from the 'men's rights' perspective which, as was discussed in Chapter 2, is a branch of masculinities theory which sees boys as a uniform group whose experiences of schooling and education are all exactly the same. As such, this perspective does not recognise the differences experienced by boys because of their diversity in terms of social class, ethnicity, culture, sexuality, religion or age. Because 'men's rights' advocates believe, as do evolutionary psychologists, that there is an *essential* nature to men then the predominance of female teachers, and indeed, single-parent (mother) families, tend to restrict or repress 'maleness'. Thus, boys have become the victims of feminist progress and the way forward to curb the downward slide of boys is to recognise, encourage and reward conventional manifestations of 'boyness' (hence those writing from the 'poor boys' and 'boys will be boys' perspectives recommend competitive sports and teaching pedagogies, and awarding boys positions of responsibility within school organisation and management practices).

The initial New Labour conceptions of 'how boys are', that is as 'problem boys' and/or ' "at risk" boys', were evident in educational policy documents in the late 1990s but were less to the fore than is now the case. At that time, government ministers paid greater attention in their comments to the manifestation of boys' underperformance in relation to girls (in that they failed to achieve the same levels), than discussing the potential causes. For example, the then Chief Schools Standards Minister, Stephen Byers spoke of 'the laddish anti-learning culture' of boys (Byers, 1998). Here references to 'laddishness' placed the responsibility for disinterest and underachievement in education, anti-social behaviours such as vandalism, drug and alcohol misuse, and general 'cheekiness' both in and outside schools, squarely at the feet of the boys themselves. As one of us (Francis 2000a: 95), pointed out:

> . . . the issue of 'boys' underachievement' has typically drawn on discourses of 'poor boys', which blames schools, teachers, feminists and/or teaching and examination practices for boys' underachievement compared with girls. Yet now blame was apparently being reassigned to boys themselves.

In 2003 educational policy documents suggested that greater attention was again being given to the potential underlying factors that the government feels explain the causes of boys' apparent disinterest and motivation in education, and their behaviour at school. Together, the anti-social, anti-schooling attitudes and behaviours of some boys and the idea that some boys take up these behaviours because they are vulnerable through feeling they do not or cannot fit in with others or at school, and so forth result in boys being seen as socially excluded.

To see how boys, as a group, are positioned as socially excluded requires some definition of what social exclusion actually means. The following is a list of characteristics drawn up to identify socially excluded people that appeared in a report published in 2000 by the Library and Information Commission:

- Experiencing or perceiving alienation
- Isolation
- Lack of identity
- Low self-confidence
- Low self-esteem
- Passivity
- Dependence
- Bewilderment
- Fear
- Anger
- Apathy
- Low aspirations
- Hopelessness.

Each of these descriptors has been used by writers in recent literature on boys and their attitudes, motivation for, and achievement in, schooling. This literature includes reports in daily newspapers and professional press for example the *Times Educational Supplement* and also books recommended by the DfES on their gender and achievement website such as Lucinda Neall's (2002) *Bringing the Best Out in Boys* and Kevan Bleach's (1998) *Raising Boys' Achievement*. Also, the literature which has been selected to illustrate the relationship between the language of social exclusion and boys and schooling is not the more academically informed literature on masculinities and schooling but the more popularist books aimed at parents as well as teachers. This literature provides 'commonsense approaches' to understanding and tackling boys and their educational experiences which seems to be more readily embraced in government agendas. The point here is that not all current publications outlining the issues related to boys and schooling and the strategies suggested for working with boys adopt the same position – however, those that are written from a 'men's rights' perspective are the ones that are informing current government policies. The following selected examples illustrate the way in which those characteristics identified with social exclusion are alluded to in the boys and schooling literature.

Experiencing or perceiving isolation
For many boys . . . it is not surprising that school comes to represent 'a system of hostile authority and meaningless work demands' (–). . . . Little exists to counter their alienation and so they seek refuge in a hegemonic masculinity . . .

(Bleach, 1998a: 12)

Low self-esteem and fear
Boys' self esteem as learners is far more fragile than that of most girls . . . boys resort to bravado to cover over the shame they would experience if they actually showed their fears about not messing up.

(Pollack, 1998: 238)

Passivity
Boys are now quieter than girls – that zest for life they once had barely produces a pulse nowadays.

(Mills quoted in Browne, 2004: 95)

Bewilderment
In my own experience, I often find boys expecting to be 'attacked for who they are' . . . Boys believe that teachers prefer girls, are more interested in girls, and think they are smarter. Yet boys are told that we live in a patriarchy in which men are unfairly in control of our country, our businesses and our schools . . .

(Hoff Sommers, 2000: 98)

Anger
So when they (boys) are upset or afraid they feel ashamed: sometimes the shame is buried deep and the boy gives the impression of being unaffected; sometimes the shame kindles anger which is self-directed and turns inward, possibly leading to depression; at other times the anger is outwardly expressed through kicking, fighting, shouting, destroying something or being rude.

(Neall, 2002: 85)

If boys, as a group, are being defined in educational discourses in the same terms as those associated with social exclusion then where does this lead us? In particular, what is the thinking underpinning New Labour policy initiatives and interventions into boys' underachievement? As has been said, a cornerstone of Third Way political agendas is the issue of inequality and, as Giddens (1998: 102) indicates 'the new politics characterises equality as *inclusion* and inequality as *exclusion*'. A problem, however, for the New Labour government is that Third Way theorists have the ideology worked out but the suggestions for how to achieve these are rather broad and too woolly to be easily translated into practical initiatives (Leigh, 2003). So, a key term associated with social inclusion/exclusion, that is, 'self-esteem' has provided the basis for the development of practical strategies and initiatives in the workplace, and in the education and welfare systems and so forth.

As several writers have suggested, the focus on individuals' feelings of self-esteem is part of a 'therapeutic ethos' that allows governments to bond with an increasingly fragmented public (Nolan, 1998; Furedi, 2004; Ecclestone, 2004a; 2004b; 2005). In relation to education, a concern for people's feelings and their self-esteem is evident in, if not fundamental to, the educational rationales of a growing number of initiatives such as schemes to encourage non-traditional entrants to higher education and personal mentoring programmes for disaffected, 'hard to reach' young people (Ecclestone, 2004a). However, this policy approach assumes that any educational strategy that promotes high self-esteem is a 'good thing' but as Kathryn Ecclestone (2004a; 2004b; 2005) indicates in a series of articles on the increasing investment of the British and other Western governments in therapeutic approaches, this fails to take into account the lack of theoretical clarity in the concept and lack of conclusive evidence for its effects on life opportunities and experiences. Yet, despite this, the notion of self-esteem has a central place in the government drives to improve boys' underachievement and Chapter 7 considers the implications of these in order to ascertain what kind of boys are anticipated to emerge as a result of these pedagogical approaches. For now, we want to concentrate on how a therapeutic ethos, as constituted within New Labour political agendas, shifts attention to the emotional and psychic well-being of boys and in such ways that suggest boys need to be made 'better' because they are currently 'unwell'. That is, school boys are not physically but psychologically 'ill' in that their *feelings* about themselves as boys are manifested in vulnerable/aggressive (social/self-harming) behaviours.

The medicalisation of school boys

The two educational discourses 'problem boys' and '"at risk" boys' locates them as both victims and threats to others. 'Problem boys' are a threat *to* society: '"at risk" boys' are made vulnerable *by* society when it fails to tackle (traditional) forms of masculinity. Put simply, trying to be a boy in today's society places them under a great deal of pressure to act in particular ways and in so doing creates psychological struggles and tensions – that is, it makes them 'ill'. The idea of 'illness' is used here in accordance with Furedi's (2004) description of the medicalisation of everyday life. That is, those things which were once just accepted as part of the human experience from birth, marriages and deaths to everyday emotions become seen as psychologically damaging making people mentally distressed and ill. As such these psychic and social hazards are seen as requiring professional support and guidance. For example, to help with the birth of a child there are parenting classes; to assist with emotional problems with a husband, wife or live in partner there are relationship counsellors. In the same way, what were once seen as aspects of individual personalities or larger social problems are given medical labels – for example, lack of self-confidence is described as 'social phobia'; violence against women is referred to as 'battered women's syndrome'; sexual predators are regarded as 'sex addicts', and people with short attention spans may be described as suffering from 'attention deficit disorder' (where 'phobia', 'syndrome', 'addiction' and 'disorder' are all medical terms). Certainly attention has been drawn by the media to an increase in the use of prescribed drugs to treat such disorders as hyperactivity/attention deficit disorders.

This 'medicalisation' of being a schoolboy is most clearly illustrated in the government's 2003 document, the *Using the National Healthy School Standard to Raise Boys' Achievement*. The National Healthy School Standard was published in 1999 and its aim is to provide both a physical and social environment that is conducive to learning. The image of a boy produced in this booklet is one where there is tension for boys between an inner, caring, vulnerable person which is competing with the outward manifestation expected of a boy – a 'laddish boy'. Thus this image brings together both the 'problem boys' and ' "at risk" boys' discourses. As such the strategies recommended to schools are those which take on this particular and specific idea of what 'being a boy' is all about. For example:

> Highly competitive or 'macho' departments tend to confirm many boys' suspicions of what being a man is all about, and will do little to help create a caring masculinity.
>
> (*Using the National Healthy School Standard to Raise Boys' Achievement*, 2003: 35)

> . . . school assemblies and tutorial time are used to address issues related to developing a 'caring masculinity' (exemplified by sensitivity and consideration . . .) (talk about) the way they need to reject violence, talk out aggression and openly express feelings without fear of embarrassment. In this way a culture is being developed that enables a boy to be himself, rather than having to live up to a tough male stereotype.
>
> (*Using the National Healthy School Standard to Raise Boys' Achievement*, 2003: 14)

Both quotations refer to a 'caring masculinity' so we might infer that this is New Labour's 'new man' and the model they anticipate boys will aspire to. We discuss the notion further in Chapter 7, which explores the construction of the 'ideal pupil' (and 'ideal boy') emerging in the education literature. Presumably one consequence of a 'caring masculinity' would be that boys' academic performance improved because they 'cared' about doing well. Or perhaps they might cease any disruptive behaviour because they 'cared' about the needs of their classmates and teacher. But as the implication is never spelt out, we can only speculate.

Conclusions

The policies of various countries in the Western world on gender in relation to education show both similarities and disparities. Back in the 1970s the feminist movement impacted upon state policy in the USA, Canada, Australia and the UK (see for example, Sex Discrimination Act, 1975; Title IX of the 1972 Education Amendments) and, to greater and lesser extents, influenced girls' educational opportunities. It is fair to say that at the time of second wave feminism during the 1970s and the subsequent policies effecting girls' educational achievement that these were enacted on the basis of social justice. Within a few years the national and international context had shifted and the move towards a globalised economy and the concomitant shift towards individualisation has encouraged countries in the Western world to place greater emphasis on 'standards' and 'achievement'. And these were to be judged on the basis of tests and various other forms of measurement. Thus the recent emergence of 'boys' as the 'newly disadvantaged' in education has taken place in a very different climate from that surrounding girls' education and schooling in the 1970s. Today, nation states are concerned that they are going to lose out on a pool of potential participants in the global market-place – and feminists would add that of equal, if not more, concern to governments is the fact that this pool is one which has traditionally been the (male) leaders, entrepreneurs, business executives, politicians and lawyers of a nation state and their potential absence rocks their very foundation.

The questions this chapter raises are, first, given the drive in countries across the Western world to address the gender gap in performance, what are the differences between the achievements of boys and girls? Second, what is the likely future for boys and girls in our schools given current policies which regard boys as a group 'socially excluded' and, by definition, 'psychically ill'? These will form the basis for consideration in the following chapters.

Chapter 4

Evaluating 'boys' underachievement'

As we spend a considerable amount of time throughout this book talking about boys' underachievement it might seem unnecessary to then devote a specific chapter to the subject. However, the reason for doing so is to allow us to directly ask and answer the question 'are boys underachieving?' We have shown at various points how debates and discussions about boys' underachievement pervade government and media discourses, and how the topic has inspired interest, concern and critique amongst educationalists, reporters and pro/feminist academics. What we do in this chapter is scrutinise the information that has been used to spark off the 'crisis of boys and schooling' debate and assess what the valid and invalid arguments are. To do this the first section will look at data from national and international studies of pupil achievement. Here it will be shown that despite the widespread contention that *all* boys are underachieving in *all* subjects, many boys in the UK are, in fact, doing well in examinations.[1] At the same time, large cohorts of boys in the UK – and indeed across the world – are failing to acquire necessary language and literacy skills and that this is one area that requires the attention of policy-makers and educationalists.

The second section examines the statistical case for boys' underachievement. Certainly in the UK the government has underpinned its efforts to raise awareness in schools about the underachievement of boys by repeatedly pointing out the statistical differences in the performance of boys and girls in public examinations. We will begin by setting out what precisely we know about boys from their performance in public examinations.

Gender and achievement in examinations

The intention in this discussion of gender and achievement in public examinations is to focus on the performance of boys and girls in England. Where, and as, appropriate we will make reference to the situation in other countries in order to draw attention to those particular factors that affect pupils' achievement in England. We want to begin by looking at the data produced by the DfES and published on its 'Gender and Achievement' website. We are aware that how the statistics we refer to in this section have been arrived at and subsequently 'read' have been open to significant criticism (see detailed discussion in Connolly, 2004) but our purpose here is to survey the information in the form that it is made available by government agencies to teachers and parents. The following three tables show boys' and girls' performance at ages 11 years (Key Stage 2), 14 years (Key Stage 3) and 16 years (GCSE/GNVQ). We have added our own table drawn from DfES figures to illustrate specific performance at 16 (Key Stage 4) in mathematics, science and English for 2003.

The commentary accompanying Tables 4.1–4.3 on the gender and achievement website and reproduced below clearly notes that boys are underachieving in English.

The key trends to emerge are:

• Girls progress more than boys on average in English throughout school.
• At Key Stage 2, the difference between boys' and girls' attainment (of the expected level) in English is 11 percentage points, but at Key Stage 3, this difference increases to 14 percentage points.

Table 4.1 Key Stage 2: analysis of performance in SATs by gender (2001–3)

| | Percentage of pupils who achieved level 4 or above at Key Stage 2 | | | Percentage of pupils who achieved level 5 or above at Key Stage 2 | | |
	English	*Mathematics*	*Science*	*English*	*Mathematics*	*Science*
Boys in 2003	70	73	86	21	32	40
Boys in 2002	70	73	86	24	29	38
Boys in 2001	70	71	87	22	26	34
Girls in 2003	81	72	87	33	26	41
Girls in 2002	79	73	87	34	25	37
Girls in 2001	80	70	88	35	23	33

Source: standards.dfes.gov.uk/genderandachievement/understanding/analysis/

Table 4.2 Key Stage 3: analysis of performance in SATs by gender (2001–3)

| | Percentage of pupils who achieved level 5 or above at Key Stage 3 | | | Percentage of pupils who achieved level 6 or above at Key Stage 3 | | |
	English	*Mathematics*	*Science*	*English*	*Mathematics*	*Science*
Boys in 2002–3	62	70	68	28	49	41
Boys in 2001–2	59	67	67	25	45	34
Girls in 2002–3	76	72	69	42	50	40
Girls in 2001–2	76	68	67	41	45	32

Source: standards.dfes.gov.uk/genderandachievement/understanding/analysis

Table 4.3 Analysis of GCSE/GNVQ results by gender (2000–3)

| | Percentage who achieved at GCSE/GNVQ | | Percentage who achieved at GCSE/GNVQ | | |
	5 + A*–C	5 + A*–G	1 + A*–C	1 + A*–G	No passes
Boys in 2002–3	47.9	86.6	70.7	93.7	6.3
Boys in 2001–2	46.4	86.9	70.4	93.6	6.4
Boys in 2000–1	44.8	86.9	69.1	93.5	6.5
Girls in 2002–3	58.2	91	80.7	95.9	4.1
Girls in 2001–2	57	91.1	80.2	95.7	4.3
Girls in 2000–1	55.4	91	79.2	95.6	4.4

Source: DfES, 2004: standards.dfes.gov.uk/genderandachievement/understanding/analysis/

Table 4.4 GCSE results in mathematics, science and English by gender (2003, England)

| | % Achieved grades A*–C | | |
	All pupils	Boys	Girls
English	60	52	68
Mathematics	51	50	52
Any science	52	52	53

Source: Information for table obtained from DfES '2003 GCSE/GNVQ National Summary Results'

- Girls progress more than boys in mathematics and science, although the differences are smaller than those in English.
- At GCSE/GNVQ, girls continue to progress more than boys. The difference between boys' and girls' attainment (5 + A*–C) at GCSE/GNVQ is as much as 10 percentage points.

> (Source: DfES, 2004: standards.dfes.gov.uk/
> genderandachievement/understanding/analysis/)

However, a point they do not make but which is also clear is that the gender differences in mathematics and science are extremely slight (indeed, where the DfES tables tend to focus on percentages around grades awarded, an exploration of their data shows that more boys than girls were *entered* for GCSEs in science and mathematics in 2003).

In concentrating the discussion simply on the differences between girls and boys overlooks how the interrelationship of ethnicity and social class with gender impacts upon achievement. When examining a detailed breakdown of the Key Stage exams by ethnicity it is clear that not all boys are underperforming and not all girls are successful. Key Stage 1 results in reading, writing and mathematics

Table 4.5 Achievements at Key Stage 1 level 2 and above in 2003, by ethnicity and gender

| Key Stage 1 | Mathematics | | | | | |
| | Eligible pupils | | | % Achieving | | |
	Boys	Girls	Total	Boys	Girls	Total
White	238,822	226,793	465,615	90	92	91
White British	230,868	219,473	450,341	90	92	91
Irish	1,168	996	2,164	89	93	91
Traveller of Irish heritage	187	183	370	48	56	52
Gypsy/Roma	355	356	711	62	58	60
Any other White background	6,244	5,785	12,029	88	89	89
Mixed	9,299	8,863	18,162	90	92	91
White and Black Caribbean	3,238	3,209	6,447	88	92	90
White and Black African	859	857	1,716	91	90	90
White and Asian	1,893	1,748	3,641	92	94	93
Any other mixed background	3,309	3,049	6,358	90	91	91
Asian	20,244	19,377	39,621	85	87	86
Indian	6,253	5,906	12,159	91	93	92
Pakistani	8,525	8,186	16,711	81	84	83
Bangladeshi	3,528	3,506	7,034	83	83	83
Any other Asian background	1,938	1,779	3,717	88	91	89
Black	10,870	10,416	21,286	82	85	84
Black Caribbean	4,072	4,003	8,075	82	87	84
Black African	5,616	5,282	10,898	81	84	83
Any other Black background	1,182	1,131	2,313	85	86	86
Chinese	852	907	1,759	95	96	96
Any other ethnic group	2,545	2,364	4,909	85	86	85
Unclassified[1]	9,998	9,358	19,356	84	87	85
All pupils	292,630	278,078	570,708	89	91	90

Source: National Curriculum Assessment and GCSE/GNVQ Attainment by Pupil Characteristics in England (DfES 2002 (final) and DfES 2003 (provisional)(http://www.dfes.gov.uk/rsgateway/DB/SFR/S000448))

Note:
1 Includes information refused or not obtained.

show that the highest overall performers in each of the tests are Chinese girls followed by mixed race (White and Asian) girls (see Table 4.5 below and Appendix 1). The highest overall achievers amongst the boys are Chinese boys also closely followed by mixed-race (White and Asian) boys. Certainly in terms of reading and writing, girls are doing better than boys generally but this does not mean that there are not boys who are successful or girls that are failing. For example, we can see from Table 4.5 that Chinese, mixed-race and Indian boys particularly perform better than many groups of girls.

Mathematics is traditionally a 'male' subject and as we have already seen, the DfES state that girls progress better than boys. However, we want to emphasise that the gender differences here too are marginal. The statistics of achievement at Key Stage 1 across ethnic groups indicates the diversity of achievement. Again Chinese girls and boys score the highest (96 per cent and 95 per cent respectively) followed by Chinese boys (95 per cent), then mixed-race (White and Asian) girls (94 per cent), Irish and Indian girls (93 per cent), and in joint place, White and Black Caribbean girls, mixed-race (White and Asian) boys and White British girls (92 per cent).

Tables of achievement at Key Stages 2 and 3 and GCSE/GNVQ by gender and ethnicity are reproduced in Appendix 1 and readers should look at these to note the pattern across the years of compulsory schooling. One significant point to observe is that percentage scores decrease for the majority of both boys and girls irrespective of ethnic group at each stage of the tests. It is interesting to note that the DfES do not make any comments on this in their reporting of the statistics! For example, Chinese girls scored 93 per cent for reading and writing at Key Stage 1; their grade is 87 per cent for English at Key Stage 2 and has gone down to 86 per cent at Key Stage 3. The drop is even more spectacular for some of those located in the 'mid-range' – mixed-race (White and Black African) boys achieved 91 per cent in mathematics at Key Stage 1. In Key Stage 2 tests their score was 72 per cent and at Key Stage 3 it was 63 per cent. However, some of the achievements of both boys and girls did appear to increase but only amongst those who were underperforming the most and it might be that the positive reading was just a 'blip'. The lowest achieving boys and girls in reading, writing and mathematics at Key Stage 1 are travelling children and those from Gypsy/ Roma backgrounds. They are also the lowest achieving pupils at Key Stage 3. While the scores of Gypsy/Roma children show the same downward pattern as other ethnic groups the achievements of traveller children of Irish heritage indicate a drop from Key Stage 1 to Key Stage 2 but an increase in reading at Key Stage 3 and a return to around the same grades in mathematics as when they started school.

Socio-economic class is another factor that we know impacts upon achievement in exams (Sammons, 1995; Tinklin, 2003; Connolly, 2004). As we will see when we look at the findings detailed in the OECD Report (2003) the impact of socio-economic status on academic success is a particular feature of the UK rather than being a universal feature. The effect of socio-economic factors on pupil achievement is judged by relating examination success to children who take free school meals (FSM). The information provided in Table 4.6 below adds support to the argument that the more socially and economically disadvant-aged the pupils, the less well they do in examinations. What also appears to be the case from these statistics is that the gender gap is wider amongst the less advantaged pupils in literary subjects but is roughly the same for mathematics and science as for those not taking FSM. The percentage point gap between girls and boys in reading at Key Stage 1 who are not taking FSM is 7 per cent

Table 4.6 Achievements at Key Stage I level 2 and above by FSM and gender

| Key Stage I | Reading | | | | | |
| | Eligible pupils | | | % Achieving | | |
	Boys	Girls	Total	Boys	Girls	Total
Non FSM	239,104	226,544	465,648	84	91	88
FSM	52,395	50,398	102,793	63	75	69
Unclassified	1,127	1,131	2,258	45	56	51
All pupils	292,626	278,073	570,699	80	88	84

| Key Stage I | Writing | | | | | |
| | Eligible pupils | | | % Achieving | | |
	Boys	Girls	Total	Boys	Girls	Total
Non FSM	239,109	226,548	465,657	80	90	85
FSM	52,395	50,399	102,794	57	72	64
Unclassified	1,127	1,131	2,258	39	54	46
All pupils	292,631	278,078	570,709	76	86	81

| Key Stage I | Mathematics | | | | | |
| | Eligible pupils | | | % Achieving | | |
	Boys	Girls	Total	Boys	Girls	Total
Non FSM	239,108	226,548	465,656	92	94	93
FSM	52,395	50,399	102,794	79	82	80
Unclassified	1,127	1,131	2,258	59	64	62
All pupils	292,630	278,078	570,708	89	91	90

Source: National Curriculum Assessment and GCSE/GNVQ Attainment by Pupil Characteristics, in England, (DfES 2002 (final) and DfES 2003 provisional) (http://www.dfes.gov.uk/rsgateway/DB/SFR/S000448)

but rises to 12 per cent amongst those who take FSM. By Key Stage 3 the gender gap in English is 13 per cent for non FSM pupils compared to 16 per cent for those taking FSM (see Appendix 2). When comparing the results reported in Table 4.6 above to those in Table 4.5 we can see that the perform-ance figures for boys and girls receiving FSM are lower than those produced by all the noted ethnic groups apart from travellers and Gypsy/Roma which demonstrates the huge impact of social class on educational performance in

Table 4.7 Examples of GCE A level examination results of 17-year-old students in all schools and colleges by subject, gender and grade in 2002–3 (for full table see Appendix 3)

								Revised figures	
17-year-olds[1]	*Males*								
	Grade obtained								
	A	*B*	*C*	*D*	*E*	*U*	*Other grades*	*A–E (%)*	*Total entries*
Biological sciences	2,990	2,943	3,073	2,746	2,225	1,063	14	92.8	15,054
Chemistry	3,698	3,150	2,519	1,938	1,351	567	16	95.6	13,239
Physics	4,867	3,754	3,393	3,020	2,208	1,001	10	94.5	18,253
Mathematics	10,347	5,425	4,465	3,372	2,338	1,235	61	95.2	27,238
English	4,510	5,403	6,288	4,566	1,885	313	58	98.4	23,023
Art & Design	2,063	1,959	2,118	1,731	959	376	26	95.6	9,232

17-year-olds[1]	*Females*								
	Grade obtained								
	A	*B*	*C*	*D*	*E*	*U*	*Other grades*	*A–E (%)*	*Total entries*
Biological sciences	5,760	5,375	4,966	4,082	2,952	1,158	27	95.1	24,320
Chemistry	4,444	3,611	2,670	1,843	1,140	379	15	97.2	14,102
Physics	1,682	1,231	951	692	481	163	*	96.8	5,202
Mathematics	6,388	3,544	2,481	1,804	952	454	29	96.9	15,652
English	10,873	14,605	15,706	10,799	3,587	483	65	99	56,118
Art & Design	6,499	5,294	4,873	3,062	1,360	401	52	97.9	21,541

Source: National Statistics, First Release SFR 01/2004 (DfES 14 January 2004)

Note:
1 Age at the start of the 2002–3 academic year i.e. 31 August 2002.

England. Further tables of achievements at Key Stage 2, 3 and GCSE/GNVQ of pupils receiving FSM are provided in Appendix 2 and here again we can see the downward progression in scores as pupils move through the age range.

So far we have seen that although girls generally are doing better than boys in literacy other factors such as ethnicity and social class have a strong influence and, therefore, making generalisations about boys and girls can mask much more fundamental factors that have a negative impact on achievement. The fact that pupils' scores appear to decline progressively as they pass through schooling irrespective of gender, ethnicity and social class would seem to be a major cause for concern. Before exploring such differences in any more detail we should note what the patterns are once pupils' interests determine the subjects they choose to study.

Examining gender and achievement at A Level, there is a substantial differ-ence in the number of females entered for A levels (325,659 of those aged 17

Table 4.8 Percentages of 17-year-old students in all schools and colleges entered gaining 'A' grades and 'Ungraded' results for GCE A level, by gender, 2002–3

	Females		Males	
	A	U	A	U
Biology	24%	5%	20%	7%
Chemistry	32%	3%	28%	4%
Physics	32%	3%	27%	5%
Mathematics	41%	3%	38%	5%
English	19%	1%	20%	1%
Art & Design	30%	2%	22%	4%

Source: Secondary analysis of data supplied by National Statistics, First Release SFR 01/2004 (DfES January 2004)

at the beginning of the academic year) and the number of males entered (273,466). The figures indicate that of *those taking up* the A level exams, 97 per cent of girls achieved an A level (grades A–E) in contrast to 96 per cent of boys; a very comparable performance.

Traditional gender subject choice continues to be strikingly apparent with vastly more boys taking A levels in mathematics and physics (though interestingly, no longer in chemistry), and girls more often taking language, art and social science subjects (with the exception of economics). These gendered choices have consequences for the type of career that students are able to pursue (Thomas, 1990; Francis, 2002; DTI, 2004; EOC, 2004). More than twice as many girls as boys take English A level, but the number of male entrants seems large considering the extent to which boys' underperformance at English in compulsory education might be expected to deter them.

As we can see from Table 4.8, the statistics tell us that, regardless of whether the subject is a traditional 'masculine' subject such as physics or a 'feminine' subject such as biology, the trend among those entered is for proportionately more girls to obtain the qualification and be successful in gaining the highest grades. There is an argument that says when girls opt for non-traditional subjects like mathematics and science they do well because 'they tend to be particularly bright and, therefore, do well, as well as being highly motivated' (Gipps and Murphy, 1994: 243). The A level results depicted in Table 4.8 support this, with fewer females entered at mathematics and physics but those entered doing proportionately better than their male counterparts. However, this pattern does not seem to be borne out for males, as the fewer males entered equal female performance for English, but are outperformed by females at other traditionally feminine subjects such as biology and art. However, before moving the discussion on to examine the complexities of making sense of the statistical data on examination performance it is worthwhile looking at the choices and results of those who go into higher education.

Table 4.9 Qualifications obtained by students on HE courses in the UK by gender and subject area

| | First degree | | | |
| | 2002 | | 2003 | |
	Female	Male	Female	Male
Medicine and dentistry	3.3	2.8	3.3	2.8
Subjects allied to medicine	16.8	4.1	18.1	4.2
Biological sciences	11.6	6.6	15.2	8.0
Veterinary science	0.4	0.2	0.4	0.1
Agriculture and related subjects	1.4	1.0	1.3	0.8
Physical sciences	4.9	7.3	5.2	6.9
Mathematical sciences	1.6	2.4	2.1	2.9
Computer science	3.0	10.8	4.2	13.4
Engineering and technology	3.0	16.8	3.1	15.7
Architecture, building and planning	1.7	4.5	1.8	4.5
Total science	47.8	56.4	54.6	59.4
Social, economic and political studies	13.3	8.5	14.7	9.9
Law	6.2	3.7	7.2	4.2
Business and administrative studies	18.0	14.6	21.2	17.5
Librarianship and information science	3.3	2.0	4.6	2.6
Languages	11.5	4.0	14.6	5.2
Humanities	5.4	4.4	7.4	5.7
Creative arts and design	14.1	8.9	16.0	10.1
Education	9.6	2.9	7.5	1.8
Combined	19.2	13.4	5.4	3.9
All subjects	148.2	118.8	153.1	120.3

Source: Information derived from HESA/JACS, 2004

(Appendix 4 contains two tables which provide further information: 'HE qualifications obtained in the UK by mode of study, domicile, gender and subject area 2001–2' and 'Qualifications obtained by and examination results of higher education students at higher education institutions in the United Kingdom for the academic year 2002–3' (HESA, 2004).)

If we focus exclusively on the statistics provided above we can see that a majority of pupils in UK schools are reaching the prescribed levels in mathematics, science and English. We can also see that boys and girls are performing roughly equally at mathematics and science, with minor yearly fluctuations, although girls make progress far more rapidly in English. When the element of choice in what subjects to study is introduced at GCSE/GNVQ and A level then traditional stereotypical subject preferences are evident.

The advantages of females at school now appear to be making their way into higher education. Female home students form the majority of graduates with first degrees although they have yet to catch up with men when it comes to gaining higher degree qualifications. Researchers have observed that men obtain more first class, third class and unclassified degrees than women (Francis, Robson and

Read, 2001). As can be seen (from the table in Appendix 4) substantially more women than men gain second class (particularly 'upper second') degrees, although in terms of the (smaller) proportion of men undertaking undergraduate study men are only slightly less likely to obtain a second class degree than are women.

It is important to note here that whilst women undergraduates outnumber males and tend to graduate with better degrees the institution they choose to study in can affect the ways in which they are expected to present their assessed work. Moreover, research suggests that university culture continues to elevate masculine values (Harding, 1991; Martin, 1997; Hey, 2003). For example, the style of essay expected at first class level – one which is assertive, intrepid, confident and argumentative (Martin, 1997) is a style associated with masculine approaches to essay writing and one which is likely to be more highly rewarded in the academy (Francis *et al.*, 2003), possibly especially at traditional 'elite' institutions, such as Oxbridge (Martin, 1997). Francis *et al.* (2001) found that the writing of men and women undergraduates shows more similarity than difference, but that men do tend to use more 'bold' or assertive sentences in their essays than do women, and that these, where qualified/supported with references according to academic convention, may fit the (gendered) criteria for a first class award (Martin, 1997). Yet such 'bold' statements, where unsupported/unqualified may be particularly penalised due to the break with academic convention, and hence may make such male undergraduates more likely to be awarded lower grades, thus helping to explain the gendered patterns of degree award. In spending time talking about the possible reasons why female graduates at Oxbridge do not receive the proportionate number of first class degrees obtained by their female counterparts in other universities, may appear to be somewhat avaricious on our part given that they are increasingly successful at university. And also, we have not given similar considerations to why males are more likely to get third class degrees in any institution let alone at Oxbridge. The reason for doing so is to highlight a point we wish to raise in Chapter 5; that is, the gendered, situated nature of academic values and assessment processes. The relationship between anomalies in gender and achievement patterns at Oxford and Cambridge and their different assessment methods illustrates how different approaches to assessment can produce different results. For now, we want to continue the examination of where gender differences emerge in achievement and choices in the higher education sector.

Both male and female undergraduates opt for degrees that will enable them to enter the professions but there are gender differences in their choices of programmes to study. As can be seen in Appendix 4 amongst the most popular courses for females are those in subjects allied to medicine (such as nursing and physiotherapy) and education, although business and administrative studies intercepts these. For men, business and administrative studies is the most favoured subject at degree level followed by the traditional male preferred areas of engineering and technology, and computer science. The most difficult places to secure at university are those in medicine and veterinary science. In both cases females obtain more degrees in these subjects (in medicine 4.9 per cent of women and 4.3 per cent of men; in veterinary science, 0.5 per cent of women and 0.2 per cent of men (HESA, 2005)).

While the information on males and females in higher education demonstrates a marked shift towards increased achievement by women it remains to be seen when and if this feeds through into the labour market. The figures used here are based on information relating to the graduation class of 2003. Yet statistics produced by the Equal Opportunities Commission for the same year show that female employees working full time earned on average 18.8 per cent less than the average hourly earnings of male full time employees (EOC, 2003). Reports show how occupational segregation (where men enter traditionally masculine occupations and women feminine occupations, guided of course by their different subject choices in compulsory and then post-compulsory education) leads to pay inequalities between men and women, and also to skills gaps in particular areas of work (Rees, 1999; EOC, 2004; Miller et al., 2004). And these different career trajectories and resulting inequalities are of course closely linked to the different choices young men and women make in their pursuit of different subject areas in post-compulsory education and training (EOC, 2004).

What we have shown here in this section is how, based on the stark information made available to the public, females are outperforming males across all sectors of education. At the same time, there is only one area where there is a very evident and worrying gender gap and that is in the area of literacy and English. Furthermore, there is one feature of this general use of statistical evidence to illustrate the gender gap in pupil performance which should have attention drawn to it – that is, the way in which it considers only those boys and girls who are successful. The discussions always centre on, say, the gender gap between boys and girls achieving level 4 at Key Stage 2 SATs or the outperformance of girls gaining five A*–C GCSE/GNVQ. Little or no attention is given to gender gaps in terms of those boys and girls who just pass or who opt out of GCSE/GNVQ and A level. Chapter 5 will look in detail at some of the various explanations for these gender differences in performance and particularly boys' underachievement. However, here we have concentrated on the achievements of pupils in UK schools and to understand the cultural context of these more fully we need to look at them from a global perspective. To do this we will consider the findings of the OECD PISA Report 2003.

Gender and achievement in the UK – findings of the OECD PISA Report 2003

PISA is an internationally standardised assessment in reading, mathematics and scientific literacy which is administered to 15-year-olds in schools in participating countries. The survey takes place every three years and for the purposes of the 2000 assessment (which will be discussed here) 43 countries were involved with 4,500 to 5,000 pupils in each country taking part in the tests.

As is evident from the findings of the report, the marginal gender gap in mathematics and science we see here in the UK is *not* a global phenomenon. This points to the significance of cultural, social and economic contexts in the achievement profiles of different countries.

There are two significant factors to emerge from our consideration of the UK statistics on gender and achievement:

- Boys' underperformance in literacy skills
- The underachievement of pupils from lower socio-economic backgrounds (i.e. those on FSM).

The findings of the PISA assessment showed that boys' underachievement in literacy is an international problem. The average better performance of females in reading is 32 points – in the UK the gap is smaller with females 26 points ahead in literacy.

A breakdown of the reading literacy assessment into retrieving information, interpreting texts, and reflection and evaluation shows that boys, internationally, are at their weakest on the reflection and evaluation scale. This part of the reading literacy assessment is where pupils have to relate a text to their personal experience, knowledge and ideas. The OECD report speculates that these findings may be associated with the types of reading materials that males and females are presented with or that which they tend to favour. For example, male pupils who took part in the assessment made much greater use of comics, newspapers and website pages than females. Also, males were less likely to say that they had an interest in reading with about a half of them declaring they read only when they had to. One of the findings of the PISA assessment data, in keeping with a significant amount of other research studies of reading, is that there is a close relationship between the interest pupils have in a subject and how successful they are at it (Millard, 1997; Maynard, 2002; Rowan, *et al.*, 2002; Marsh, 2003). Thus, 'the different habits and interests of females and males may have far-reaching consequences for learning that educational policy needs to address' (OECD Report, 2003).

What is good news for the UK is that teachers and parents must be doing something right in terms of getting boys engaged with reading. In fact, the OECD PISA Report (2003) notes that in comparison with other countries, pupils in UK schools do rather well and the gender gap is relatively small:

> In reading literacy . . . the United Kingdom achieves both high average scores and limited gender differences. In mathematical literacy . . . the United Kingdom achieves both high average performance and small gender differences.
> (OECD PISA Report, 2003)

The same situation applies to pupils' reading literacy in Korea, Ireland and Japan. However, whilst in the UK there are no variations in gender differences between the other subjects examined in the PISA research (that is, where girls do very well at some subjects and boys very well at other subjects), in Korea,

Table 4.10 OECD PISA Report 2003 (Executive summary: home different results by gender, p. 1 of 2)

A *Reading literacy: females do better in all countries*		B *Mathematics: males do better in half of the countries (in other countries, no statistically significant difference)*	
Females		Austria	27
at least half a proficiency level ahead		Brazil	27
Latvia	53	Korea	27
Finland	51	Portugal	19
New Zealand	46	Spain	18
Norway	43	Luxembourg	15
Iceland	40	Denmark	15
Russian Fed.	38	Germany	15
Italy	38	Switzerland	14
Czech Republic	37	France	14
Greece	37	Ireland	13
Sweden	37	Liechtenstein	12
Poland	36	Czech Republic	12
		Norway	11
Females		Canada	10
less than half a proficiency level ahead			
Germany	35		
Australia	34		
Belgium	33	C *Science: females do better in three countries*	
Canada	32		
Hungary	32		
Liechtenstein	31	Latvia	23
Switzerland	30	Russian Fed.	14
Japan	30	New Zealand	12
Netherlands	30		
France	29		
Ireland	29		
United States	29	C *Science: males do better in three countries*	
Luxembourg	27		
Austria	26		
United Kingdom	26		
Denmark	25	Korea	19
Portugal	25	Austria	12
Spain	24	Denmark	12
Mexico	20		
Brazil	17		
Korea	14		

(Columns A and B labelled: Average score advantage (points) females *and* Average score advantage (points) males; *Science tables labelled* Average score advantage (points), females *and* Average score advantage (points), males*)*

Source: http://www.pisa.oecd.org/dataoeed/1/60/34002216.pdf

which has the lowest gender differences in literacy, boys are 27 points ahead of girls in mathematics. This information is noteworthy on two counts: first, because gender differences do not vary according to subjects other than literacy in the UK it suggests that the learning experiences of pupils are similar; that is, in those countries, such as Korea, where boys do better at mathematics and science and

Table 4.11 Pupil performance on the retrieving information, interpreting texts, and reflection and evaluation scales by gender

	Retrieving information						Interpreting texts						Reflection and evaluation					
	Males		Females		Difference[1]		Males		Females		Difference[1]		Males		Females		Difference	
	Mean score	S.E.	Mean score	S.E.	Score dif.	S.E.	Mean score	S.E.	Mean score	S.E.	Score dif.	S.E.	Mean score	S.E.	Mean score	S.E.	Score dif.	S.E.
Australia	523	(4.3)	551	(5.0)	−28	(5.7)	511	(4.1)	545	(4.9)	−34	(5.7)	507	(4.0)	548	(4.7)	−42	(5.5)
Austria	495	(3.3)	510	(3.6)	−16	(5.4)	497	(3.1)	520	(3.8)	−23	(5.3)	493	(3.5)	532	(3.8)	−39	(5.5)
Belgium	504	(4.7)	529	(5.4)	−25	(6.6)	498	(3.9)	529	(4.7)	−31	(6.1)	475	(5.2)	522	(5.3)	−47	(6.4)
Canada	519	(1.9)	543	(1.8)	−25	(1.8)	518	(1.8)	547	(1.7)	−29	(1.6)	521	(1.8)	566	(1.7)	−45	(1.3)
Czech Republic	467	(4.7)	495	(2.8)	−27	(5.4)	483	(4.1)	517	(2.6)	−34	(4.6)	457	(4.3)	511	(2.6)	−54	(4.5)
Denmark	491	(3.4)	506	(3.2)	−14	(3.5)	485	(3.1)	506	(2.9)	−21	(3.4)	480	(3.2)	523	(3.3)	−43	(3.6)
Finland	534	(3.4)	578	(3.1)	−44	(3.4)	529	(3.3)	579	(3.2)	−51	(3.1)	501	(3.0)	564	(3.1)	−63	(2.8)
France	503	(3.8)	527	(3.0)	−23	(3.6)	492	(3.5)	519	(2.7)	−27	(3.3)	477	(3.7)	515	(2.9)	−39	(3.9)
Germany	471	(3.0)	497	(4.0)	−26	(5.2)	472	(2.9)	505	(3.8)	−33	(4.8)	455	(3.5)	503	(4.2)	−48	(5.3)
Greece	435	(6.7)	466	(5.0)	−32	(5.6)	459	(5.5)	492	(4.2)	−33	(4.6)	468	(6.8)	522	(5.4)	−54	(6.1)
Hungary	465	(6.0)	491	(4.8)	−25	(6.3)	466	(5.1)	494	(4.1)	−28	(5.4)	460	(5.7)	503	(4.5)	−43	(5.8)
Iceland	485	(2.4)	517	(2.2)	−32	(3.3)	497	(2.1)	535	(2.1)	−38	(3.0)	476	(2.0)	529	(1.9)	−54	(2.8)
Ireland	514	(4.2)	536	(3.6)	−22	(4.7)	513	(4.3)	541	(3.6)	−27	(4.7)	515	(4.0)	552	(3.3)	−37	(4.5)
Italy	474	(5.7)	504	(4.0)	−31	(7.8)	470	(4.6)	509	(3.3)	−39	(6.4)	460	(5.5)	507	(3.8)	−47	(7.6)
Japan	512	(7.0)	539	(5.8)	−27	(6.8)	505	(6.3)	530	(5.3)	−25	(6.1)	508	(7.2)	551	(5.5)	−42	(7.9)

Korea	527 (4.1)	533 (4.3)	−6 (6.9)	521 (3.7)	530 (3.6)	−9 (5.9)	514 (3.7)	541 (3.5)	−27 (5.8)
Luxembourg	424 (2.6)	444 (2.5)	−20 (4.0)	433 (2.6)	460 (2.6)	−27 (3.9)	423 (3.0)	464 (2.8)	−40 (4.5)
Mexico	396 (5.0)	408 (4.4)	−12 (5.1)	410 (3.8)	427 (3.3)	−17 (3.9)	428 (4.9)	463 (4.5)	−35 (5.6)
New Zealand	516 (4.7)	555 (4.1)	−39 (7.1)	506 (4.3)	549 (3.9)	−43 (6.6)	502 (4.2)	559 (3.9)	−57 (6.4)
Norway	490 (3.9)	523 (2.9)	−32 (4.0)	487 (3.7)	527 (2.7)	−40 (3.8)	479 (4.0)	539 (2.9)	−60 (4.1)
Poland	461 (6.6)	489 (6.2)	−28 (7.8)	465 (5.5)	500 (5.5)	−35 (6.6)	451 (6.4)	504 (5.8)	−53 (7.4)
Portugal	447 (5.5)	464 (5.0)	−16 (4.2)	461 (4.7)	485 (4.3)	−24 (3.5)	461 (5.1)	497 (4.5)	−36 (4.8)
Spain	477 (3.7)	493 (3.1)	−16 (3.8)	481 (3.3)	502 (2.8)	−21 (3.4)	487 (3.5)	526 (2.9)	−39 (3.5)
Sweden	501 (2.7)	532 (2.9)	−30 (3.2)	505 (2.5)	540 (2.5)	−34 (2.8)	486 (2.7)	536 (2.5)	−51 (2.6)
Switzerland	487 (5.2)	510 (4.7)	−22 (4.7)	484 (4.8)	510 (4.4)	−26 (4.2)	465 (5.4)	511 (5.1)	−46 (4.5)
United Kingdom	515 (3.1)	534 (3.4)	−19 (4.4)	503 (2.9)	527 (3.5)	−24 (4.3)	522 (3.0)	557 (3.4)	−35 (4.4)
United States	486 (8.8)	512 (6.5)	−26 (4.5)	491 (8.4)	518 (6.4)	−27 (4.2)	488 (8.4)	524 (6.3)	−36 (4.5)
OECD total	*485 (2.4)*	*508 (2.1)*	*−23 (1.8)*	*485 (2.3)*	*512 (2.0)*	*−26 (1.6)*	*483 (2.3)*	*523 (2.0)*	*−40 (1.8)*
OECD average	*486 (0.9)*	*510 (0.8)*	*−24 (1.1)*	*487 (0.8)*	*516 (0.7)*	*−29 (0.9)*	*480 (0.8)*	*525 (0.8)*	*−45 (1.6)*
Brazil	360 (4.3)	370 (4.0)	−10 (4.5)	393 (3.8)	408 (3.5)	−14 (4.1)	404 (4.2)	429 (3.7)	−25 (4.3)
Latvia	428 (6.1)	474 (6.0)	−46 (4.9)	434 (5.0)	485 (5.0)	−51 (3.8)	423 (5.7)	493 (6.1)	−71 (4.5)
Liechtenstein	484 (8.2)	504 (7.7)	−20 (12.3)	474 (7.8)	497 (6.9)	−23 (11.6)	447 (8.9)	492 (8.6)	−45 (13.5)
Russian Federation	434 (5.5)	468 (4.8)	−34 (3.7)	450 (4.4)	486 (3.9)	−36 (3.1)	431 (4.2)	480 (4.0)	−49 (2.8)
Netherlands[2]	537 (5.4)	559 (4.4)	−22 (6.6)	519 (5.0)	551 (4.1)	−32 (6.1)	508 (4.3)	543 (3.5)	−35 (5.4)

Notes:
1 Positive differences indicate that males perform better than females, negative differences indicate that females perform better than males. Differences that are statistically significant are indicated in italic.
2 Response rate is too low to ensure comparability (see Annex A3).

girls at reading it is likely that the learning experiences they are offered differ according to gender. Second, the fact that boys' and girls' performance in subjects vary across countries adds weight to the idea that learning and assessment are socially and culturally situated and, therefore, amenable to change.

The socially situated conditions relating to assessment within individual countries leads to the second bullet point noted earlier: the underachievement of pupils from lower socio-economic groups. In the UK it is 'common knowledge' that the lower down the socio-economic scale an individual or family is the less able they are to access or make full use of educational opportunities. This common knowledge is backed up by research studies providing evidence of the differential experiences of working-class and middle-class pupils. In practical terms this means, for example, parents are less likely to be able to get their children into the 'best' schools or to liaise assertively with teachers on behalf of their children or to help with decisions about a university education (Ball and Gewirtz, 1997; Reay, 1998; Reay et al., 2001). Then there is the psychic influence of social class whereby, for example, working-class girls believe they have to work extremely hard but are unlikely to do as well as middle-class girls (Plummer, 2000) and middle-class girls feeling they too have to work hard but whatever they achieve is never good enough (Walkerdine et al., 2001). However, this underachievement of pupils in lower socio-economic groups is not an international phenomenon and only applies to pupils in some countries, the UK being one of them. As the OECD Report (2003) states:

> Advantaged students perform better by similar amounts at different levels of advantage, but socio-economic background does not determine performance.
> (OECD PISA Report, 2003, *The Relationship Between Socio-Economic Background and Student Performance*, p. 1 of 3)

In fact, several countries (Canada, Finland, Iceland, Japan, Korea and Sweden) demonstrated that it is possible to have students who perform well from a variety of socio-economic backgrounds. The report noted that 'High performance does not have to come at the expense of inequalities as some of the countries with the best levels of performance have relatively gentle gradients' (OECD Report, 2003, *The Strength of the Socio-Economic Effect in Different Countries* p. 3 of 7). In contrast to those countries that combined a high degree of achievement with equality between socio-economic groups, the UK (as well as Australia and Belgium) has a high quality of performance combined with above average *inequality* between advantaged and disadvantaged socio-economic groups. Thus the UK seems to have made little progress in eliminating, or even reducing, the effects of social class on a person's life chances or opportunities.

Related to the above is what the OECD PISA survey refers to as 'home background' citing this as the key to educational success. We take this to mean what Bourdieu refers to as social capital whereby wealth is not the most important factor but knowledge of, and access to, cultural capital is. Thus the OECD PISA research found that parental occupation is strongly associated with pupils' performance in assessments, for example, those whose parents have higher status jobs demonstrated higher literacy performance. Also, it was students from homes that had the most cultural capital that typically achieved very well; that is, pupils who had access to literature, and so forth. In some countries the differences were particularly marked and, certainly in the UK, pupils in the top quarter of cultural participation were at least 70 points ahead of pupils in the bottom quarter (likewise for the US, Belgium, Germany and Spain).

The impact of single-parent (mother) households on a child's educational achievements has been the subject of debate and discussion in the UK and US with the general finding that this type of family composition has a negative influence (Milne *et al.*, 1986; Mulkey *et al.*, 1992; Ermisch and Francesconi, 2001; Nelson *et al.*, 2001). The findings of the OECD PISA survey support the evidence of previous studies where it discovered a 12 point difference in performance in reading in students from single-parent families but in the UK, US and Netherlands, the gap exceeded 28 points or more. The report noted that 'not only is living in a single-parent family more common in the United Kingdom and the United States, but the consequences for student performance are also more pronounced' (OECD Report, 2003). Now a resounding 'but' needs to be interspersed here. It is not because children live in single-parent households that causes their lack of progress. Rather, and indeed as the OECD PISA Report points out, there are other factors involved. We have already seen that socio-economic factors play a huge part in achievement in the UK as does the occupational status of the parents. This discussion about the significance of socio-economic factors in the UK on achievement is not gender specific because the OECD PISA survey did not obtain information about gender differences in achievement between boys and girls who came from single-parent households, or who had the least cultural capital. Some commentators have argued that boys from single-parent (mother) families are more 'at risk' in terms of educational progress, and particularly in reading, because of the absence of a father (Fluty, 1997; Buckingham, 2002). However, we would add the caveat, although speaking generally and recognising that this is not applicable to all single-parent families, many of them are headed up by the mother who frequently does not occupy a high status job and does not have access to, or cannot provide, the cultural capital also shown to be significant to achievement.

Summary

What we have pointed out in this section is that the government has provided the public with information on boys' underachievement which is based on statistics gleaned from performance in school examinations. Using the same sources of information three factors have emerged:

1   Across OECD countries boys are underachieving generally in relation to girls but this is largely caused by the significant gap in achievement at literacy. In the UK, the differences are slight with the exception of literacy.

2 However, the achievement/underachievement of any group of pupils is extremely complex and it is not possible to say 'all boys are underachieving' when we can see that some groups of boys are doing very well when compared to other groups of girls.

3 The OECD PISA data shows that factors relating to achievement cannot be taken as a 'given' or universal, but are particular to the social, economic and cultural aspects of life in any one country. This means that assessment and achievement are socially situated (see discussion in following section).

Chapter 5 will look at the critiques of and explanations for the current boys' underachievement debate.

Boys' underachievement: the statistics

As we show throughout this book, there are numerous factors that affect achievement and numerous perspectives have been applied to understanding these. Here we want to focus on what has been seen as a key issue: the interpretation and presentation of the statistics.

The evidence to demonstrate that boys, as a group, are underachieving comes from the production of statistical tables and graphs. Stephen Gorard and his colleagues (1999; 2000), have argued that these statistics have been simplistically, and consequently misleadingly, read. The point Gorard et al. make is that the information the public is provided with relies on *percentage point* differences between the scores of boys and girls. However, they suggest that a realistic picture can only be gained by looking at the *achievement gap*; that is, the *percentage increase* in boys' and girls' performance from the previous year. For example, Connolly (2004) compares the differences between boys' and girls' successes in GCSE (A*–C) in 1991–2 and 2001–2 using the two different ways of reading the statistics.

A reading of *percentage points* clearly suggests that the gender gap has widened over the course of the ten years with boys doing increasingly worse than girls. Yet these critics argue when a more sophisticated mathematical reading is undertaken then it becomes obvious that boys have reduced the gender gap.

Table 4.12 Comparison of the proportions of boys and girls in England gaining five or more GCSEs grades A*–C between 1991–2 and 2001–2

Year	% boys	% girls	% point gap	Increase for the boys (%)	Increase for the girls (%)	No. of boys per 100 girls
1991/2	34.1	42.7	8.6	–	–	79.9
2001/2	46.0	56.6	10.6	34.9	32.6	81.3

Source: Connolly, P. (2004: 12) *Boys and Schooling in the Early Years*

Table 4.13 Comparing 'percentage point' gap with 'achievement gap': one school's Key Stage 2 results

	Girls	Boys	Percentage point gap	Achievement gap
2000	80	60	20	33.3
2004	94	72	22	30.6

Gorard *et al.* (1999) point out, we cannot just compare two year groups – we have to consider the proportions of girls and boys who achieve the benchmarks in any particular examination. Connolly (2004) provides an example when he says that if 10 per cent of girls and 5 per cent of boys passed a GCSE examination then the percentage point difference would be five and this would be the same if 95 per cent of girls and 90 per cent of boys passed the examination. Now if we looked at that proportionately it means that, in the case of 10 per cent of girls and 5 per cent of boys, girls are twice as likely to pass the examination. But, in the case of the 95 per cent versus 90 per cent, the girls are only slightly more likely to pass than the boys.

To arrive at the figure indicating the *achievement gap* (that is, the comparison of proportions of boys and girls achieving the relevant benchmark in an assessment) means carrying out a simple sum ascertaining the number of successful boys per 100 successful girls. Let us take another example, this time of the Key Stage 2 results of a fictitious school.

If we divide the number of girls that were successful in 2000 by the number of boys we can see that boys were 0.75 times as likely as girls to reach the required level 4 (that is, $60 \div 80 = 0.75$). In 2004 boys had a slightly better chance of reaching the required level thus reducing the gap between them and the girls (that is, $72 \div 94 = 0.77$). To look at this gender gap in another way, and using a different mathematical formula, Table 4.13 shows that the percentage point gap between girls and boys had increased in the years from 2000 to 2004 i.e. increased from 20 per cent to 24 per cent. However, if we ask 'how much better did the boys have to do to catch up with the girls?' we can see the gender gap actually reduced. In 2000 boys would have had to improve their performance by 33.3 per cent to catch up with girls but by 2004 they would only have had to do 30.6 per cent better in their test scores. (To arrive at the achievement gap divide the percentage point gap by the boys' score and multiply by 100 (percentage point gap $\div$ boys' score $\times$ 100).)

Further, we have pointed out that the DfES formulations of data focus on the *achievement* percentages of pupils at various key stages rather than on the numbers entered for the exams, or on numbers or percentages of those who fail at these exams. The lesson these critics provide is that the way in which the statistical data on examination performance is read, and subsequently presented to the public can be misleading. Having said this, one recent argument is that such critiques of the presentation by the government of statistics on achievement is itself misconceived and that the picture we are given is more, rather than less, accurate (Connolly, 2005), and this debate is bound to continue. We hope to have shown how what is focused on, and what goes 'unsaid' in the presentation of government statistics, reflects political preoccupations.

Whatever the rights and wrongs of the presentation of the statistical data are, however, the fact remains that here in the UK the underachievement of boys has been identified by the government as a fundamental predicament for education and described by the media using the language of crisis (Griffin, 1998; Arnot *et al.*, 1999; Smith, 2003). Explanations for why and how the discussions on boys' underachievement have taken on the form of a 'moral panic' have been widely discussed, particularly by feminists/pro-feminists. For example, improvements in girls' examination results have meant they are taking up places in prestigious university courses (such as medicine) which were once the preserve of middle-class boys (Yates, 1997). Thus the 'status quo' is being destabilised and inroads by females into traditionally male areas is experienced as threatening. We will return to the discourses around boys and schooling in greater detail a little later on and, for now, we want to clarify what we are saying here. We have shown that the interpretation of statistical data to prove that boys are underachieving misrepresents the actual situation. We are not saying that boys are not underachieving as they most certainly are in literacy, and this is a universal phenomenon. In other subjects boys, as a group in the UK, do tend to trail slightly behind girls, but this is not to say they are '*under*achieving' – the OECD PISA data demonstrated that the UK has above average levels of attainment. Rather the information on achievement in the UK needs to be looked at in perspective to obtain an accurate reflection. In adopting such an approach one of the most significant factors to emerge is the gendered and socio-culturally specific and socially situated nature of assessment conception and practice.

Chapter 5

Explaining gender differences in achievement

Introduction

While statistics have been used to prove that many boys are underachieving in relation to girls, several different reasons have been given for how this situation has come about. The explanations for why, where and how boys and girls achieve differently in schools depends on the point of view a person holds (see Chapter 2). Those people who strongly believe that gender is in-born will tend to see any inequalities in achievement as a consequence of hormonal, chromo-somal or brain differences. Similarly those who believe that gender is 'fluid' will argue the case that what it means to be a 'schoolgirl' or 'schoolboy' is diverse and differentiated and will appear differently in each educational setting. Then there is the idea that schools, particularly primary schools, are 'feminised'. For example, it has been argued that the predominance of women primary teachers has resulted in male teachers avoiding working in this sector and therefore depriving boys of necessary male role models. Or again, the fact that the major-ity of teachers are women has meant that there is a tendency to favour 'girls' learning styles' and the kinds of learning behaviours associated with females such as cooperation and studiousness. And, in the same vein, it has been sug-gested that, however well meaning they are, women teachers simply have not recognised the particular difficulties faced by boys in learning how to be boys (Pollack, 1998; Gurian, 2002).

The intention in this chapter is to explore and evaluate the reasons put forward to explain the 'gender gap' in the UK. The arguments we will discuss are that:

- Boys and girls are naturally different and this explains discrepancies in achievement.
- Boys and girls have different learning styles.
- Schools are feminised and this disadvantages boys.
- Assessment procedures are biased towards girls.
- Pupils' constructions of gender produce different behaviours which impact on achievement.

Each of these explanations are explored as sub-sections of this chapter. The first claim, that gendered patterns of achievement are the result of 'natural' differences between males and females, is based on gender essentialist views of biological sex differences producing different abilities and behaviours in the sexes. These views are drawn on by subscribers to the other explanations too, but these other explanations are all based on hypotheses concerning social relations, and hence contain social constructionist elements (to greater and lesser extents).

EXPLANATION 1: BOYS AND GIRLS ARE BORN WITH DIFFERENT INTERESTS, MOTIVATIONS AND ABILITIES

Ascertaining the links (if any) between gender and sex of a body and how these relate to education continues to be widely debated (Halpern, 1992; Head, 1999; Baron-Cohen, 2004). 'Gender' is usually accepted to refer to cultural constructions of masculinity and femininity (what it means to live out being a male or female in our daily lives); and one's 'sex' refers to male/female physiology (which are biological constructions of the body – although this 'taken-for-granted' notion of male/female bodies has also been challenged; see Kessler and McKenna, 1978; Butler, 1990).

As we indicated in Chapter 2, many commentators, particularly those sub-scribing to evolutionary psychology/'brain difference' perspectives, believe that gendered patterns of educational achievement are explained by inherent differences between males and females. And others see gender differences in educational performance as entirely due to socially constructed factors. Can we give a definitive answer as to whether the research indicates that there is no, some or unquestionable evidence that gender is innate? The answer is a disappointing 'no' but we can, at least, clarify this unhelpful response. The reason being that we, individually, hold different beliefs and the research is simply not conclusive enough for either of us to convince the other of our alternative points of view. As we said in Chapter 2, people uphold those theories that are the closest match to what they believe, and, as such, we will take it in turns to present our individual interpretation of the evidence. Christine Skelton starts from the premise that gender is predominantly socially constructed but she sees that recent research into brain structure offers some potential explanation as to why there are more boys who are autistic, have special needs, or even why boys generally are less adept at literacy than girls. Becky Francis supports the view that gender is completely socially constructed.

Christine Skelton writes

The advocates of innate explanations for gender differences cite a variety of biological sources for these from hormonal to chromosonal to brain structure

(Kimura, 1992; Moir and Moir, 1999; Gurian, 2002). The most widely cited text, and one which continues to be considered the most authoritative overview of the research, is Diane Halpern's (1992) *Sex Differences in Cognitive Abilities*. Halpern's views on her interrogation of the research findings have been quoted variously as saying that biological explanations 'are unlikely to provide an adequate account of gender differences in academic performance' (Arnot *et al.*, 1998) but, alternatively, 'once she had studied all the evidence, she admitted she had been wrong . . . "there are real, and in some cases sizable, sex differences"' (Moir and Moir, 1999: 117). Clearly, Halpern's work is used by some to prove that gender differences are socially constructed and by others to justify their argument that they are innate! It is important to note that her own initial beliefs at the beginning of her research were that 'it seemed clear to me that any between-sex differences in thinking abilities were due to socialisation practices, artifacts and mistakes in the research, and bias and prejudice' (Halpern, 1992: xi). Her conclusions after completing the research were that, when the evidence is considered together, both 'nature' and 'nurture' contribute to shaping cognitive abilities in males and females:

> Socialization practices are undoubtedly important, but there is also good evidence that biological sex differences play a role in establishing and maintaining cognitive sex differences.
>
> (Halpern, 1992: xi)

Of course, as Halpern found, much of the evidence is not convincing but she did conclude that one of the strongest hypotheses was that 'there are important differences in the way cognitive abilities are organized within each hemisphere' (1992: 170). It is the argument that apparent cognitive differences between males and females may be explained by how the brain communicates which is attracting particular attention (O'Boyle, 2000; Geake and Cooper, 2003; Baron-Cohen, 2004). What is of interest to note in this literature is what some neuroscientists have to say which dispels some of the claims made about brain and gender differences. For example, some educationalists claim that the brain is wired differently according to gender with boys using the right side of their brains and girls the left (Biddulph, 1997; Gurian, 2002). This is supposed to explain why girls tend to be better at language and communication skills and boys at spatial tasks. However, as Northen (2004) writes in a report in the *Times Educational Supplement*, the idea that the left hemisphere deals with language and vocabulary is rather too simplistic as, while the left side might be concerned with the production of speech and the technicalities of grammar, the right side is at work too by tackling meaning and inference. Thus, the majority of brains use both hemispheres to process a task so being 'right' or 'left' brained is not seen as an advantage. At the same time, the idea that girls are 'left brained' is erroneous as John Geake, chair of the Oxford cognitive neuroscience and education forum, has pointed out that 'Girls seem to have many of their modular functions more distributed around the brain and boys tend to have them more extremely lateralised – either on one side or the other' (Northen, 2004: 19). The explanation for how this comes about has been attributed to the release of testosterone in males during foetal development which acts more on the right hemisphere, inhibiting the development of the left hemisphere. It apparently also strengthens the corpus callosum which is a large bundle of nerve fibres that connects the two cerebral hemispheres. One might assume from this that a strengthening of the corpus callosum via male hormones should advantage boys, if an important function of the corpus callosum is to facilitate use of both sides of the brain. There seems then to be mixed messages when we are told that in girls, the corpus callosum is both thicker and broader which facilitates use of both sides of the brain (e.g. Gurian, 2002).

Neuroscientists such as John Geake, Michael O'Boyle and Simon Baron-Cohen (see Northen, 2004) are not claiming that these brain differences in the corpus callosum of boys and girls, with girls showing a stronger connection between the two hemispheres, means that girls are bound to outperform boys in intellectual abilities. The question then has to be 'Why not?' when their argument is that girls' brains are advantaged in relation to those of boys. These neuroscientists argue the idea that girls are more likely to use both sides of their brain, however, they say this does not make them better than boys and we cannot make generalisations. Having said that, Professor O'Boyle has said that the right-side development of boys' brains is both a blessing and a curse. He cites research which showed that the right hemispheres of those boys who processed information using *both* sides of their brains were in 'tip top' condition and facilitated by the transfer of data across the corpus callosum. Other boys, according to Professor Geake, whose right-sided brain dominance leaves them at a disadvantage in terms of processing language tasks are left behind by the educational system. For example, Geake and Cooper (2003) argue that exchanging depth of curriculum knowledge and understanding for breadth of curriculum reduces opportunities for repetition; that is for going over the same concepts, knowledge and so forth over and again and in different ways. It is opportunities for repetition that those in the field of neuroscience advocate as beneficial in 'exercising' the brain.

What does need to be borne in mind is that the brain is a tensile organ and responds to external stimuli (Sacks, 1993 quoted by Paechter, 1998; Baron-Cohen, 2004). This is an extremely important issue as the danger of talking about 'brain differences' leads to the conclusion that there is nothing to be done about it. Just because there are gender differences between the connectivity of the two halves of the brain in males and females does not mean it is a 'done deal' with girls as the 'doing well plodders' and boys as the 'dullards' or 'geniuses'. Baron-Cohen (2004) notes that by identifying the faster development of the right hemisphere in male foetuses he is not inferring that it does not develop in females. As he says, he is aware of many men with empathetic brains and many women with a gift for systemising but to understand this 'we must refer to their particular biology *and* experience' (Baron-Cohen, 2004: 183, my emphasis).

It is important that we do not go down the line of ascribing gender differences exclusively to biological causes, first because, as neuroscientists have argued, some females are as good mathematicians, scientists, and so on, as right hemisphere dominated males; and, second, and more importantly, there is a danger that the identification of why boys may not be as able as girls at literacy, show more cases of autism and are more likely to have special educational needs, could lead to 'biological excuses' for other sorts of behaviours. For example, an acceptance that biology might have a part to play in boys' development (albeit the acquiring of language skills) could serve to reinforce ideas that male aggressive behaviours are 'natural' and, therefore, understandable, if not even excusable (Mahony, 1998).

Becky Francis writes

Christine has already outlined some of the key findings concerning a tendency towards gender difference in patterns in brain activity. Applying my social constructionist perspective to these findings, I should like to reiterate two of her points and to add a third (which I come to later). The first is that there is as much difference within sex groups as between them. As Slavin (1994: 130) observes:

> The most important thing to keep in mind about this debate is that no responsible researcher has ever claimed that any male-female differences on any measure of intellectual ability are large compared to the amount of variability within each sex. In other words, even in areas where true gender differences are suspected, these differences are so small and so variable that they have few if any practical consequences.

And second, there is as yet no evidence to show that these (extremely slight) tendencies to difference in the brain are related to gendered patterns in educational achievement – whereas the evidence that achievement is affected by social factors is overwhelming. That gendered expression is, to some extent, socially constructed is incontrovertible – even the most die-hard evolutionary psychologists are forced to admit that some constructions of gender and gender difference change over time and between different cultures and social groups. As we have seen, the changed patterns in gender and achievement are one example of this – it is not that girls have grown more innately intelligent; rather social conditions that were previously inhibiting their achievement have altered somewhat, impacting on their performance. Yet debates continue as to whether or not gender differences in achievement are at all affected by biological factors, and in recent years there has been a re-emergence in arguments supporting 'brain difference' theses.

In the feminist tradition, I am going to draw on some of my own experiences ('the personal') as a parent to provide illustration for my arguments that gendered achievement patterns express 'nurture' not 'nature'. Many self-professed feminist mothers maintain that the arrival of their children was a turning point in their beliefs regarding this debate – that the gendered behaviours of their children in the face of 'feminist parenting' finally showed them that gender differences are inherent and inevitable (for examples of such reflections, see some contributions to Steven's *Between Mothers and Sons* (1999); for discussion of how and why children take up these behaviours irrespective of parental values see Grabrucker, 1988; Davies, 1989). Before I had children I was told time and again that my social constructionist views on gender would change once I became a mother.[1] However, ironically, rather than demonstrate to me that gender is innate, parenthood has strongly affirmed my social constructionism. I have been acutely aware of how I have compromised my beliefs in deconstructing gender stereotypical positions for fear of stigmatising my young sons (see Davies, 1989; 1993 for discussion of how non-conformity to gender positions can risk marginalisation by other children and/or ridicule from parents). Protection of them from ridicule and stigmatisation has meant that in innumerable minor instances I have facilitated their constructions as 'boys', rather than disturbing or challenging these. Social graces also require this (e.g. not wanting to hurt relatives' feelings by querying their choice of clothes and toys – predominantly gender-marked – for my sons).

These seemingly minor instances quickly build up, and precipitate consequences. For example, that people tend to assume boys are, or will be, interested in particular things has meant that my sons are given particular toys, books and resources as presents. As a result vehicles and technical resources are disproportionately represented among their toys and books. Many of these encourage further engagement and perpetuate learning in that area (for example, many of my sons' books on diggers and trains are incredibly technical and informative, meaning that I have learnt more about these vehicles and their mechanisms in the space of three years than I had previously picked up in a lifetime). Hence my 3-year-old son has not only learnt that this kind of information is appropriate for him (as a boy) to know and expand, but also *has* gained an extensive knowledge and interest in this field (what might appear to you or I to be a 'digger' is for him 'a backhoe loader with hammer attachment', or similar!). A cyclical process has gained momentum: his demonstrable knowledge and interest in these mechanical and technical areas in turn impress friends and relatives, who therefore buy him more such toys and resources – hence feeding his interest and compounding his expertise further. Meanwhile, aspects of play which emerge when playing with dolls and the like (socially creative explorations of human interaction, emotion and so on) are foreign territory. One can see how already children not much older than toddlers are expert in different (gendered) types of play by noting how perturbed some children are as to what to do with certain toys they are confronted with if these are absent from their home environment. Gendered interests are subtly taught and encouraged, and are later actively picked up and drawn on by children themselves to delineate their gender construction as boys or girls (Davies, 1989; Francis, 1998). So I am arguing that in even very young children gendered abilities and interests can be explained by social factors; and these trends are exacerbated as a child grows older.

These processes have been extensively documented by Kessler and McKenna (1978), Archer and Lloyd (1982), Grabrucker (1988), Lloyd and Duveen (1992) and others, who have shown how adults interact with babies differently according to their gender from the moment a baby's sex is identified (i.e. pre-birth, in many cases). The differing interests and expertise consequently encouraged in boys and girls via countless subtle (and not-so-subtle) messages and resources are likely to impact on their skills and abilities, and hence to impact on their achievement. For example, many proponents of 'brain difference' maintain that girls are 'naturally' disposed to be better at communications skills (which impacts beneficially on their achievement in literacy and languages). But is it not likely that if girls are from birth talked to and engaged in conversation more frequently than boys (Kessler and Mckenna, 1978; Archer and Lloyd, 1982), and encouraged to articulate themselves and their emotions, and to consider the needs of others (Gilligan, 1982), they will be advantaged at communications skills?

Similarly, it has become a truism that boys tend to possess superior spatial skills. For example, Hoff Sommers (2000) cites spatial differences between girls to demonstrate that there are innate sex differences. Actually, these tendencies to difference are slight, as even she admits. (Males score higher than females in areas of mechanical reasoning and mental rotation; there are no gender differences according to abstract reasoning or spatial visualisation – see for example Kimball, 1989; Feingold, 1992.) But I would argue that these too are explainable by social factors. One experiment which is frequently used to illustrate girls' and boys' different abilities (and boys' superior spatial skills) is that of drawing a bike. Groups of boys and girls are asked to draw bikes. The results reveal girls tend to draw aesthetically pleasing but mechanically incorrect bikes, and boys tend to produce less 'pretty' bikes, but bikes that would 'work' mechanically. However, if we reflect on the above discussion of my 3-year-old son's technical expertise, and the complete absence of technical and mechanical development aspects in girls' toys and resources, I would argue that these differences in bike-drawing are exactly what we would expect from a social constructionist perspective, with no need to recourse to biological essentialist explanations.

A further important point is that evidence has shown how social stimuli effect brain development (see Chapter 2 for discussion). As neuroscientist Rogers (2000) observes, even hormones may be affected by environmental factors. So even if a relation were eventually to be found between patterns of brain difference and gendered patterns in educational achievement, these gender differences in the brain might still be the result of social experiences rather than innate (and unalterable) factors. It is often noted that the brain is a muscle. It is possible that girls' brains may tend to develop slightly differently from boys' because of their different behaviours and modes of expression. In this case, directing pedagogies to meet the apparent brain predilections of one sex or another might exacerbate differences further.

Reaching a conclusion?

Finally, we would both like to raise a couple of points of reflection in concluding this section. Many of the proponents of brain difference as an explanation for 'boys' underachievement' draw on 'poor boys' discourses to make their arguments, maintaining that boys' narrower corpus callosum and consequent lesser ability to use both sides of the brain mean that they are currently disadvantaged by teaching and/or assessment methods, and that their needs must be taken into account (e.g. Hoff Sommers, 2000; Gurian, 2002). Hoff Sommers (2000) accuses feminists of pathologising boys, but it is hard to imagine an argument more pathologising than one which claims boys are less able to use both sides of their brain than girls, and are therefore in need of extra help and attention! And there is a further contradiction, in that some proponents of innate gender differences in ability are keen to apply these theories to *girls'* underachievement to claim that girls are inherently less able. See for example Moir and Moir (1999: 119):

> The hardline feminists simply refuse to entertain the idea that boys just might be plain better at higher mathematics than girls. They insist that girls are scared out of being good at it, though they never really explain why anyone should want to frighten girls away (except to claim, of course, that there is a male conspiracy to keep women down). Their explanation makes no sense to conspiracy theorists, and the accumulated evidence from years of research demonstrates that the sex difference in higher mathematics, however regrettable, is firmly in the biological domain.

Yet these arguments are never extended to boys – it is hard to imagine anyone suggesting that the male 'underachievement' which commentators assume to be so pervasive shows that girls 'just might be plain better' at academic work, and we should stop wasting time on the issue! Yet this might be the obvious conclusion of 'brain difference' theories. The apparent brain differences that Hoff Sommers cites, for example, suggest that girls are better at communication and boys more aggressive – which might indicate the conclusion that girls are 'naturally' predisposed to be better scholars? But these theories are instead used to argue that boys' needs must be met and facilitated – maintaining that boys are more needy, but never that they are less able. Such apparent inconsistency will come as no surprise to feminist educational historians, who have documented such constructions through the ages. For example, Cohen (1998:

25) explains of thinking on gender and educational ability in the eighteenth century:

> If little girls were quicker and generally more advanced than boys of the same age, this was not, Bennett (1784: 30) argued, because they were cleverer. On the contrary, it was because boys were thoughtful and deep that they were slow and appeared dull: 'gold sparkles less than tinsel'. Thus, as the eighteenth century came to a close, girls' brightness, construed as inferiority, and boys' dullness, construed as potential, were woven into the fabric of gender difference.

It would appear that some discursive constructions endure the test of time.

We have here presented our overview of the polarised 'nature–nurture' debates which have a long history in discussions of education, ability and achievement, and are consistently raised in any conversations about boys' underachievement. What we have attempted to show through our differing perspectives is how the 'natural' differences stance forecloses any discussions on gender, power and knowledge. In Chapter 8 we provide illustrations of ways in which schools can, and have, made progress in enabling achievement through the tackling of essentialising attitudes, expectations and behaviours of both staff and students.

EXPLANATION 2: BOYS AND GIRLS HAVE DIFFERENT LEARNING STYLES

One of the most frequently expressed 'commonsense' views used to explain gender differences in achievement is the one that says boys and girls have different learning styles (Duffy, 2003; Maby, 2004). This viewpoint is most strongly advocated in the branch of boys' underachievement informed by evolutionary or men's rights theoretical perspectives. The basis for this argument being that, if boys are naturally different from girls because of their biological make-up then it follows they will have different approaches to learning (Noble and Bradford, 2000; Gurian, 2002). In the previous section we saw how some commentators believe that gendered brain differences make boys and girls pre-disposed to greater ability at different curriculum subjects. Many believe that an orientation towards different subjects reflects boys' and girls' tendency to approach learning differently. For some, these different 'styles' are a natural manifestation of their inherent brain differences. Feminists have dismissed such essentialist arguments by pointing out that should biological imperatives dictate how boys and girls learn then we would have no female mathematicians or male writers. But even in these circles, there is a recognition of gendered tendencies in pupils' preferred ways of learning, even if these are seen as the result of social constructions of gender identity rather than 'brain differences'. However, as with

theses, the very notion of gendered learning styles is controversial and
d.

Various curriculum subjects have traditionally been seen as either 'masculine'
or 'feminine'. Areas of the curriculum traditionally seen as masculine have been
science (particularly physics), mathematics and information technology and
feminine subjects have been English and modern languages. And there are
those practically based subjects which, despite some repackaging, remain highly
gendered in their form and practices such as physical education, music and
design technology, with the latter incorporating what was once home economics
(Paechter, 2000). These associations between curriculum subjects and gender
are not exclusively due to gendered preferences: 'masculine' subjects such as
maths and science have been invested with high prestige, and historically women
have been excluded from their study. But traditionally-gendered subject preferences remain strong among pupils and students. Research shows that these
associations have decreased somewhat in recent years (Wikeley and Stables,
1999; Francis, 2000a), and also are influenced by 'race' and social class (Mirza,
1992; Lightbody, 1997; Francis and Archer, 2005), but that gendered tendencies remain in place in terms of enjoyment and pursuit of different subjects, and
perceptions of certain subjects as masculine/feminine (Arnot et al., 1999; Francis,
2000a; Francis et al., 2003).

The reasons attributed to why boys and girls have favoured respectively math-
ematics/science and English/humanities subjects have included the idea that there
are different, gendered learning styles and these are matched up by the demands
of the particular subject. So boys favour a learning style that involves memorisa-
tion of rules and abstract facts (see Arnot et al., 1998a) and will provide episodic,
factual and commentative detail (Murphy, 1989). This mode of response is the
one demanded by maths and science tasks. Alternatively, girls appear to prefer
open-ended tasks which are related to real situations and tend to respond in
ways that are elaborative and provide a broader context. English and humanities
subjects demand precisely this form of response from pupils in written assessment.
Thus, different subjects make different learning demands to which boys and
girls respond differently. As Madeleine Arnot et al. (1998a: 28) suggest,

> Boys show greater adaptability to more traditional approaches to learning
> which require the memorisation of abstract, unambiguous facts and rules
> that have to be acquired quickly. They also appear to be more willing to
> sacrifice deep understanding which requires effort, for correct answers
> achieved at speed.

They go on to say that girls are more likely to achieve well on 'sustained tasks
that are open-ended, process-based, related to realistic situations and that require
pupils to think for themselves' (Arnot, et al., 1998a: 28).

There has been work on gendered learning preferences which argues that
girls tend to prefer collaborative group-work activities, reflection and discussion

(Spender, 1982; Belenky *et al.*, 1986); while boys relish competition and prefer whole-class teaching than small group work (Pickering, 1997; Noble, 1998). Researchers such as Lucey *et al.* (2003) have discussed how these preferences may relate to factors such as social class as well as gender, but are supportive of the notion that certain pedagogic/learning practices are gendered.

It would seem then that in spite of varying beliefs amongst educationalists as to why boys and girls appear to have different preferred learning styles they agree these tendencies do exist, at least to some extent. Should then the response to this be for teachers to develop strategies which cater for these different learning styles? Certainly the issue demands reflection, but caution is also crucial. The extent of these gendered tendencies in learning style remains highly contested (Elwood and Gipps, 1998; Younger *et al.*, 2005). Even Gurian (2002), author of *Boys and Girls Learn Differently*, admits there is as much difference between boys and between girls as between boys and girls. As teachers themselves point out, many pupils buck the trend in terms of learning preferences, and many teachers are adamant that gender differences in learning are non-existent or superficial (Francis *et al.*, 2004). But other authors refer to 'gender specific preferred learning styles' (Davison and Edwards, 1998) as though this area is unproblematic and differences 'taken-as read'. As Swan (1998) asserts, 'It has become starkly obvious to us that boys and girls learn very, very differently' (p. 167). Yet she provides no evidence to support this claim, going on instead to expand on boys' disruptive behaviours (which presumably are not their approach to learning)!

We would suggest that teachers should be aware of pupils' preferred ways of learning but these should not be tagged with a 'gender label' – adopting the strategies recommended in some of the literature will only entrench traditional masculine and feminine stereotypes of boys and girls as learners. To explain this we need to say a few words about learning styles. There is a real appeal for policy-makers and educationalists in knowing more about how learners learn in order to more accurately direct policy and teaching interventions. At the same time, underpinning the 'lifelong learning' initiatives of the New Labour government is the role of individuals in their own development and included in this is for everyone to recognise their own strengths and weaknesses. Thus, a part of the teachers' role is not only to target their teaching but to help pupils understand the ways in which they approach learning situations in order to enable them to become more independent. So what do we know about learning styles?

In a recent research study of learning styles, Coffield *et al.* (2004) showed that the field is not unified, and also complex. They point out that the research on learning styles emerges from a number of different disciplines and that 'evidence about learning is guided by contrasting and disputed theories from psychology, sociology, education and policy studies' (p. 1). As a result there is little 'cumulative knowledge' coming out of the various studies undertaken from different theoretical perspectives. Perhaps not surprisingly, as a consequence of this, the findings of the Coffield *et al.* (2004) study suggest that current strategies for targeting 'boys' learning styles' are misplaced. For example, teachers are told to ensure their lessons are 'energetic and full of quick changes' (Maby, 2004); to make them 'active' (Noble and Bradford, 2000); to provide opportunities for competition (Gurian, 2002); to keep boys stimulated and challenged (Neall, 2002); and to give 'quick feedback' and 'plenty of praise' (Duffy, 2003). Furthermore, teachers are constantly exhorted to match their teaching style to their (male) pupils:

> We really do believe that the teacher who takes the trouble to find out the learning preferences of pupils and acts upon the results will be vastly increasing his or her effectiveness and job satisfaction . . .
>
> (Noble and Bradford, 2000: 31)

> Improvement in boys' performance does involve fresh teaching methods . . . For change to be made, there needs to be a clearer identification of children's learning styles, so teaching methods fit more than one type of personality.
>
> (Maby, 2004: 4)

The crucial idea here is the notion of 'match' i.e. that teachers should 'match' their teaching styles to boys' and girls' learning styles. The importance of 'match' between teacher and pupil within current educational policy discourse is also to be found in the drive by the DfES and TTA to improve boys' achievement by increasing the number of male primary teachers (and similarly increasing numbers of ethnic minority teachers to encourage ethnic minority pupils to do well). However, in the same way that there is no evidence to indicate that matching teachers and pupils by gender will have a positive impact on boys' and girls' motivations and attitudes towards school, the findings of the Coffield *et al.* study indicate there is no effective outcome in matching teachers' teaching and pupils' learning styles:

> The one implication for practice which is repeated throughout the literature on learning styles is that it is the responsibility of teachers, tutors and managers to adjust their teaching styles to accommodate the learning styles of their students or staff members . . . Despite the strong convictions with which the ideas are promoted, we failed to find a substantial body of empirical evidence that such strategies have been tried and found successful.
>
> (Coffield *et al.*, 2004: 43)

We would argue that the 'gender dimension' of pupils' various approaches to learning has been allowed to obscure broader questions about effective teaching and learning. So we are given the impression that it is partly the result of 'boring teaching' that has caused boys' underachievement:

...everyone I met agreed that boys were far less prepared to stomach boring lessons than girls.

(Maby, 2004: 4)

What can be perceived as bad behaviour is often just boys using their imaginations to make things more interesting...Boys can get bored if teachers say too much...They can also get bored or distracted if they spend too long on a task.

(Neall, 2002: 144)

Many classes simply aren't taught in a way that boys find captivating.

(Pollack, 1998: 246)

However, it is not the case that being 'bored' in the classroom is the prerogative of boys but the preoccupation with boys' disaffection encourages teachers to focus on this group. The quotation above by Maby implies that girls are not affected by 'boring' lessons. But girls' learning *is* influenced by the content and delivery of the teaching:

Boredom, and poor quality of explanation of tasks, were the factors girls said most often deter them from learning generally, and from doing their homework (although teachers saw the situation somewhat differently).

(Francis *et al.*, 2002: 3)

Other studies report girls saying they become bored in lessons when classmates (boys) become disruptive and the teacher spends all the time trying to manage their behaviour (Cruddas and Haddock, 2003). These recent studies are reflecting the findings of earlier projects that discovered female pupils are far from immune when it comes to 'tuning out' of schooling but they do so differently from boys (Fuller, 1980; Riddell, 1989). By choosing to pass notes to each other at the back of the classroom or doodle on pieces of paper or give attention to their personal appearance (for example, doing their nails), girls are absenting themselves from learning. The point here is that rather than attempts being focused on boys to capture their interest and motivation, any teaching strategies should be developed in terms of effective teaching for all pupils.

This section has considered the arguments that suggest girls and boys' different learning styles partly explain why boys fail to do as well as girls at school. The most recent research on learning styles indicates the complexity of the field and notes there is no evidence, as yet, to suggest that matching teaching styles to learning styles brings about any improvement in achievement. This is not to argue against seeking out pedagogical approaches which enable the learning of pupils but these should be based on what is known about effective teaching rather than essentialising boys and girls.

EXPLANATION 3: SCHOOLS ARE 'FEMINISED' AND THIS DISADVANTAGES BOYS

A frequently made assertion about why boys underachieve is that it is a consequence of the 'feminisation' of schools and education. As Francis (2000a) and Burman (2005) have pointed out, the meaning of the term 'feminisation' is rarely identified by those adopting it, and it is often applied in different ways. So what is meant by the 'feminisation' of education? As one Australian author has observed 'it is possible to interpret the label of teaching as "feminised" at several levels, and it seems that those who refer to teaching as feminised also assume different meanings' (Smith, 1999: 3). It is possible to identify three distinct ways in which the phrase is used although there are overlapping, influential factors:

- Numerical (women teachers outnumber men teachers particularly in the primary sector).
- Cultural (where the teaching environment and practices are seen to be biased towards females).
- Political (the tensions between feminist and anti-feminist perspectives on gender inequalities in schooling).

What we also need to ask is whether the idea that schools are 'feminised' accurately reflects the situation in schools, particularly in the primary school sector which is where there is a predominance of female teachers, and to which arguments about 'feminisation of schooling' are most frequently applied.

Statistics and the 'feminisation of teaching'

One of the main features of schools that is drawn attention to in the boys' underachievement debate is the predominance of women teachers in relation to the number of men teachers (Lewis, 2000; Hutchings, 2001). When Ralph Tabberer, Chief Executive of the Teacher Training Agency said, 'Many would-be male primary teachers are dropping out of training or leaving the profession because they feel isolated in schools where nearly all the staff are female' (*Independent*: 23 April 2002) he seemed to be implying that there was a time when this was not the case and the UK had equal numbers of men and women teachers. However, females have always made up the majority of the primary teaching force. Although at the time of the Forster Education Act 1870 which introduced state education to the UK there were equal numbers of men and women teachers, their roles were stratified so that men teachers predominantly taught in boys' public schools and women in state elementary schools (Partington, 1976). However, as Steedman (1982) and Walkerdine and Lucey (1989) document, throughout most of the twentieth century (and into the twenty-first), primary

Table 5.1 Teachers in service 1997–2002, FTE teacher numbers[1] in the maintained schools sector: 1997 to 2003 by country and phase

	England and Wales						
	1997	1998	1999	2000	2001	2002	2003
England							
Nursery, primary and secondary	393,800	391,970	396,280	402,140	410,150	417,010	418,140
Special and education not in schools[2]	18,980	18,830	19,000	19,160	19,610	20,090	20,220
Total	412,790	410,800	415,280	421,290	429,760	437,100	438,360
Wales							
Nursery, primary and secondary	26,960	26,410	27,240	27,100	27,310	27,750	27,870
Special and education not in schools[2]	830	760	750	780	820	830	840
Total	27,790	27,170	27,990	27,880	28,130	28,570	28,710
England and Wales							
Nursery, primary and secondary	420,760	418,380	423,520	429,230	437,460	444,750	446,010
Special and education not in schools[2]	19,820	19,590	19,750	19,940	20,430	20,920	21,060
Total	440,580	437,970	443,270	449,170	457,890	465,670	467,070

Source: DfES annual 618G survey and National Assembly for Wales stats3 survey.

Notes:
1 Includes occasional teachers.
2 Includes pupil referal units and those employed by local education authorities but not teaching in schools or primary and secondary establishments, e.g. home tuition services. Excludes non-maintained special schools.

teaching has been seen as an 'ideal job for a woman' – and indeed women have been positioned as 'naturally able' at this job because of their supposedly inherent nurturing qualities. What has occurred over recent years is a decline in the (already low) numbers of men entering this sector whilst the number of women teachers demonstrates a slight but steady increase.

Women primary teachers outnumber men by roughly 5:1, but it continues to be the case that males are disproportionately represented at headteacher level. Table 5.2 shows the distribution of headteachers in 2002 across primary and secondary schools. Whilst it appears that female headteachers outnumber male headteachers in the primary school and the reverse for secondary schools this does not give an accurate representation of the likelihood of obtaining a headteacher's position. Male teachers in both sectors are statistically far more

Table 5.2 Headteachers in maintained primary and secondary schools 2002

Headteachers	Nursery and primary (000)	Total number of teachers (000)	Secondary	Total number of teachers (000)
Men	6.6	26.6	2.6	82.3
Women	10.6	142.4	1.2	99.2

Source: Statistics of Education: School Workforce in England 2003 (published by DfES 2004)

likely to become headteachers than are their female colleagues (Hutchings, 2002).

Clearly there are substantially more female primary teachers than male. There is not such a large gender difference in the teaching population of secondary schools and the secondary sector is, therefore, less open to accusations of numerical 'feminisation'. For some, the under-representation of men as primary school teachers is an issue in itself regarding gender and achievement, the argument being that boys of an impressionable age are denied appropriate male educational role-models. We return to look at this idea more closely below.

If we take it that the 'feminisation of teaching' means more than who actually does the job of teaching then different definitions of the term are required. One of these is the idea that the curricula, assessment, management and ethos of schools are 'feminine' in nature.

Culture and the 'feminisation of teaching'

The predominance of female teachers has been argued to have had a fundamental impact on primary school pedagogy and culture. This includes ideas such as the adoption of daily routines and practices which favour females; female teachers demonstrating they have low expectations of boys' abilities; the absence of male role models which creates problems for boys in terms of motivation, discipline and social interaction; and, the way in which the curriculum is delivered and assessed favours girls' learning styles (Delamont, 1999).

Where 'feminisation of teaching' is used to denote management and pedagogical practices that are supposed to favour girls, there are two different strands of argument. On the one hand, some texts aim to help teachers address the problems of boys' underachievement but avoid attempting to apportion blame for this situation on the changes in women's position (Bleach, 1998a; Noble and Bradford, 2000). These texts offer a range of explanations for the causes of boys' underachievement including genetics and changes in society and the family (as well as looking at possible bias towards 'the feminine' in school organisation and practices). On the other hand, some writers frame discussion of the 'feminisation of teaching' in terms that imply that feminism has created a shift towards the privileging of female learning styles, assessment practices, modes of discipline and so forth (Redwood, 1994; Gurian, 1998). This articulation of the 'feminisation of teaching' is a feature of the political usage of the term.

Political usage of the term 'feminisation of teaching'

There have been significant changes to the perceptions and reality of women's lives in the last 30 years. Arnot *et al.* (1999) document how economic developments have precipitated social changes and transformed expectations, particularly in relation to women and work. Second-wave feminism played a key role in identifying inequalities (for example, in terms of the education they received, their access to careers, health matters, issues of sexual harassment and expectations of family commitments and obligations, to name but a few). But social changes have created a climate of uncertainty and resentment in certain areas and for particular groups which, in turn, has given rise to 'backlash politics'. For some, the advances for women brought about by feminism have contributed to this climate of uncertainty by creating a challenge to conventional sources of male power such as paid work, access to and ownership of knowledge production, and privileges in the home. For example, the decline in traditional jobs for working-class males focused around apprenticeships and skilled and semi-skilled work has been replaced by an increase in part-time, 'client centred', and low-paid, jobs in 'feminine' areas (such as call-centres and the leisure industry). Feminism has not *produced* backlash politics but is one of a range of factors associated with it. As Lingard and Douglas (1999: 127–8) have argued:

> In one sense, merit has become more important than gender or ethnicity as a determinant of opportunity; the overall result is more competition for jobs with careers attached, and greater and more pervasive uncertainty. Even those who access the 'good' jobs with career prospects are in a more uncertain position. Insecurity abounds and has been a significant factor in the emergence of backlash politics, including backlash national chauvinisms and anti-feminism . . .

In addition, the move towards increased credentialism has resulted in greater competitiveness to access the 'good jobs', or indeed any job, and inevitably some people get 'left behind'. This has largely affected working-class and minority ethnic boys and girls whilst, according to some commentators, white middle-class boys have been challenged by the increased achievements of middle-class girls to their 'natural/normal/rightful' places in high status university courses (Yates, 1997). However, as has been argued, the gains in public testing made by girls at school are relatively minor especially when these successes do not translate into well-paid careers with salaries commensurate to that of males (Mahony, 1997; Epstein *et al.*, 1998). For others, feminism has gone 'too far' and has generated a swing towards the 'feminisation of teaching' whereby circumstances are set up for girls to succeed and boys to fail (Browne and

Fletcher, 1995; Pollack, 1998). For these commentators, the 'feminisation of teaching' is used as a political attack on feminism.

While the political use of the 'feminisation of teaching' is evidently employed in a pejorative way, it is a tendency that is also apparent in the other two definitions. In all three usages, the 'feminisation of teaching' is portrayed as something which 'carries negative connotations, and assumes that the trend is a worrying one which needs to be reversed' (Smith, 1999: 3). Francis (2000a) points out that the phrase 'feminisation of the workplace' implies that the men in it have lost a degree of power and security as they have been reduced to the same level as the female workers. But by calling such processes 'feminisation' rather than 'disenfranchisement of the work force' (or any similar term), females are implicated as somehow responsible and to blame for these processes. These negative perceptions of what 'feminisation' means are themselves indicators that feminism still has a lot of work to do, and leads us to eschew any application of the term 'feminisation' ourselves. But the question here is whether it can be claimed with any accuracy that primary schools are 'feminised' in terms of their culture and values.

The feminisation of primary schools?

Primary schools are supposedly feminised because the teaching staff is predominantly female and, as a consequence, the practice and delivery of the curriculum, management strategies and teacher expectations favour girls. This, however, is a simple reading of a complex situation. There are two main questions that are generally unasked (for exceptions see Francis, 2000a; Mahony and Hextall, 2000; Haywood and Mac an Ghaill, 2001): what would a truly feminised primary school look like? And, if the 'feminisation of the teaching profession' (O'Connor, 1999) generates 'feminised' school practices then can only females 'do' femininity and males display masculinity? In agreeing with this, we would be taking a step backwards into sex role socialisation theory of the 1970s and 1980s which has been rigorously challenged for its limitations (Connell, 1987; Davies; 1989; Walkerdine, 1990). Each of these questions will be considered in turn.

A feminised primary school

If a 'feminised primary school' is taken to be one where daily organisational practices and management routines are based on conventional feminine characteristics and respond to ascribed female needs and desires then, according to the literature on female management styles, the following features would be observable:

- care and attention given to the provision of adequate and flexible child-care facilities for staff and parents (Francis, 2000a);
- a non-hierarchical management structure where decision making occurs on a democratic basis (Powney and Weiner, 1991);

- more inclusive approaches to the organisation of teaching and learning and, correspondingly, less emphasis on individualism (Adler *et al.*, 1993);
- school agendas that are informal and flexible (Ozga, 1990);
- emphasis on the improvement of educational opportunities for all with particular attention given to disadvantaged groups (Wyn *et al.*, 2000);
- emotional labour given priority (such as the sponsoring of younger [female] staff by older [female] staff) (Al-Khalifa, 1989).

However, the reality is that, far from becoming more progressively 'feminised', primary schools are increasingly 'masculinised' in terms of management regimes (Mahony and Hextall, 2000). But, it is a different form of 'masculinised school-ing' from that identified by feminists in an earlier period. Research in the 1980s demonstrated that opportunities to centralise and prioritise boys and masculinity were widespread in the primary school: for example, teacher expectations where boys were seen as more confident and able learners (Clarricoates, 1980); teach-ing resources such as reading schemes which stereotyped girls (Stones, 1983) whilst science and history books ignored female contributions (Walford, 1980; Cairns and Inglis, 1989); male teachers being responsible for discipline in the school and teaching only the oldest pupils (Aspinwall and Drummond, 1989). The more subtle manner in which 'masculinised primary schooling' was enacted through liberal child-centred pedagogies was perhaps more significant but less well debated (see Walkerdine, 1983).[2]

In the same way that major global changes in terms of the breaking down of traditional family forms, economic national boundaries, and conventional social relations, together with deindustrialisation and the subsequent effect on labour markets, has given rise to a 'new' form of politics as in the 'New Right' and 'New Labour', so a 'new' or 're-masculinisation' has emerged in schooling (Haywood and Mac an Ghaill, 2001). As we saw in Chapter 3, the 1988 Education Reform Act (ERA) brought to an end the concept of education as a means of developing economic growth and fostering equality of opportunity and social justice, replacing this notion of education with one that enabled individual aspirations through market competition. Since coming to power in 1997, New Labour have maintained support for this 'politics of difference' as opposed to the more traditional left adherence to a 'politics of redistribution' (Fraser, 1995).

In this context, the teacher's role has become increasingly focused on ensur-ing pupils achieve prescribed stages at certain ages in public tests whilst the 'job' of pupils is to become proficient in the subjects set down in a state regulated curriculum. Haywood and Mac an Ghaill (2001) have argued that one conse-quence of a restructured authority system, together with intensified surveillance, disciplinary codes, curriculum and testing stratification technologies, subject allocation and knowledge selection, has been to re-masculinise schooling. They go on to outline how this re-masculinisation emerges in school structure and organisation:

A legacy of the restructuring of state schooling . . . is the masculinization of the administrative functions that have come to predominate school life. High status has been ascribed to the 'hard masculine' functions of the accountant, the Key Stage tester, the curriculum coordinator, and the Information and Communication Technology expert. At the same time, female teachers are associated with and directed into the 'soft feminine' functions of profiling and counselling.

(Haywood and Mac an Ghaill, 2001: 28)

What is important here, as Haywood and Mac an Ghaill make clear, is that these masculine and feminine functions of teachers' roles are not characteristics or properties of male and female bodies. Rather, they are masculinised and feminised discourses which are woven into current policies on, and practices of, primary schooling.

'Doing' masculinity in the primary school

Calls for more men teachers in primary schooling can be heard by governments in Britain, North America, Australia, New Zealand and across Europe. The implicit message is that men teachers are needed to provide positive *masculine* images for boys and, to a lesser extent, girls. A lack of male teacher 'role models' is seen to be contributing to boys' lack of identification and consequent disaffection with schooling. For example, Noble (1998: 29) remarks with concern that,

. . . there are a large number of boys who may not come across an authoritative adult male until they reach secondary school. Only 12 per cent of primary teachers are male, many of them heads. Eleven years is a long time to be denied a role model of what you might be when you grow up.

It seems odd to discount headteachers as possible authoritative role models. Moreover, Noble goes on to ask what the 8-year-old boy thinks he will grow up to be, commenting that 'He knows he is not going to be his mother' (p. 29). But of course neither is a child going to 'be' his father! Are role models inevitably gendered? Are those frequently held up as international role models (Nelson Mandela, for example) only admired by one sex? Of course not. In which case we might reasonably ask whether a female teacher cannot provide a role model for boys just as well as a male teacher? Certainly all the evidence suggests that gender does not feature strongly in either boys' or girls' preferences for particular teachers (Lahelma, 2000; Ashley, 2001). It is true that liking someone or feeling they are good at teaching (aspects which have not been found to depend on gender) is not the same as seeing them as 'a role model'. And that boys are less likely to see themselves in the roles occupied by females than girls are those of males (Davies, 1989). But there is as yet no evidence to show that pupils of either gender *do* see their teachers as 'role models' (indeed, research has found that pupils' perceptions and aspirations are in any case rather more complex than notions of 'role modelling' suggest; Francis, 1998). And if pupils are not more likely to relate to or prefer teachers of the same gender, it seems unlikely that they would have a greater tendency to see same-sex teachers as role models. Further, as our own research has shown, men teachers are not themselves immune to the pressure to construct their masculinity in 'laddish' ways – hence in some cases they may reinforce 'macho' and anti-schooling constructions of masculinity in the classroom rather than providing 'alternative models' (Francis and Skelton, 2001. See also Connolly, 1998; Skelton, 2003).

The understanding of gendered identities reflected in ideas about male role models is based on essentialist notions of gender which recent theories, informed by post-structuralist perspectives, have challenged (Davies, 1989; Walkerdine, 1990). As Connell (1995: 230) has pointed out: 'Though most discussion of masculinity is silent about the issue, it follows from both psycho-analytic and social construction principles that women are bearers of masculinity as well as men'. An example of this occurred in research carried out in a primary school in the North East of England (Skelton, 2001a). The school was located in an area that was dominated by the activities of groups of young men in their mid- to late teens and it, together with the teachers, were often the targets of physical and verbal attack. The form of control exercised by the 'lads' was that of intimidation and aggression. In exercising classroom control, both male and female teachers emulated the same modes of masculine authority as the 'lads' thereby demonstrating that women can 'do' masculinity as effectively as men.

The way in which women, as well as men, might well be coerced into taking up what are traditionally 'masculinising behaviours' is indicated by Mahony and Hextall (2000) in their discussion of management in education. They begin by noting the masculinist language employed in the National Standards for Head-ship (TTA, 1998) and how they create an image of today's headteacher which is resonant of that associated with traditional male hierarchical management models. For example, headteachers are portrayed as leading and controlling others; so they 'lead by example' and 'ensure that all those involved in the school are committed to its aims' (p. 9). The personal characteristics of headteachers are those connected with hegemonic masculinities (Kenway and Fitzclarence, 1997) such as 'energy, vigour and perseverance', 'self confidence and intellec-tual ability' (p. 8). It may well be that the Teacher Training Agency were unaware of their gendered articulation of what a headteacher is and does but the use of such language might prove encouraging to men and discouraging to women. However, more importantly, Mahony and Hextall say that:

> . . . the problem goes far beyond the presence or absence of women and even beyond the relative positioning of women to men . . . If success in management is defined in masculinist terms then women (and men) will be

pressured to conform to its dictates in ways which may create tensions between their values and their power to act in collaborative ways.

(p. 119)

Furthermore, Mahony and Hextall go on to quote Kanter (1993) who has pointed out that when women move up the hierarchy they begin to identify more with the masculine model of managerial success and eventually discard any female managerial traits they may once have supported (see also Thompson, 2001).

There would seem, then, to be substantial support in research findings for the idea that, far from schools being increasingly 'feminised', there are strong indicators that in terms of educational policy-making they are becoming masculinised – or re-masculinised – in ways that are commensurate with global, new managerialist ideologies (Lingard and Douglas, 1999; Ashley, 2001).

EXPLANATION 4: ASSESSMENT PROCEDURES AND TEACHING PRACTICES ARE BIASED TOWARDS GIRLS

Assessment and achievement

Experts in the field of assessment have drawn attention to the complexity of 'testing' and the many and varied ways in which unfairness and inequity arises (Harlen et al., 1992; Gipps and Murphy, 1994; Broadfoot, 1996; Black and Wiliam, 1998; Ecclestone, 2002). As Gipps and Murphy (1994: 273) conclude 'there is no such thing as a fair test, nor could there be: the situation is too complex and the notion simplistic'. As we have seen, one of the preoccupations of those concerned with boys' underachievement has been that pedagogical practices in the UK, particularly in relation to English, have not been conducive to boys thus resulting in boys' poorer performance (Ofsted, 2003b). Methods of assessment have been identified particularly frequently as a key factor in this bias against boys. An explanation for boys doing less well at GCSE and A levels was the amount of coursework that was assessed with the argument being boys did less well in this aspect because of their preferred learning styles. Girls are seen to do better with sequential assessment methods that rewards consistent application (what Bleach (1998) controversially terms the 'diligent and plodding approach that is a characteristic of girls': 14). Girls do less well at 'sudden death' exams (timed exams previously unseen by the candidate) which require self-confidence and rely on last-minute revision. This latter form of assessment has been argued to favour boys (Bleach, 1998a), and were the model upon which O levels (the exams that preceded GCSEs in Britain) were based.

Hence in expressing concerns at 'boys' underachievement' some commentators in the British media have called for a return to more 'masculine' assessment techniques. But the assumptions behind this argument are rejected by the evidence. As Arnot *et al.* (1999) point out, girls tended to gain more O levels than boys too – it was just that as these awards were often in less prestigious subject areas than those taken by boys the point did not then raise concern. And Bleach (1998a) observes that girls' results were already improving *before* the GCSE assessment model was introduced. Moreover, Arnot *et al.* (1999) describe how a reduction in coursework in public examinations in the 1990s did little to alter the pattern of gender achievement. Bleach (1998a) cites educational bodies to show that girls currently outperform boys in both coursework *and* 'sudden death' examination components (see for example NEAB, 1996 cited by Bleach 1998a). Hence this evidence strongly contests the idea that gendered assessment models explain any gender gap in achievement at school.

Recent research suggests that one factor possibly having a negative impact on boys' performance is a self-fulfilling prophecy brought about by the media and government emphasis on 'boys' underachievement'. Teachers are receiving loud and frequent reminders that they need to be alert to and tackle the lower achievement in, and disinterest of boys for, education. Thus, it is not surprising to see research studies reporting that teachers are beginning to respond accordingly.[3] In their study of gendered classroom behaviour in relation to achievement, Younger *et al.* (1999: 327) report:

> While it is clear that in terms of quantitative measures, boys dominated student–teacher interactions, our data nevertheless suggests that growing numbers of teachers may be increasingly defining their 'ideal student' as female.

And later:

> Similarly, some teachers may be increasingly prone to take for granted the 'normality' or even the inevitability of increasing gender differentiation in girls' favour. In such cases, their behaviour towards boys may all too easily generate a self-fulfilling prophecy.

In their paper on gender and performance at 14, Elwood and Murphy (2000) considered how pupils are entered for GCSE mathematics. Since the introduction of GCSE in 1988 pupils have been allocated to one of three tiers for mathematics with the idea being that it increases reliability and is beneficial to pupils. Mathematics is comprised of three tiers: a foundation tier (grades D–G), an intermediate tier (grades B–E) and a higher tier (grades A*–C). As in the studies above, Elwood and Murphy (2000) discovered that teacher views and perceptions were influenced by boys' (and girls') attitudes and behaviours. Hence, more boys than girls were likely to be entered for the foundation tier on the basis that they were less motivated (and, as a consequence, were often not entered for GCSE mathematics). More girls than boys were entered for the intermediate level because teachers perceived girls to be less confident about their mathematical abilities. Boys dominated in the higher tier as teachers saw them to be highly competitive and expectant of good grades.

The behaviour of boys, or rather teachers' perceptions of boys' behaviours was also a feature in Harlen's (2004) report on 20 years of research into assessment. This report found, amongst other things, that teachers' judgements of boys' academic abilities were informed by their behaviour and, as they tended to misbehave more than girls, they were more likely to lose out on good assessment grades. Thus, unruly boys were given worse marks by teachers than their abilities warranted because they were not seen as good or hard workers (Mansell, 2004). These practices are of course inflected by issues of social class and ethnicity, as well as gender. A body of work has shown how many teachers read the behaviours of pupils differently depending on 'race' and social class (e.g. Sewell, 1997; Wright et al., 2000; Reay, 2001b). Although such gendered evaluations were not conscious judgements by teachers they provide a firm indication of the impact of social and cultural expectations on assessment.

It is worth noting, as indicated in the Elwood and Murphy (2000) research, that it is not only boys who are experiencing negative consequences of the situated nature of assessment. In terms of the segregation into tiers for GCSE mathematics, girls' perceived lack of confidence by teachers means their abilities are constrained as, in effect, they are obtaining more of their grades B and C from their position in the intermediate tier. Hence, 'there is a disproportionate number of girls whose participation in mathematics is marginalised' (Elwood and Murphy, 2000: 5). A similar occurrence was found by Lucey et al. (2003) in their longitudinal study of the teaching and learning of numeracy in primary schools where girls were progressing less well. The reason for this was partly attributable to girls' and boys' ways of interacting in maths classrooms, with the maths, with the teacher and with each other, which were 'surprisingly familiar, traditional even' (Lucey et al., 2003: 54).

Assessment experts tell us that assessment practices and evaluation of pupils' responses in tests need to take into account a range of contextual, and structural (gender, social class, ethnicity) factors. Alienation from the content knowledge needed to answer questions, familiarity with assessment materials and resources, and a recognition of preferred response styles can all introduce a bias into the assessment procedures and subsequent results (Gipps and Murphy, 1994). Furthermore, factors specific to a country should be recognised as, for example, when the OECD PISA (2003) data tells us that single-parent family background is an issue – but in the UK not in other countries – and that home background is a key, as is cultural capital and the job status of parents. All of this complex information needs to be factored in to any judgement about the impact of gender on assessment outcomes, but the evidence allows us to conclude at least that attributing girls' out-performance of boys to 'feminised assessment tools' is unfounded.

EXPLANATION 5: PUPILS' CONSTRUCTIONS OF GENDER PRODUCE DIFFERENT BEHAVIOURS WHICH IMPACT ON ACHIEVEMENT

Researchers have explored the way in which gender identities are socially con-structed in interaction, and an extensive body of work has applied these findings and approaches to research in educational settings. Hence researchers have shown how children actively construct their own gender identities as relational (masculinity being what femininity is not, and vice versa), and adopt different behaviours to express these oppositions (Davies, 1989). Although these beha-viours might be seen as a matter of choice, research has shown the strong penalties for children who fail to conform to gender norms (Davies, 1989; 1993; Connolly, 2004); and also the way in which these modes of being are taken on at a psychic level (Walkerdine, 1990; Walkerdine *et al.*, 2001). These gendered behaviours have variously been found to manifest in different ways at different stages of schooling. For example, researchers of early years education have documented gendered aspects of play at pre-school and early years levels (Davies, 1989; Lloyd and Duveen, 1992; MacNaughton, 2000; Connolly, 2004). Researchers in the primary school have shown how by this age boys are already tending to verbally and physically dominate classrooms (Reay, 1990; 2003; Skelton, 1996; 2001a), and how girls adopt helping and facilitating roles in efforts to delineate their femininity (Belotti, 1975; Walkerdine, 1990). Francis (1998) maintains that primary school girls construct themselves as 'sensible and selfless' in contrast to the boys, whose demanding behaviours they position as 'silly and selfish'. But she observes that their consequent facilitating behaviour meant frequently deferring power to the boys during mixed-sex interaction. Renold (2000; 2003) and Connolly (2003) have documented the sexualised behaviours evident among primary school children and shown how within these heterosexual tropes, male dominance and even sexual harassment are practised.

In all of this, the peer group is of central importance. As any teacher knows, given the choice pupils usually sit in same-gender groups, and, typically, friend-ship groups are composed of pupils of the same gender (Thorne, 1993; Adler and Adler, 1998). Davies (1989) and Lees (1992) show in detail how primary and secondary pupils respectively police and regulate the gendered behaviour of their peers, and punish failure to conform. Hence even during the early years modes of acceptable gender behaviour are firmly established among peer groups. These develop and change in aspects of their expression, and recent research has attended to the ways in which these expressions are produced differently according to social class and ethnicity (Connolly, 1998; 2004; Reay, 2001a; 2001b; 2003; Ali, 2003). But central features remain in place into adulthood, such as, the verbal and physical dominance of education spaces by boys (Howe, 1997; Younger *et al.*, 1999; Francis, 2000a; Warrington and Younger, 2002); the construction of femininity as sensible/mature and self-effacing; and the contrasting construction of masculinity as demanding and assertive.

It has been argued by many researchers that a particular construction of masculinity is invested with high peer-group status in the secondary school (and even in the later years of primary schooling). This construction is what has commonly been referred to as the 'laddish' construction of masculinity. For those outside the UK, the concept of the 'lad' may require some explanation. As Francis (1999c) discusses, the term was traditionally applied to young men and boys, and has gradually taken on a particular meaning around being 'one of the lads'. This term evokes a group of young males engaged in hedonistic practices (including 'having a laugh'; disruptive behaviour; alcohol consumption; objectifying women; and an interest in pastimes and subjects constructed as masculine). The concept tended in the past to be used in relation to white working-class youths (see Willis, 1977). But as Francis (1999c: 357) recounts,

> in the 1990s, a backlash against 'political correctness' led to a defiant resurgence of traditional 'laddish' values in the media, typified by the men's magazine *Loaded* and the popular sit-com 'Men Behaving Badly'. Thus, the values of 'lads' were appropriated by and popularised for middle-class (and often middle-aged) men, and the term has gained a new prominence in popular and media culture.

The key point in relation to gender and educational achievement is that the 'laddish' construction is seen as 'anti' academic application, hence having a negative impact on achievement. Some commentators see this by inference due to the conflict between 'laddish' values and school culture (Francis, 1999c; 2000a). In this sense 'laddish' behaviours have a negative affect on the achievement of the boys concerned and of their classmates due to the 'lads' disruptive and distracting behaviours, and prioritisation of other interests over schoolwork (Salisbury and Jackson, 1996; Francis, 2000a; Skelton, 2001a). Other writers see 'lads' as *specifically* 'anti-swot', and 'anti-work' (Willis, 1977; Mac an Ghaill, 1994; Martino, 1999): school work, diligence and application are constructed as feminine and hence some boys seek to disassociate themselves from it in efforts to bolster their constructions of masculinity. Martino (1999) maintains that where previously it had been particularly working-class boys who saw academic application as feminine and consequently sought to disassociate themselves from learning, these attitudes are now as well being adopted by some middle-class boys. Francis and Archer (forthcoming) have shown how constructions of 'laddism' itself may differ according to pupils' 'race' and social class.

There is though, another hypothesis which suggests that some boys act out laddish behaviours as a result of their negative schooling experiences and subsequent disenchantment (Bleach, 1998b; Jackson, 2002b; 2003). In this view, boys take up 'laddish' expressions of masculinity as an alternative method of building their self-worth or 'self-esteem', which has been damaged by their experiences of schooling. This assumes, like certain policy documents reflecting the discourse of 'at risk boys' (see Chapter 3), that boys tend towards having 'low self-esteem'. For example, commenting on his finding that boys said they would be unlikely to try hard if teacher feedback on their work was bad, Bleach (1998b: 45) maintains, 'This *fragility of ego* manifested itself in admissions of "stupidity" and "embarrassment", and in the desire to give up or, at least, maintain a low profile' (our emphasis). But as we shall see in the next chapter, the evidence shows that boys tend *not* to maintain a 'low profile' in the classroom. Hence there is a contradiction between research showing that boys have *higher* self-confidence and belief in their ability than girls, and the idea that they have 'low self-esteem' and low confidence, and retreat into 'laddism' as a result. Both views are represented within Kevan Bleach's edited collection: on one side there is Davison and Edwards (1998) noting that 'boys have an overconfidence in their own ability and a willingness to blame others, particularly teachers, for their failure' (p. 129), and Ryder (1998: 145) referring to boys' 'notorious and ill-judged optimism' about their work. Then conversely in the same book Terry and Terry (1998) reflect, 'It seems that more boys in our schools opt out of the academic race through fear of failure' (p. 110), and Bleach (1998b) concludes from boys' interview responses that to ask questions in class is 'to expose oneself to potential ridicule', hence boys 'lie low and avoid attention' to avoid the derision of their peers (p. 48). Bleach argues that such strategies have 'worrying implications' for boys' learning. Yet we know from classroom observational studies (Howe, 1997; Younger *et al.*, 1999; Warrington *et al.*, 2000) that boys ask far more questions in class than girls, as well as tending to produce more attention-seeking behaviour – so to see them as avoiding asking questions and 'lying low and avoiding attention' appears misplaced.

A slightly different view is the argument that some boys take up disruptive behaviours if they are not doing well in their schoolwork as a result of their competitive behaviours, rather than due to their 'low self-esteem' (e.g. Salisbury and Jackson, 1996; Epstein, 1998). In other words, such boys adopt the attitude that 'if they can't win then no-one will'; or they look for other competitions to excel in (e.g. being 'the most rebellious'; or the best at sport, etc.). This view sees boys as needing to depict power and 'success' of one sort or another as an aspect of their masculinity; but this is quite different from seeing boys as having 'low self-esteem'.

While we remain sceptical about boys' low self-esteem *per se*, a substantial body of work has shown how boys' constructions of masculinity which are high-status among secondary school peers are likely to have a negative impact on attainment (their own, and sometimes that of their classmates) (Salisbury and Jackson, 1996; Pickering, 1997; Epstein, 1998; Martino, 1999; 2000; Younger *et al.*, 1999; Francis, 2000a; Warrington *et al.*, 2000; Skelton, 2001a; Martino and Pallotta-Chiarolli, 2003; Younger *et al.*, 2005). These various studies have illustrated how constructions of gendered behaviour constitute a key explanation for a 'gender gap' in achievement. As with other explanations for gendered achievement patterns, it is extremely difficult to ascertain the *extent* to which boys' 'laddish' constructions of masculinity negatively affect their achievement –

for example, some boys appear adept at achieving in spite of 'laddish' behaviours – and few of the studies have examined the behaviours of individual boys in relation to any impact (or otherwise) on their educational attainment. However, the evidence presents a convincing explanation for the comparative under-attainment of some boys, and this is the only explanation that has not been discredited or challenged by counter-evidence.

Given this explanation about boys' constructions of masculinity having a potentially negative impact on their learning (and on that of their peers), there are different views of how to address this. Some commentators suggest what we have termed 'pragmatic approaches' (Francis, 2000a; Skelton, 2001a); which play on boys' constructions of masculinity. These include, for example, Noble's (1998) suggestion that competitive approaches to learning are foregrounded by teachers in order to engage boys; and Swan's (1998) advocacy of separate reading boxes for girls and boys (containing books appropriate to gendered tastes, and allowing boys to see their reading box as something not for girls and hence acceptable for them to peruse). Swan (1998) acknowledges, 'Some teacher colleagues would baulk at this manipulation of gender stereotypes, but others see it simply as a means of differentiation enabling both boys and girls to feel confident' (p. 169). However, we have argued that these approaches are likely to reinforce limiting stereotypes and to exacerbate gender differences in ability and expertise (Francis, 2000a; Skelton, 2001b). Others have argued rather that instead of pandering to constructions of difference which risk perpetuating the gendered behaviours seen to be impacting on achievement, schoolboys' constructions of high-status masculinity – and particularly those which position academic learning as feminine – need to be challenged (e.g. Salisbury and Jackson, 1996; Epstein et al., 1998; Francis, 2000a; Skelton, 2001a; Lingard et al., 2002; Martino and Pallott-Chiarolli, 2003). Particularly, Lingard et al. (2002) and Younger et al. (2005) and Warrington et al.'s (forthcoming; see also Warrington and Younger 2002) extensive studies of strategies being used to raise boys' achievement (without being detrimental to the achievement of girls) have conclusively shown that of the various approaches they monitored, the reduction in 'gendered classroom cultures' has the most profound impact on raising boys' achievement (Younger et al., 2005). Indeed, Warrington and Younger (2002) argue that decreasing gender difference and expectations around differentiated gendered behaviours is a vital prerequisite and first step before any other strategy may be fruitful. We shall explore these various approaches in relation to 'what works' in raising the achievement of boys and girls in more detail in Chapter 8.

Chapter 6

What has happened to the girls?

Introduction

Discussion of the notion of 'boys' underachievement' has punctuated the preceding chapters as we have tried to unpick the discourses and evaluate claims concerning gendered exam performance. In this chapter we turn instead to a group who constitute half the student population, yet have been largely ignored in the popular debates on gender and achievement – girls.

Some feminists have criticised 'celebratory discourses' around girls' improved exam performance as masking the extent to which such female achievement is differentiated by social class and ethnicity (e.g. Lucey, 2001; Walkerdine *et al.*, 2001). But although some liberal feminists may talk up girls' success, such 'celebration' has in fact been scarce, particularly among media commentators and policy-makers. In the scramble to analyse 'what has happened to the boys', girls' achievement, and the issues around it, have largely been ignored. Indeed, it is worse than this – to say that girls have been 'ignored' implies that their framing in the literature has been less pernicious than is actually the case. Girls are absent in the popular debates, *except* where to complain that boys have been disadvantaged, and girls aided by the 'feminisation' of assessment methods. This argument subtly implies that as well as disadvantaging boys, so-called 'girl-friendly' methods of assessment such as coursework are 'namby-pamby' and insufficiently 'rigorous'. Francis (2000b; Francis *et al.*, 2003) has shown how particular subjects and methods of study are constructed as gendered on the basis of the following dichotomy:

Male	*Female*
rationality	emotion
objectivity	subjectivity
science	nature
'hard'	'soft'
'the sciences'	'the arts'
male logic and focus	indecision and lack of focus
self-confidence	self-doubt
content	communication/presentation

Binary dichotomies produce power and lack. We suggest that the above dichotomy is evident in the discourse of disparagement concerning the 'feminisation of assessment'. The discourse equates 'sudden-death' tests with toughness, robustness, assertive confidence, 'hard' curricula. So 'sudden-death' tests are constructed both as masculine and as academic (conflating the two), in opposition to coursework which is positioned as gentle, easy, nebulous, mediocre, not properly academic, and feminine. And of course as we saw in the previous chapter, in blaming '*femini*sation' of assessment, the discourse unsubtly blames *females* for boys' apparent underperformance.

But apart from these arguments about assessment, girls are largely absent from the mainstream debate. Although 'boys' underachievement' is obviously nominally being compared to an unspoken 'girls' achievement' (or even 'girls' *over*achievement'), girls' performance itself is rarely discussed. The very fact that the debate is coined as '*boys*' underachievement' (rather than 'gender and achievement') demonstrates the focus of attention. For example, few researchers or policy-makers have analysed the improved attainment of girls in some areas or examined possible explanations for it. Moreover, while some research projects continue to explore girls' classroom experiences, these are vastly outnumbered by research projects on boys (particularly in terms of funded research); the latter of which also gain far more attention from media and policy-makers. The lack of discussion of girls, then, constitutes an absence, a silent gap in the discourse. This gap reveals the marginalisation of girls, how their school performance is seen as peripheral to that of boys, how they *do not count*. Some feminist educationalists have observed that when *girls* were perceived to be the underachieving group during the 1970s and 1980s there was far less attention to their plight, or funding to remedy the situation (Griffin, 1998; Arnot *et al.*, 1999).

Therefore in this chapter we want to spend time discussing 'what has happened to the girls' in terms of their achievement and educational experiences. We shall investigate the extent to which girls are 'achieving' in the education system, examining differences according to variables such as social class and ethnicity. We will discuss explanations as to changes in girls' achievement patterns. We shall highlight and illustrate the fact that not all girls are achieving (and that there is some evidence that the policy focus on boys' achievement is further marginalising these underachieving girls). And finally we shall draw attention to the fact that irrespective of their exam performance, evidence demonstrates that actually very little has changed for girls in mixed-sex schools over the last three decades in terms of their actual (gendered) classroom experience.

Girls' changed ambitions

As we have seen in Chapter 4, the achievement of girls *as a group* at GCSE examination has increased. The exam performance of both boys and girls is improving year on year in Britain. Girls' overall performance at A level and at degree level has increased too. More women than men now enter higher education, and more of these women undergraduates are acquiring 'good' degrees than are their male counterparts (Francis *et al.*, 2001). So what has led to these patterns of achievement for girls? It is often assumed that girls used to underachieve at exams marking the end of compulsory education, and that this situation has now 'turned around'. For example, that when the final year of British compulsory education was marked by O level exams, as it was until 1987, girls performed badly in comparison with boys. But that since the 1980s, and particularly since the introduction of the GCSE examination, girls have gradually been increasing their performance and have now eclipsed boys. But as we saw in Chapter 5, this is a misrepresentation. Girls' achievement at O level had not been recognised because it tended not to be in prestigious subject areas. With the introduction of the National Curriculum in England and Wales in 1988, boys and girls were forced to take the same core subjects for the first time. Following that introduction girls very quickly caught up with boys at mathematics and science, while boys have failed to catch up with girls at English and modern languages. Hence Arnot *et al.* (1999) argue that in England and Wales it is the introduction of the National Curriculum that has made the most significant contribution to the changed patterns in gender and achievement since the 1980s.

But, given that girls' achievements have improved as a group even since the introduction of the National Curriculum, it is important to consider what might have led to these changes, as well as to look more closely at *which* girls are achieving. As we saw in Chapter 5, there is scant evidence to suggest that girls' increased performance over recent decades is due to changes in methods of assessment. However, there is a body of work which demonstrates that girls' social views and aspirations have altered considerably during this period, and some have suggested that these changes may be impacting on girls' educational motivation. As David (2003) catalogues, the period since the 1980s in Britain and the Western world generally has been one of particularly marked social change. Accepted gender norms have shifted along with a raft of other dramatic changes affecting the fabric of social life (see Chapter 3). We have discussed how theorists of these changes have argued that society is 'individualised', and how this perspective additionally positions individuals as responsible for their security and fates in this individualised world, deflects responsibility away from the state and on to individuals themselves (Sampson, 1989; Lucey, 2001; Reay *et al.*, 2001; Walkerdine, 2003; Bauman, 2005; Skelton, 2005).

Interestingly, as Lucey (2001) has observed, it is women whom Beck (1992) sees as embodying this new vision of individualised selfhood. They are held up as 'setting the pace of change'. Yet it is actually just middle-class women who are being constructed in this way (Walkerdine, 2003). And as Walkerdine and Lucey's joint and separate bodies of work show, social class (and other social variables such as ethnicity) continue to have a profound impact on educational outcomes. Unfortunately the *experience* of such failure as *individual* is illustrated all too clearly in the data from their young women respondents who often feel inadequate and responsible. We shall return to the impact of social class and ethnicity in relation to girls' educational performance later in this chapter. But before that we want to look at girls' own views of their futures and how this may relate both to the recent patterns of gender and achievement and to girls' future trajectories in post-compulsory education and the adult workplace.

Schoolgirls' occupational aspirations have broadened considerably and become more ambitious over the last three decades. Researching in the 1980s, Spender (1982), Gaskell (1992) and others found that girls planned to work until they were married, and then to stop work or assume the role of secondary breadwinner. But findings in the primary and secondary school now show that girls have since become far more career-oriented (Sharpe, 1994; Francis, 1996; 2002; Miller and Budd, 1999). The majority appear to see their chosen career as reflecting their identity, and see it as a vehicle for future fulfilment, rather than as simply a stopgap before marriage (Riddell, 1992; Wilkinson and Mulgan, 1995). And whereas Spender (1982) and others found that secondary school girls largely aspired to a very narrow range of stereotypically-feminine, non-professional jobs, more recent research has found secondary school girls choosing a much broader range of occupations, including some stereotypically masculine jobs (Wikeley and Stables, 1999; Sharpe, 2004). Closer inspection of these choices shows that gendered preferences remain evident in the attributes of the jobs selected by girls, which tend to be categorisable as caring or creative (Francis, 2002; Francis et al., 2003). Yet it is certainly the case that as a group girls have higher aspirations than used to be the case: many girls now choose jobs which normally require a degree, demonstrating a high level of ambition (Lightbody and Durndell, 1996; Francis, 2002). This raised ambition represents a dramatic change over the last three decades. This change has been facilitated by the economic transformations that have led to different working practices and expectations, and the resulting changed discourses around acceptable behaviour for men and women, with an accelerating effect as the greater representation of women in diverse areas of work offers examples of future possibilities to school girls. Such 'choices' are not equally open to all girls, however. 'Choices' are limited or facilitated by young people's particular environments, institutional barriers, and the sorts of routes and aspirations which they consequently see as appropriate or achievable for 'people like me' (Archer and Yamashita, 2001). Francis (1996; 2002) found girls from the largely working-class and ethnically mixed London schools in her sample to be highly ambitious and diverse in their choices of future occupation. But findings from Warrington and Younger (2002) and Francis et al.'s (2004) research with wider samples suggest that ethnicity and locality are influential, as the white working-class girls in their studies that included non-urban areas provided a less ambitious and more gender-stereotypical range of occupational choices. This supposition is supported by Mirza's (1992) finding that girls of African-Caribbean origin were more ambitious and more ready to opt for non-gender-traditional jobs than were white girls; and findings by Lightbody (1997) and Francis and Archer (2004) that British South Asian and Chinese pupils are more likely than other groups to opt for professional careers.

Girls realise that in order to achieve their increased occupational ambitions, they need qualifications. This is particularly true of upper-middle-class girls, who, as Arnot *et al.* (1999) observe, are invested in by their (independent) schools and families in order to turn social capital into economic capital. But girls from other social groups are also increasingly aware of the importance of educational credentials. Francis (2000a; 2002) shows how London working-class girls from diverse ethnic groups are highly aware of, and concerned about, continued sex discrimination in the adult workplace. They talked of having to be 'better than the boys' in order to level the employment playing field, and qualifications were seen as a way to demonstrate their ability. She maintains that girls' increased ambition, coupled with a feeling that opportunities in the workplace are skewed against them, is what has provided girls with new motivation for achievement at school. Girls are increasingly confident of their ability at schoolwork when comparing it with that of boys. There is evidence that in some schools the debate over 'boys' underachievement' has trickled down to pupils, buoying girls' confidence about the academic abilities of girls as a group (Francis, 2000b).

'Achieving' girls . . .

Expectations of 'excellent achievement' for daughters as well as sons have been the norm within middle- and upper-class families for some time. Hence Diane Reay (2001a) argues that what has changed in terms of gender and achievement is 'the gendered composition of middle-class academic success' (p. 156) – middle-class girls are now doing as well as (and in some cases better than) middle-class boys. Walkerdine *et al.* (2001) found that in some of the middle-class families in their study exam success was expected to such an extent that anything other than 'excellent' grades was perceived as failure. The longitudinal work by Walkerdine and Lucey (1989) and Walkerdine *et al.* (2001) shows that feelings and fears of 'not being good enough' characterise the talk of middle-class girls from an early age. These girls expressed high levels of anxiety and lack of confidence about their performance, despite in many cases being extremely high-performing. It was as though they could '*never* be good enough' (see also Lucey and Reay, 2000a). These findings about the pressure that some white middle-class girls are under somewhat call into question Helen Wilkinson's (1995) argument about the emergence of the 'masculinised new woman'. She maintains that these high performing young women are at ease with themselves in their acquisition of the exciting masculine attributes of competition, ambition, and 'drive'. Wilkinson's model reflects a 'post-feminist' image of 'girl power', in which gender equity is increasingly realised as the norms of gendered behaviour are challenged and changed. Clearly such a view represents a liberal perspective where a goal of 'gender equity' in terms of women's ability to be 'like men' is realised, rather than a more radical feminist challenge to the masculine values and practices which underlie all facets of our social interaction.

That aside, as Lucey (2001) maintains, such presentations of young (middle-class) women as 'having it all' and 'in control' are something of an illusion.

Indeed, even for middle-class girls, the route to 'success' is less a path than a tight-rope. Girls realise that in order to be seen as successful women in contemporary society they must be attractive, as well as high educational achievers (Hey, 1997; Walkerdine *et al.*, 2001; O'Brien, 2003). This combination is particularly difficult to negotiate, as there are powerful associations between cleverness and a-sexuality/unfemininity (Walkerdine and the Girls and Mathematics Unit, 1989; Reay, 2001a). Valerie Hey (1997) and Diane Reay (2001a) argue, therefore, that there are fundamental psychic contradictions in being an educationally achieving girl, pincered as girls are between discourses of compulsory heterosexuality that foreground gender difference and discourses of academic application which suppress difference. Being a popular or 'successful' girl depends on a particular construction or interweaving of factors such as ethnicity, intelligence, academic achievement, 'beauty', social class, knowledge of and access to popular culture, and so on (Ali, 2003). As we shall see, the achievement of such balances may be particularly challenging for girls who do not fit the 'norm' of white, middle-class girlhood. However, even for white, middle-class high-achieving girls, there are psychic tensions bound up with such balances. As Lucey (2001) and Walkerdine *et al.* (2001) show, the behaviour of these girls is tightly constrained, and the costs of the suppression of femininity and sexuality involved in being an academic achiever can lead to stress, anxiety and even identity crises. It is argued that these psychic costs can be evidenced in the increase in self-harm and eating disorders among middle-class girls (Reay, 2001a; Walkerdine, 2003).

The achievement of minority ethnic girls tends to be either ignored or problematised by commentators. As Mirza (1992) has demonstrated in her stinging critique of commentary on 'race' and educational attainment, the educational performance of British African-Caribbean girls has tended to be overlooked, due to a conflation of their achievement figures with those of British African-Caribbean boys. British African-Caribbean boys underachieve compared to their female counterparts, but this underachievement gains more attention, so that their underachievement tends to be conceived as 'underachievement of [all] African-Caribbean pupils'. High achieving groups such as British-Indian and British-Chinese girls tend to face a doubly pernicious discursive positioning. The usual narratives regarding achieving girls (they are too quiet, too diligent, achieving through hard work rather than brilliance, and via repressive learning practices rather than by approved active learning) are applied to them, arguably even in a heightened way (Archer and Francis, 2005). But they are also positioned as achieving due to a ruthlessly oppressive home culture (Siraj-Blatchford, 1993; Archer and Francis, 2005). Hence the achievement of these girls is problematised by racist and sexist discourses which 'Other' the girls and their practices in relation to an unspoken but ever-present white, middle-class masculine model.

So even for achieving girls, the occupation of the masculine position of academic achiever is fraught with difficulties and costs. Indeed, as 'natural brilliance' continues to be constructed as a male attribute, it is little wonder that the success of these girls is rarely recognised, and that they internalise feelings of 'never being good enough'. For they are not, and can never be, boys. That being said, middle-class white girls' educational success is clearly reproducing class capital in that many of these girls go on to work in careers that are relatively well-paid and high status.[1] Which is far from being the case for many girls. We turn now to girls who are not achieving high education credentials. These are predominantly white working-class girls.

... And 'underachieving' girls

As we have already seen, in Britain the social-class gap in achievement is far more significant than the gender gap (Gilborn and Mirza, 2000; Plummer, 2000; Lucey, 2001). The focus of policy-makers and media commentators on *gender* and achievement is obscuring entrenched and enduring differences in achievement according to social class and ethnicity. Working-class girls are outperforming working-class boys at school, but middle-class girls *and* boys continue to do far better (Lucey, 2001). The tendency to present middle-class girls' achievement as representative of all girls insidiously hides the underachievement of many working-class girls, thus masking continued social inequality.

The notion of 'excellence' is a trope in contemporary British education policy, with striving for, and the production of, 'excellence' (i.e. high achievement) represented as a central concern. As Lucey (2001; Lucey *et al.*, 2003) observes, the idea of 'excellence' depends on the continued presence of its opposite: failure. She describes how special programmes in Britain such as 'gifted and talented' schemes, ostensibly conceived as enabling meritocracy by providing gifted working-class children with recognition and development, actually construct working-class failure. She points out that in spite of the rhetoric it is actually middle-class children who are more likely to be chosen for such schemes, and that anyway the schemes are available only to a small number of pupils. However, by their very existence the schemes can be used to suggest that the mass 'failure' of working-class pupils is of their own making rather than due to inequality of opportunity. Her findings with Reay (Lucey and Reay, 2000) show that the 'failure' of working-class girls is set up early on in their lives, exacerbated by notional markets and theories of 'free-choice'. Middle-class girls have been found to defer to their parents concerning the decision about which secondary school to attend (Reay and Ball, 1998; Walkerdine *et al.*, 2001; O'Brien, 2003), whereas the different values and lack of 'educational capital' in working-class families means that working-class girls tend to rely on social networks rather than parents to direct their decisions around school choice (O'Brien, 2003). Moreover, working-class girls are less likely to be offered a place at their school of choice than middle-class girls (black boys have been found to fare worst in this process) (Lucey and Reay, 2000). So 'choices' are far from equal, and are strongly mediated by social class and 'race'. Walkerdine *et al.* (2001) found that the few working-class white girls in their study who had succeeded in gaining undergraduate degrees had taken extremely fragmented and diverse routes to higher education in comparison with their middle-class contemporaries. Walkerdine *et al.* set these struggles of the working-class girls against the largely homogeneous and smooth routes to higher education taken by the middle-class girls in their study to challenge Beck's (1992) claim that educational experience can no longer be understood in social class terms.

Qualitative research reveals the psychic consequences of struggle and 'failure' for working-class girls. As Maeve O'Brien (2003: 251) observes of the working-class Irish girls in her study,

> Often the price of [educational] success becomes too high for many working-class girls. Against a background of parental worry and concern, working-class girls internalise that the effort required to achieve high academic performance is too gruelling, too lonely, unsociable and stressful, and to give up the idea that they can have it all, i.e. both success and happiness.

We have already commented on the difficult battle in performing femininity simultaneously with academic success which is undertaken by successful middle-class girls, and the psychic costs involved. But at least for middle-class girls the values of the school tend to reflect those they experience at home. O'Brien (2003) reports that the middle-class culture and expectations in some secondary schools are hard for working-class girls to adjust to. For many of these girls acclimatisation into this middle-class ethos is too difficult, and the girls concerned begin to disengage; a process which O'Brien labels ' "moving out" rather than "moving on" ' (p. 251).[2] Clearly such processes impact on the self-image of these girls, particularly in light of the contemporary individualist discourses which position underachievement as the responsibility (and failure) of the individual. For example, Archer *et al.* (2003) found that those not engaged in 'lifelong learning' expressed guilt, embarrassment and shame at this 'lack', irrespective of the reasons for their non-participation. But as well as these psychic burdens as a consequence of educational underachievement, the economic implications remain enormous: particularly in the light of recent qualification inflation (Ainley, 1994), education credentials are increasingly vital in the search for a 'good' job.

As Diane Reay (2001a) has observed, variables such as 'race' and social class 'never mediate gender in formulaic or predictable ways' (p. 154). Girls from some ethnic groups do better than others in the British education system (see Chapter 4). Although it is generally the case that social class is the clearest predictor of educational achievement for all ethnic groups, and across ethnic groups (Gilborn and Mirza, 2000), this is not *always* so. For example, British-Chinese pupils from working-class backgrounds still tend to do well in the British education system (Francis and Archer, 2005). Findings by Mortimore and Whitty (1997) show that in all ethnic groups adult women are generally less qualified than men, except for African-Caribbeans where women are better qualified than their male counterparts.

The gendered nature of 'girls' achievement'

Despite the changes in overall patterns of gender performance, a closer look at the figures on gender and achievement reveals some co-existing continuities. As we have indicated in Chapters 4 and 5, strong differences remain in the types of subject pursued by young men and women, and the status accorded to these subjects. We spend some time focusing on this issue here because (a) we maintain that the gendered patterns in pursuit of different subject disciplines illustrates underlying stability in the gender order; and (b) they have been shown by the Equal Opportunities Commission to provide one of the key explanations for the continuing gender pay-gap, where in Britain men continue to earn on average more than women (EOC, 2004).

As we observed in Chapter 4, even at GCSE level, where male and female pupils have all followed the National Curriculum, fewer girls than boys are entered for GCSE exams in science and mathematics, and more girls than boys are entered for English and modern language exams. There is some evidence that girls and boys are now slightly less gender-stereotypical in their subject preferences than used to be the case – for example, Francis (2000a) found that girls *and* boys rated English as the most popular subject, and that mathematics is now popular with many girls. But in terms of least favourite subjects, a more traditional pattern remains, with girls overall tending to dislike mathematics and science more than boys,[3] and more boys than girls disliking arts subjects. Gender differences in relation to curriculum subjects are evident even in the primary school years, with girls doing consistently better at literacy, and more boys showing an affiliation with mathematics. Lucey et al. (2003) maintain that by age 11 boys' advantage in mathematics and science is already apparent, and is maintained to GCSE and A/AS level with more boys entered for these exams, and more boys gaining top grades.[4] Once subject choice is introduced at 16 young men and women continue to make highly gendered decisions – right up to degree level. As we showed in Chapter 4, far more young women than young men choose 'arts' subjects (including arts, languages, and humanities subjects) at A level and undergraduate level, and the science subjects (including subjects such as mathematics, science, engineering and IT)[5] remain dominated by men. For example, in 2003 only 3.1 thousand women gained a first degree in engineering and technology, and 4.2 thousand in computer science; compared to the 15.7 thousand men who gained a first degree in engineering and technology and 13.4 thousand in computer science. And conversely 14.6 women gained first degrees in languages; compared with 5.2 thousand men (HESA, 2004). Moreover, in the case of females, fewer of those who do take up science subjects excel at post-compulsory level. With some notable exceptions such as medical degrees (which have seen an explosion in uptake by women) these traditional, gendered patterns remain entrenched.

It has traditionally been the case that 'the arts' have been constructed as a feminine realm, while conversely 'the sciences' are constructed as masculine. This dichotomy bears a hierarchy in terms of the status attached to the subjects involved. 'The sciences' are associated with high-status (masculine) traits such as rationality and objectivity, while 'the arts' are relationally positioned as imbued with feminine attributes of emotion and subjectivity (see the binary dichotomy at the beginning of this chapter for illustration). As we have seen, the dichotomy is unequal in terms of power and status: the traits assigned to the 'feminine' are lower in social status, and are positioned in relation to the masculine as 'other' and sub-standard. In relation to curriculum subjects, not only are 'feminine' arts subjects constructed as lower-status than science subjects due to their ascribed feminine attributes such as emotion and subjectivity, but they also suffer in status due to their positioning as 'soft' (conflated, as we have seen, with 'easy'). The sciences are seen as harder, more difficult, more rigorous. This is bound up both with a construction of masculinity (masculine traits) and with gendered power (status and power residing in the masculine). So subjects which are more often pursued by young men are seen as more difficult and more important than those more commonly pursued by young women.

Why do boys and girls tend to enjoy different subjects? Explanations for this phenomenon have been diverse; for example, those of inherent sex differences (Parsons and Bales, cited in Whitehead, 1996); differences in cognitive style (see Head, 1996, for discussion); a masculinised educational environment which values the learning styles of boys over girls (Walkerdine *et al.*, 1989); and gender stereotyping, or differential constructions of gender, among pupils and teachers (Spender, 1982; Thomas, 1990; Whitehead, 1996; Francis, 2000a). We have already discussed in Chapter 5 how evidence for the influence of inherent sex difference on abilities is extremely slight, and has been extensively challenged. And although a substantial body of work has suggested that *as groups* boys and girls tend to prefer different learning styles, the extent of such differences has been debated. For example, Younger *et al.*'s (2005) study examined the visual, auditory and kinaesthetic aspects of primary and secondary school pupils' pre-ferred learning styles and found that there was little differentiation in preferred learning style between boys and girls. So although it is clearly the case that boys and girls as groups tend to behave differently in the classroom, it is not clear to what extent such differences manifest in actually different learning preferences and abilities.

A further explanation is that girls and boys may tend to be drawn to different subject areas due to constructions of the genders as different and relational. In other words, pupils and teachers may (consciously or unconsciously) see it as more appropriate for girls to study arts subjects and for boys to pursue the sciences. For example, Lucey (2001) observes that literacy and English are often constructed as 'naturally female' due to their 'feminine' curriculum content.

Girls, then, may find the study of English to be affirming to their constructions of femininity, while boys may find it challenging to their constructions of masculinity. Such gendering of pursuits and activities used to be seen as the result of gender stereotyping, so that girls and boys would pursue subjects and adopt other behaviours as appropriate to their learnt gender roles (see for example Spender, 1982). As we saw in Chapter 3, more recently feminists have drawn on postmodern theories to incorporate pupils' active pursuit of such constructions, and in many contrary cases their resistance to such gendered positioning (see Davies, 1989; 1993). For example, it has been argued that pupils draw on gender discourses to construct their own gender positions, and that different discourses are available to different children (for example, depending on their gender, social class, 'race', and so on) at different times, in different environments. As researchers such as Connolly (1998), Francis (1998), Marsh (2000) and Skelton (2002) maintain, pupils utilise particular behavioural signs (such as particular actions, dress code, interests, etc.) to delineate their gender allegiance and bolster their gender identity. Moreover, our implication in gender discourse is so subtle that behavioural difference becomes taken for granted and naturalised. Butler (1990) argues that gender is a performance, and that gender identity is maintained by the countless repetition of gendered acts. Yet these acts become completely unconscious: we are largely unaware that we are 'doing' gender. And because our gender identities are bound up both with our desires to 'fit in' and with other Enlightenment discourses of individual choice and personhood, we tend to view our behaviours as natural expressions of our personalities, rather than as the product of our (gendered) discursive positioning. Hence girls' tendencies to choose arts subjects over sciences, and boys' preferences for the sciences, may reflect both the desire of the individual to align themselves with apparently gender-appropriate subjects, and the appeal of a (gendered) subject curriculum to an individual with gendered interests.

Teachers and other adults (such as parents) may also play a part in these processes. It has been shown that teachers' expectations and perceptions of their pupils are often gendered. For example, behaviour that teachers see as acceptable in one gender is sometimes problematised in the other. Girls generally are expected to be appropriately reticent, conscientious and demure in the classroom – although such behaviour in itself is not necessarily rewarded. Walkerdine (1990) maintains that girls' helpful and obedient behaviour tends to be viewed as 'other' and even despised by primary school teachers who see such girls as lacking the demanding and 'creative' behaviour that delineates the proper [masculine] child. This tendency is exacerbated for South Asian and Chinese girls and boys, whose apparent diligence and obedience is often viewed by educators as pathological, and as reflecting 'oppressive' cultural attitudes on the part of parents (Siraj-Blatchford, 1993; Connolly, 1998; Archer and Francis, 2005).

When girls do not conform to conventional gender behaviours they invite harsh criticism from teachers. In a study by Reay (2001b) teachers spoke of girls who were misbehaving as 'a bad influence', 'little cows', 'scheming little madams' and 'spiteful' whilst similar behaviour in boys was simply seen as 'mucking about' (see also Skelton, 2002). So as Reay (2001b) argues, girls' bad behaviour is seen as indicative of a character defect, whereas such behaviour in boys is often constructed as 'natural high spirits'. These tendencies of expecting boys and girls to behave in different ways, but constructing the feminine mode as 'lacking' and inadequate, can also be seen in perceptions of ability. Studies conducted over the last three decades have shown that, irrespective of actual performance, innate academic brilliance is perceived by educators to reside in the male. Girls (and women) are viewed as 'conformist plodders' who achieve through hard work, whilst boys (and men) are seen as lazy or distracted but 'naturally talented' (Belotti, 1975; Walden and Walkerdine, 1985; Cohen, 1998; Griffin, 1998; Francis *et al.*, 2003). So, in terms of teachers' perceptions of the abilities of pupils, boys continue to be perceived as 'naturally bright but lazy'. As we suggest elsewhere (Skelton and Francis, 2003), perhaps it is the converse positioning of girls as 'not naturally bright, but hard-working' that partially explains the reluctance to celebrate 'girls' achievement'. Such perceptions by teachers open up the likelihood of self-fulfilling prophecy, providing a likely contributing explanation for the fact that boys are consistently shown to tend to over-estimate their ability and performance; while girls conversely lack confidence and underestimate their academic abilities.

So, if teachers perceive girls and boys and their approaches to, and production of, school work in different ways according to gender, it is likely that some teachers will consciously or unconsciously encourage girls and boys to pursue 'gender-appropriate' subjects. Spender (1982) and Stanworth (1981) found that teachers' expectations for pupils differed dramatically according to pupils' gender: expectations tended to be gender-stereotypical and were more ambitious in the case of boys. Similarly Benett and Carter (1981) found that careers officers tended to steer girls and boys towards gender-stereotypical occupations, and of course such routes required particular (gendered) subject qualifications. Rolfe (1999) has found that such practices are far less overt than they were in the past, but that gender equality issues are not prioritised in the careers service, and that covert or unconscious stereotyping may remain a problem on the part of careers advisors. It is clear that such gendered subject choices have an extremely strong impact on young peoples' future career trajectories in terms of job opportunities, status, and remuneration (Furlong and Cartmel, 1997; Rees, 1999).

So we have shown here how in spite of some shifts in terms of exam achievement, there is continuity in types of subjects chosen and pursued according to gender, and that these choices continue to have strong consequences for pupils future lives.

Classroom interaction and girls' experience of co-education

And what are the experiences of girls in the classroom? Feminist classroom research in the 1970s and 1980s drew attention to the ways in which girls were marginalised in the education system, and systematically belittled and undermined in the mixed-sex school classroom and playground. Education policy, curriculum, teacher expectations and interaction, and interaction with boys, were demonstrated to impact negatively on girls' classroom experience and self-perceptions. Such findings were used to argue that girls' apparent under-performance at subjects such as mathematics and science could be explained by their lack of confidence and disaffection from schooling (and from 'masculine' subjects in particular). As we have seen, girls were not actually underachieving at this time – their positioning as such was due to the application of a masculinist hierarchy of curriculum subjects prior to the introduction of a mandatory National Curriculum. Nevertheless, because girls' experiences of schooling were set up as explaining underachievement at mathematics and science, many assume that because girls have recently caught up with boys at these subjects their classroom experiences must now be equitable with those of boys; or even that the equal opportunities initiatives of the 1980s have 'gone too far' in empowering girls, and that attention now ought to be brought to bear on improving schooling experience for boys. In fact, as Arnot et al. (1999) demonstrate, equal opportunities initiatives tended to be small-scale, disparate, and undertaken sporadically rather than systematically. This was due to the fact that they were largely unfunded or under-funded, and frequently undertaken voluntarily by dedicated teachers, often in the face of outright hostility from colleagues, pupils and parents (see for example, Reay, 1990; 2003), and from the media and government (Arnot et al., 1999). Hence, valuable as these initiatives were for improving the experiences of some girls and resisting the dominant ethos, it is extremely unlikely that they were solely responsible for raising girls' achievement in mathematics and science.

However, all the evidence shows that girls' classroom experiences are actually characterised more by continuity than by change. A review of the literature of the past 30 years on gendered classroom relations demonstrates little change in three decades in the perceptions applied to girls, girls' classroom behaviour, and girls' experiences (Skelton and Francis, 2003). For the purposes of this chapter we highlight this point by focusing briefly on gendered classroom interaction in co-educational schools, attending to issues of power and control.

Boys' physical domination of the classroom and playground space has been well-documented. In the classroom, boys quite simply tend to take up more space than girls. Even when sitting at desks boys tend to sprawl more to take up more room, and when moving around the classroom their activities are more invasive of space. Such activities often involve real or jokey violence between boys: maintenance of a construction of aggressive and competitive masculinity involves constant confrontation and challenges between boys (Skelton, 2000a; 2001a). This male physicality is not only applied to other boys. Sexual harassment of girls, and sometimes of women teachers, by boys in the classroom has been reported by a variety of researchers (e.g. Herbert, 1989; Salisbury and Jackson, 1996; Mills, 2001; Renold, 2003). Such harassment can be verbal as well as physical, and homophobic verbal harassment is also rife. Misogynist and homophobic abuse has been shown to be a frequent feature in classroom exchanges, further degrading the feminine as 'other' in the classroom (Epstein, 1997; Epstein et al., 1998; Francis, 2000a; Renold, 2000; 2003; Martino and Pallotta-Chiarolli, 2003).

These gendered, controlling practices are continued in the playground. As researchers such as Thorne (1993), Skelton (2001a) and Connolly (2003) show, the activities pursued by girls and boys in the playground tend to be quite different. In Britain boys' tendency to dominate the primary and secondary school playground space is particularly enacted and illustrated by their common practices of playing football (e.g. Blatchford et al., 1990; Connolly, 1998, 2003; Skelton, 2001a). Football games usually involve a large number of boys and take up a considerable proportion of playground space, often the majority of it. As Paul Connolly (2003) reports, football games often force those not involved in the game to play on the peripheries of the playground. Girls in his study were often fearful of going near the game. Football games are also used by boys to enforce a masculinity hierarchy through exclusion of girls and less athletic boys from games (Connolly, 1998; Skelton, 2000b; 2001a). Connolly reveals how such constructions of masculinity can be racist as well as sexist: South Asian boys in his study tended to be constructed as effete by other boys, and hence excluded from football games. Such physical male-dominance of the playground and classroom has the effect of subordinating and constraining the interaction of girls and of less physically confident/aggressive boys.

Boys have also been shown to dominate verbal interaction in mixed-sex classrooms. In their landmark studies, Dale Spender (1982) and Michelle Stanworth (1981) found that boys gained far greater proportions of the teachers' time and attention than did schoolgirls in the same classes. Twenty years later, research demonstrates that, as a generalisation, boys still tend to dominate the classroom verbally (Younger et al., 1999; Francis, 2000a; Warrington and Younger, 2001). This continues through school right into higher education, where men are shown to talk more in seminar groups and where women students are often silenced in mixed-sex interaction (Thomas, 1990; Somners and Lawrence, 1992). Researchers have, however, developed more nuanced analyses of the issues at stake. Researchers have examined how social class and 'race' inflect with gender in teachers' responses to pupils (Connolly, 1998; Wright et al., 2000; Reay, 2001a; Reay, 2002b). And research has explored the nature and content of pupil–teacher interaction, revealing that boys are verbally disciplined more frequently than girls (Younger et al., 1999). But when girls do behave badly, they are penalised more heavily than boys (Spender, 1982; Connolly, 1998; Reay, 2001b).

Gendered pupil interaction can have profound implications for pupils' power positions in the classroom. Being popular and 'fitting in' are experienced as extremely important, particularly given the heavy consequences of failure (which can result in marginalisation and/or bullying). Hence taking up 'correct' gender positions is extremely important (Davies, 1989), and this involves perpetuating particular types of behaviour. Walkerdine argues that the model primary school pupil is constructed as active, dynamic, assertive, mischievous – male. Excluded from the child role, girls are forced to adopt a quasi-teacher role (see also Belotti, 1975), servicing and facilitating boys. For example, studies document how girls provide boys with equipment and services such as sorting out arguments and helping with homework (Belotti, 1975; Mahony, 1985; Thorne, 1993). This behaviour enables their construction as 'good, sensible girls'. However, Belotti (1975) observed that this 'quasi-teacher' role often meant that girls simply ended up clearing up after boys; and Walden and Walkerdine (1985) add that girls' 'helpful', 'sensible' behaviours were actually despised by the teachers that girls sought to please. Crucially, in mixed-sex interaction the girls' 'sensible selfless' behaviour often involves relinquishing power to the more demanding boys (Francis, 1998). Indeed, findings show that girls still tend to defer to boys in mixed-sex classroom interaction, and behave in ways which reinforce boys' power at the expense of their own (Francis, 2000a; Renold, 2000; Reay, 2001b). Hence their relational construction of gender holds consequences for power positioning in mixed-sex groups. Girls are also frequently directly silenced by boys, through ridicule or by sexist/misogynist abuse (Lees, 1992; Francis, 1998; 2000a; Skelton, 2001a; 2002). Of course, not all boys are able to construct themselves this powerfully. But nevertheless, research work in this area is punctuated by such examples of boys with high-status masculinity systematically excluding and ridiculing girls and less successfully masculine boys (e.g. Connolly, 1998; Francis, 2000a; Renold, 2000; Skelton, 2001b; Reay, 2003). Such ridicule and marginalisation of girls and non-'laddish' boys does much to silence girls, and to 'teach them their place' in the classroom.

So to conclude, girls tend now to aspire to careers, and to see their future jobs as indicative of their identity, in a way that was not the case 20 years ago. Their increased ambition in relation to 'career' is playing a part in driving improvement in some aspects of their achievement. Some middle-class girls, particularly, are achieving extremely impressive performance. However, such performance is not without its (gendered) costs. Working-class girls continue to underachieve in comparison to middle-class pupils of both genders (although out-performing working-class boys). Meanwhile, there is also long-term continuity according to gender in the subjects which young people pursue, and the varying status ascribed to these, as well as in classroom behaviour. The continuing gender dichotomy at work in mainstream society still devalues girls' preferences, choices and behaviours.

Chapter 7

The future for boys and girls?

(Re)constructions of gender and achievement

Thus far we have evaluated the arguments around gender and achievement, the extent of comparative 'underachievement' of some groups of boys (and girls), and the arguments used to explain the 'gender gap'. We have shown how such arguments rest on various gender discourses which position boys, girls, teachers and educational approaches in different ways. In this regard we have highlighted the development of discursive practices around boys' achievement, showing how new discursive constructions surface or become foregrounded which reflect movements in wider discourses informing social policy. This chapter aims to set out our 'reassessment' of the gender and education debates that emerge from this analysis, and to explore the implications of these discursive shifts for pupils' gender identities, developing our own reflections on the themes and conclusions emerging from our analysis in the preceding chapters. In particular we explore questions such as:

- What are the implications of the problematisation of boys?
- Is the 'ideal learner' seen as masculine or feminine?
- What do pupils themselves make of the debates around gender and achievement?
- What does society/social policy want boys to be like?
- What is our own feminist response to these constructions of gender identity in relation to achievement?

The problematisation of boys

In their earlier analysis of the field Epstein *et al.* (1998) identified the strength of the 'poor boys' discourse. As we have seen, this discourse remains powerfully represented in the arguments of the many commentators maintaining that boys' 'underachievement' is explained by factors such as a 'feminisation' of school culture and approaches to pedagogy and assessment; and a lack of fit between these educational approaches and boys' biological/cognitive needs. However, we have also observed that the 'boys will be boys' discourse now appears to be less frequently evoked in the UK than was recently the case. This discourse, which as

Epstein *et al.* (1998) documented celebrates boys' 'natural' roguishness and antipathy for diligence, has been nudged into decline by those newly ascendant discourses which position boys' roguishness and antipathy for diligence as points of grave concern. These we have branded the ' "at risk" boys' and 'problem boys' discourses. We have argued that these discourses are tied to the movement of individualist neo-liberalism within British social policy and elsewhere.

Neo-liberalism is dependent on individuals buying into notions of meritocracy (via credentialism), flexibility, individual responsibility, economic competitive-ness and so on – all of which evoke the 'good' hard-working pupil rather than the errant schoolboy 'rogue' or 'lad'. Within this ethos disruptive and low-achieving boys (or girls for that matter) are no longer to be accepted with wry amusement as an inevitable fact of life (as positioned in the 'boys will be boys' discourse). Instead they are positioned as irresponsible and inflexible, unable – or worse, unwilling – to fit themselves into the meritocratic educational system which produces the achievement vital for the economic success of the individual concerned and of the nation. In a 'something for something' social model, underachieving boys are not upholding their side of the bargain. Within these new discourses, then, 'problem boys' are positioned as not only irresponsibly impeding their own individual growth, but also that of the nation. These boys, it is insinuated, hold us all back by their selfish and anti-social behaviour. Their unreconstructed (working-class) masculinity is inappropriate for contemporary socio-economic models of the self in society (and the school). They distract their classmates and the teacher, taking resources from those better-intentioned pupils doing their best to progress. Their underachievement threatens institu-tional and governmental achievement targets, and then on leaving school these (indicatively white and black working-class) boys are likely to drain 'our' social resources still further, relying on social support and probably ending up on the wrong side of the criminal justice system. Does this sound over-stated? We maintain that this is precisely how underachieving boys are increasingly being positioned. The quotes from policy documents we highlighted in Chapter 3, and the increasingly drastic measures suggested to 'confront the "lad culture" ' in schools (School Standards Minister David Miliband, quotes in *The Times*, 2004), are testimony to this view.

' "At risk" boys' are seen as having 'low self-esteem', and in need of attention and remedy in order to save them from becoming 'problem boys'. Problem boys though, once sardonically condoned as simply expressing their natural masculinity, are now demonised as 'beyond the pale' in the policy discourse.

In this sense, the 'poor boys' discourse, which as we have seen remains highly prevalent, is closely related to and underpins the ' "at risk" boys' discourse, but the latter narrative is more specific to neo-liberal and 'Third Way' themes (bearing the preoccupations with therapeutic approaches and health of the self; inclusion/exclusion; and social/individual responsibility). However, where the 'poor boys' and ' "at risk" boys' discourses position boys sympathetically as victims in need of help, the 'problem boys' discourse reflects the less benevolent side of neo-liberal government once individuals are seen to have 'bitten the hand that feeds'. There is a preoccupation with tighter surveillance and social control, and fear of those who do not 'fit in' with the individualised ethos. Various academic commentators have analysed how new managerialist, neo-liberal approaches not only apportion blame for underachievement to the individuals concerned rather than to social structures and resulting inequalities (e.g. Rose, 1989; Walkerdine, 2003; Bauman, 2005); but also enculture the rest of us into thinking it is their individual faults as well (Davies, 2003). In this sense, neo-liberalism and its new managerialist practices perpetuate a system of discursive and material discipline which implicates us all in the perpetuation of the panopticon (see Foucault, 1977; Davies, 2003).

Yet given that as a result of the 'poor boys' discourse the focus remains very much on how boys are disadvantaged in relation to girls, and the anti-feminist implications of such arguments, how are we as feminists to read this new demonisation of 'problem boys'? Our own research has documented how the behaviours of some boys in mixed-sex schools have negative impacts on other pupils (female and male), as well as on their own achievement (Francis, 2000a; Skelton, 2001a). Hence it is not our intention to say that, simply because we have reservations about the ideology woven into the 'problem boys' discourse, the classroom behaviours of some boys are not an issue. But our analysis has made us think very carefully about how we, and others, do position boys.

How do boys present themselves?

Before going on to explore how the policy material appears to construct boys, we pause to reflect on the way in which boys present themselves. From the 'poor boys' and ' "at risk" boys' viewpoints we might expect boys to be articulating crisis; resentment at their school experiences, disillusionment, 'low self-esteem', and disempowerment. In fact, this is far from being representative of the majority of boys. Many boys are documented in the research literature as confident, assertive, and popular with peers and teachers. As Kehily and Nayak (1997) observe, humour is central to masculine classroom culture. Francis (2000a) describes how the prioritisation of 'having a laugh' ensures that many boys provide entertainment not just for themselves, but also for their fellow pupils and class teacher. The wealth of interview data provided in numerous studies portray many boys talking with confidence, clarity, humour, and often with great intelligence, reflexivity and sensitivity (see Mac an Ghaill, 1994; Connolly, 1998; 2004; Martino, 1999; Francis, 2000a; Frosh *et al.*, 2001; Skelton, 2001a; Martino and Pallotta-Chiarolli, 2003; Archer, 2003 amongst others). They do not often talk of hating school or even of hating schoolwork. As we have seen in earlier chapters, boys as a group continue to dominate the classroom interaction, and the hedonistic practices associated with the 'laddish' construction of masculinity so prestigious in the classroom hardly call to mind miserable or disempowered selves. As Reay (2003) reports, most boys (and many girls) say it is better to be a boy. The only complaint which some of the studies noted above *do* observe boys to articulate about their schooling concerns injustice around teacher practices of classroom management. These report that boys believe themselves to unfairly suffer negative discipline more frequently than girls, who are seen as 'getting away with' behaviour for which boys would be penalised (Pickering, 1997; Younger *et al.*, 1999; Francis, 2000a; Warrington and Younger, 2000). Warrington and Younger (2000) discuss these complaints in relation to classroom interaction, noting how boys' louder and more ostensibly disruptive behaviour often demands discipline.

However, within these generally 'upbeat' presentations of boys cheerfully constructing gender identities in hedonistic and self-assured ways, there are also emerging themes which do illustrate the problems which dominant constructions of masculinity can produce for some of the boys concerned. For example, boys in the studies by Francis (1999; 2000a) and Frosh *et al.* (2001) described the pressures of performing masculinity, how this impinged on their work, and constrained 'non-laddish' presentations of self. Francis (1999a) notes that where in the past girls' relationships have often been stereotyped as 'bitchy', this was not the case among some boys in her study who referred to them with wistful idealism as more open and less judgemental in comparison with the pressures of the male peer group.

Particular constructions of masculinity performed by their peers were experienced as oppressive and resented or despised by some of the boys in these studies. Researchers from Willis (1977) to Martino and Pallotta-Chiarolli (2003) have documented the complaints of some boys about the behaviour of others, which is often derided as 'macho' and 'for show' or 'to look cool'. An example is provided by Mac an Ghaill's (1994) 'Real Englishmen', who despised and resented/feared the macho construction of masculinity based on physical dominance adopted by some of the working-class boys (these middle-class 'Real Englishmen' drew on alternative masculine values to construct their own masculinity through competition and rationality). Clearly the effects of some of the constructions of masculinity, particularly those based on physical violence, intimidation and derision, have a negative impact on many of the people around them. The ways in which these oppressive behaviours are routinised among many boys (who are in turn expected to endure them and if possible 'laugh them off', or risk their own construction of masculinity) has been extensively documented (Salisbury and Jackson, 1996; Epstein, 1997; Francis, 2000a; Frosh *et al.*, 2001; Mills, 2001; Skelton, 2001a; Reay, 2002; Martino and Pallotta-Chiarolli, 2003). Diane Reay's article 'Shaun's Story' (2002) provides a particularly vivid illustration of the difficulties one working-class boy experienced in balancing school work and social expectations within the competing demands of gendered and classed discourses. And Wayne Martino and Maria Pallotta-Chiarolli's books (2001; 2003) reveal the awful consequences for some boys in their inability (for a raft of potential reasons) to achieve this balance, and the consequent emotional and physical abuse this can open them up to.

In documenting such oppressive behaviours, though, and also the often sensitive and reflective talk of some of the boys involved in perpetuating these behaviours, Frosh *et al.* (2001) identify a temptation for commentators to assume that there is a vulnerable 'inner boy' hiding within a hyper-masculine shell. The perception that the masculine behaviours are 'all for show', and that such macho dressing, when stripped away, will reveal a 'real', authentic, boy who is sensitive and probably frightened. Frosh *et al.* (2001) point out that such conceptions rest on humanist beliefs of a 'true self', which are not in keeping with those perspectives influenced by postmodernism or psychoanalysis. But this is of course precisely what many commentators believe to be the case, and is a view increasingly reflected in educational policy. As we saw in Chapter 3, for example, the DfES booklet 'Using the National Healthy School Standard to *Raise Boys' Achievement*' juxtaposes a fragile 'inner boy' with an external, macho presentation (and frequently advocates the development of 'caring masculinity'). As we saw in Chapter 3, it recommends that, 'school assemblies and tutorial time are used to address issues related to developing a "caring masculinity" ', and recommends that teachers talk with boys about 'the way they need to reject violence, talk out aggression and openly express feelings without fear of embarrassment. In this way a culture is being developed that enables a boy to be himself, rather than having to live up to a tough male stereotype' (p. 14). Here 'talking' about emotions and developing a 'caring masculinity' are explicitly set up as methods to 'enable a boy to be *himself*' (our emphasis). The implication is two-fold: (a) that boys have an inner, 'real' self – which is sensitive, but does also appear to be innately aggressive, as boys have to 'talk out aggression'; and (b) that boys themselves cannot be relied on to produce this 'real' self, but must be supported and facilitated in this endeavour by pedagogical practices. A contradictory stance which oscillates between essentialism (the real boy) and mistrust of essentialism (in spite of being 'real', this expression of the real may never manifest if not facilitated).

Other writers suggest that it is the vulnerability of this central male self or ego which leads to hyper-masculine behaviours. For instance, Bleach (1998a) maintains that some 'shattered male egos' (shattered by the reconfiguration of the socio-economic landscape) 'seek sanctuary in a hardened 1990s construction of masculinity' (p. 11). This notion of a movement *toward* hyper-masculinity by men who feel their masculinity threatened is reminiscent to the notion of 'flight from femininity' (Whitehead, 1998), which suggests that as women move into areas traditionally defined as masculine, men 'flee' into more masculine areas and/or modes of expression to maintain the relationality of gender.

But more often the notion of the vulnerable inner boy adopting a hyper-masculinity *because* of his vulnerability emerges as an explanation for these behaviours in the classroom. Particularly, it is often suggested that boys use constructions of hyper-masculinity in the classroom to compensate for the loss of self-esteem they endure via their underachievement at schoolwork. Bleach (1998a) cites a headteacher of a school in Jarrow as commenting that boys believe that 'it is better to be famous for being a clown or a toughie than working hard and being a failure . . .' (Williams, 1996, cited in Bleach, p. 11). This is similar to the premise that boys adopt 'laddish' behaviours 'as a self worth protection strategy' (Jackson, 2002b; 2003). In this view, rather than boys adopting 'laddish' behaviours simply because they express a particularly high status version of masculinity (as suggested by the likes of Martino, 1999; Younger *et al.*, 1999; Francis, 2000a; Warrington *et al.*, 2000, and Skelton, 2001a), they adopt them as a strategy to heal and protect their damaged egos. The end result is the same in terms of behaviour produced, but the causes are read differently.[1]

Quite apart from the point that laddish behaviour is by no means exclusive to underachieving boys (Martino, 1999; Francis, 2000a), we dispute any inference that there is a 'real', total personality lurking beneath contradictory behaviours. For us, expressions of masculinity and femininity are expressions of self-hood for a self which is always developing in social interaction. The values of the 'lad' are not the sole property of underachieving boys, but are elevated by popular culture at large, and are often admired by teachers as well as pupils (Francis, 2000a; Francis and Skelton, 2001; Skelton, 2001b). But this is not to deny that boys can experience the demands to perform masculinity as painful, or that girls and boys are not tyrannised by these practices. We are not attempting to support the status quo. In terms of achievement, too, *boys themselves* tend to support the view that boys' 'laddish behaviour' in schools impedes their achievement (Francis, 1999; Francis and Archer, forthcoming). Very many of them talk of the pressure to perform a style of masculinity which is antithetical to learning, and in which academic application and achievement is constructed as the effete preserve of the 'boffin'/swot (Francis, 1999a; Martino, 1999; Younger *et al.*, 1999; Warrington *et al.*, 2000; Reay, 2002). A majority of boys support the thesis that these behaviours damage the achievement of the boys concerned (although boys frequently and justly protest that these behaviours are not representative of *all* boys). And the explanation these boys most frequently provided for the perpetuation of such behaviours was the pressure from, and expectation of, peers (Francis, 1999a; 2000). These arguments were made even more forcefully by girls discussing their male peers in coeducational schools (Francis, 1999c; Frosh *et al.*, 2001).

The gender of the 'ideal pupil'

One of the key questions raised is, what do educationalists want boys to be like? We have observed how individualism valorises flexibility, responsibility and diligence. By no coincidence, these characteristics are also some of those of the 'good' and achieving pupil. Arguably, they are also traits ascribed as feminine. Critiquing Beck's work on the individualised society, Walkerdine *et al.* (2001) and Walkerdine (2003) have maintained that the model for the neo-liberal subject is female (though, Walkerdine observes, a specifically *middle-class* female) precisely because flexibility, conscientiousness, etc. are feminine traits. The project of upward mobility via education and work constitute 'the feminine site of production of the neo-liberal subject' (Walkerdine, 2003: 238). In this sense, Walkerdine and her colleagues argue that femininity is currently being refashioned. Although the developments and reconfigurations of femininity around education and work in contemporary times have been catalogued (e.g. Smith, 1998; Francis, 2000a; Walkerdine *et al.*, 2001), commentators do not speak of any such changes as representing a 'crisis of femininity'. Indeed, it is these very changes in dominant constructions of femininity which are seen as precipitating a 'crisis of masculinity'. Arguably, this is because most commentators hold middle-class, liberal values, and read the reconstructions of femininity as incorporating educational and career 'achievement' as positive and beneficial. The psychic implications of such changes are seen as relating to men, rather than for women themselves.

So what are the attributes which Walkerdine suggests represent the 'neo-liberal subject'? Drawing on her theoretical paper on social class mobility (2003), they appear to be as follows:

Industrious
Diligent
Responsible and self-regulating (and self-blaming)
Introspective
Flexible and self-transforming
Reflective
Caring

She maintains that as well as a middle-class conservatism the neo-liberal values include those of 'emotionality, caring and introspection – the values of a psychology and interiority usually ascribed to women' (p. 242). Clearly the attributes above can all be seen as feminine, with the possible exception of 'industrious' (which evokes 'industry' – masculine – as well as less gendered 'achievement through hard work'. This latter becomes gendered when the achievement is seen to be *exclusively* through hard work rather than talent or daring – 'plodding' diligence, which is seen as feminine). Clearly, these various attributes listed as indicative of the neo-liberal subject also represent those of the achieving schoolgirl.

So is the (middle class) feminine construction of self now positioned as the 'ideal' version of identity in terms both of producing educational achievement and as being the expression of selfhood most suited to the neo-liberal political and economic climate? Walkerdine appears to imply this to be the case. She is deeply critical of the values of neo-liberalism itself, and of the psychic stress that it produces in people immersed in its systems (as, like the high-achieving middle-class young women in Walkerdine *et al.*'s 2001 study, they can 'never be good enough'). But her view that neo-liberalism valorises the feminine is clear – she claims that the female worker is projected as 'the mainstay of the neo-liberal economy' (p. 238).

We challenge the view that the female is now represented in public discourses as the archetype for either the 'ideal learner' or the 'ideal subject'. As we saw in Chapter 6, girls' achievement continues to be constructed as problematic, even in their out-performance of boys (as the talk is all of 'boys' underachievement', rather than 'girls' achievement'). They tend to be constructed as performing through diligence rather than talent (and hence this diligence continues to be pathologised, even as educationalists urge boys to be *more* diligent, see Francis and Archer, 2005), and as insufficiently questioning and challenging in their learning – as insufficiently masculine to be 'ideal students' (Walkerdine, 1990; Cohen, 1998; Francis *et al.*, 2003). Girls themselves have been found to internalise these perceptions, tending to have less confidence in their abilities than boys, and even when achieving highly often feeling that their performance is still inadequate (Walkerdine *et al.*, 2002). As Archer and Francis (2005; Francis and Archer 2005) have shown, such constructions of high achieving groups as pathological also extend to some minority ethnic groups such as British-Chinese (and Indian) pupils, who are also produced in a Western educational construction as *too* diligent and conformist (i.e. insufficiently masculine). They produce the following binary dichotomy to suggest the way in which these raced and gendered discourses work in a Western context to produce British-Chinese pupils as Other:

Masculine/West	*Feminine/East*
Naturally talented	Diligent (achieving via hard work)
Innovative	Conformist
Leaders	Followers
Questioning and challenging	Deferent and unquestioning
Assertive	Unassertive
Independent	Dependent
Active	Passive
(Normal)*	(Other)*

(*As with all structural dichotomies, power is located one side and the 'other' marginalised or pathologised)

(Francis and Archer, forthcoming)

Hence traits stereotyped as 'Chinese' are consigned to the feminine, and consequently position British-Chinese boys as 'not proper boys'. The grouping of the masculine/Western traits, many of which are associated with 'laddism', may provide the key to explain why boys' comparative underachievement at GCSE is rarely conceived as due to their lower ability – they are constructed as naturally able but lazy.

Crucially, the feminine characteristics referred to by Walkerdine (2003) in her discussion of the neo-liberal self (listed above) are only *some* of those demanded of selfhood in a neo-liberal context. A number of masculine attributes are central to neo-liberal ethos and subjecthood, but are omitted from her discussion. Walkerdine herself refers to Du Gay's (1996) description of the neo-liberal subject as the 'entrepreneur of oneself'. This term effectively evokes the entrepreneurial values of neo-liberal individualism and the neo-liberal self – risk, self-sufficiency, individual rather than social fulfilment, competition, assertion, etc. – which are highly masculine. Francis and Archer's work shows how such masculine values also permeate constructions of the 'ideal student', meaning that girls and minority ethnic boys are positioned as lacking in relation to this phantasy.

On the other hand, perhaps because insufficient numbers of boys either are managing to adopt these attitudes, or are adopting them but not producing high achievement, the beam of surveillance has now fallen on boys too, and they are also being problematised. We suggest that the neo-liberal political and economic climate has permutations for constructions of gender which make the relationality of gender difficult to maintain. For example, the neo-liberal subject must be invested in independence, competition, 'risk' and so on, but must also embody feminine traits such as flexibility, conscientiousness and re-flexivity. Holding these often opposing attributes together raises tensions which may have particularly problematic psychic implications for the self that is its own 'entrepreneur' (Du Gay, 1996). Arguably, this requirement for both masculine *and* feminine traits is inherent too in the new discourses on gender and achieve-ment (which indeed provide a particularly illustrative case). The attributes set out on the masculine side of Francis and Archer's dichotomy (see above) have been shown to be insufficiently enabling to boys' achievement in terms of educational credentials. Studying for and doing well at examinations requires application, diligence and obedience. But a Western model in which an autonomous 'seeker of knowledge' learns by active and critical engagement with information renders such feminine traits on their own inadequate. To paraphrase Walkerdine's (1988) commentary on girls' approaches to learning maths, these traits do not express the 'proper way of learning'. Hence the ideal *achieving* pupil must incorporate traits from both sides of Francis and Archer's dichotomy, perhaps displaying in particular behaviours ascribed acceptable to a pupil's construction of gender, or in ways which do not jeopardise securing educational credentials.

The notion that we are witnessing a reconfiguration of gender identities, or an accelerated period in the ongoing development of gender identities, is sup-ported by the proliferation of discussion of masculinity in the mass media, particularly centring on the notion of crisis. But as we have seen, dominant constructions of femininity too have been changing. Girls' constructions of femininity differ depending on other aspects of identity such as ethnicity and social class, yet as a group girls are more career oriented than was the case in the past (Francis, 1996; 2002; Lightbody and Durndell, 1996), and less afraid to be seen as clever (Francis, 2000a). Although the extent of these changes are often over-stated in a media presentation of young (middle-class) women as 'having it all', greater assertion and confidence among young women are celebrated in popular culture (McRobbie, 1999). Although such changes as we have seen 'fit' with the neo-liberal model and tend to be read as positive by commentators, there are elements of concern at particular manifestations of this new more self-assured femininity. For example, we have been subjected to recent moral panic in the press concerning the 'binge drinking' of female 'laddettes', their associated promiscuity, and the apparent increase in young women being jailed for violence. Whitehead (2002) provides an illuminating account of how concepts of 'manhood' (masculinity) have developed and altered throughout the centuries, showing how changing socio-economic conditions influence the development of gender identities in a particular direction. The present time appears to be one of these key moments in the history of gender identities where the socio-economic climate is precipitating a modification. The issue of gender and educational achievement provides a prominent case in which these shifts are being developed and played out. Certainly neo-liberalist social policy-makers demand (a) high educational achievement (purely conceived as credentials, as opposed to more broadly/alternatively); and (b) appear to demand a particular kind of masculinity which is able to incorporate behaviours and values that result in academic achievement. Hence it may be that we are seeing a hiatus and reconfiguration in discursive productions of 'acceptable' masculinity within education. So what might this look like?

'Caring masculinity'

As we saw in Chapter 3, education policy-makers now frequently allude to a 'caring masculinity'. This is a particularly intriguing term due to the multiple contradictions the joining of these two words manages to achieve. 'Caring' is one of the most gendered traits, traditionally unequivocally stereotyped as feminine. It is often associated in a triad construction with nurturing and emotion, which are seen as quissessential attributes of the female (Walkerdine and Lucey, 1989). Hence the placement of this trait next to 'masculinity' causes a jarring in itself. For many social constructionist feminists, masculinity is constructed in *relation* to femininity – traits ascribed masculine are opposite to those ascribed feminine. From this position, the evocation of a 'caring' (feminine) masculinity is nonsensical. This is not to say that men are unable to care – of course most men can be very caring. But rather, that their 'caringness' is not part of their construction/performance of masculinity. Indeed, it could be said that when a man is behaving in caring ways (or expressing other traits ascribed to the feminine) he is not constructing himself as masculine, or that his expression of caring destabilises his construction of masculinity, by expressing the feminine. Such issues are not articulated by those using the phrase, who often appear to imply that 'caring masculinity' could simply be a different kind of (sensitive) masculinity, perhaps which would allow boys' sensitive 'inner selves' to be expressed.

In any case, the phrase alludes to boys behaving in caring ways as part of their repertoire of behaviour. Yet it is hard to see how boys' adoption of caring behaviours will impact positively on their achievement. Any rationale for this leap between caring behaviour and academic outcomes is never articulated. We speculate that the 'caring' in the phrase 'caring masculinity' is a sort of associative trigger word used to evoke femininity generally – the inference being that boys who are less masculine, or adopt feminine behaviours (and some would see this as one and the same, Francis, 2000a), are more likely to academically achieve than are, say, 'laddish' boys.

The persistence of misogyny

So do policy-makers want boys to be more like girls? Hoff Sommers (2000) claims this to be the case, but as we have shown, girls continue to be problematised, and are not held up as models of good practice in the policy literature. Certainly nobody ever says openly that boys ought to emulate girls' behaviour – indeed arguably phrases such as 'caring masculinity' demonstrate the extent to which commentators will go to advocate more feminine behaviour in boys *without* openly advocating that they behave like girls. As we have seen, strategies aimed at addressing boys' apparent underachievement often stop short of promoting 'feminine' approaches to learning. They tend instead to look at the practices of teachers, recommending pedagogical styles and strategies which are believed to be preferred by boys (e.g. whole-class teaching, short-term target-setting, etc.). In fact, rather than encouraging boys to behave 'more like girls', many strategies actually seem to encourage boys to behave 'more like boys', playing on (and hence potentially exacerbating) established expressions of masculinity. These include the advocation of separate, 'gender appropriate' resources for girls and boys; an elevation of sport; and the promotion of competition. Possibly the nearest any British strategy for 'raising the achievement of boys' has come to advocating girls' practices as a model has been the suggestion of boy-girl seating practices and work pairings in the classroom:

> A few schools or departments had set out to address the underachievement of boys by seating boys and girls alternately and there was evidence that this helped attitudes to learning, especially among boys. In these schools, the boys often acknowledged that they worked better when they were not allowed to sit with male friends.
>
> (Ofsted, 2003b: 27)

The suggestion here is that by working with girls, boys may emulate their learning styles as well as avoiding distractions from male friends. However, even in this case exponents never articulate outright the controversial notion that boys ought to adopt feminine working practices. Why might this be? We argue it is because that would mean advocating boys becoming more effeminate.

It is worth reflecting on reaction prompted by the word 'effeminate'. It is constructed as wholly pejorative, negative. Yet it simply implies a lack of the masculine, more of the feminine, in a male (in some psychoanalytical perspectives femininity is anyway simply the 'lack' of masculinity, although we contest this theoretical position). One might argue that the notion of the 'effete' or effeminate male is stigmatised by its association with homosexuality. But of course, as Jordan (1995) argues, gay men are feared and ridiculed by many heterosexuals precisely because, in uncoupling the heterosexual binary which underpins dominant gender relations and power inequalities, they have undermined traditional binaries and rendered themselves 'not real/proper men' (and hence 'like women'). This is compounded by the rejection by some gay men of aspects of traditional performances of masculinity, this 'lack' of masculinity making them even more 'like women'. So the social misogyny that denigrates the feminine is a strong element in the homophobic associations which problematise the notion of effeminacy.

These values are entrenched in classroom interaction. As we saw in the previous chapter, homophobia is one of the key ingredients in the construction of heterosexual masculinity, and consequently homophobic and misogynist abuse is rife in the classroom (Lees, 1992; Salisbury and Jackson, 1996; Epstein, 1997; Skelton, 1997; Mac an Ghaill, 1999; Martino, 1999; 2000). The feminine/female continues to constitute a point of scorn. Yet, what many under-achieving boys need to raise their achievement is to read more, listen and attend more to teachers and other pupils, work harder (greater diligence), be more conscientious and take more pride in their work, work collaboratively, and articulate themselves better in all aspects of communication. Evidently, these are all aspects of learning/working which are constructed as feminine, and which are stereotyped as adopted by girls. As we discussed in Chapter 5, research has contested the extent to which girls and boys adopt gendered learning styles, and moreover classroom behaviours depend on a host of other aspects of identity as well as gender – not all girls adopt these 'feminine' approaches to learning, and even those that do may not adopt them all, or with any consistency. But as generalisations research has found, girls do tend to read more than boys (Millard, 1997; Pickering, 1997; QCA, 1998; Ofsted 2003a), and the achievement figures in language and literacy show girls' marked out-performance of boys in these areas. It has also been shown to be the case that learning and academic achievement is not so socially stigmatised for girls as it is for many boys (Francis, 1999a; Martino, 1999; Younger *et al.*, 1999; Warrington *et al.*, 2000), and hence they are less deterred from application by social considerations. The bodies of work on boys' approaches to literacy and on the impact of dominant constructions of masculinity (particularly 'laddish' personas) in the classroom strongly indicate that it is by adopting more traditionally-feminine behaviours and approaches that these boys could improve their school work.

So why do policy-makers recoil from vocalising this point? Clearly it is for all the reasons noted above (the pejorative associations of notions of femininity and 'effeminacy'). But as we have begun to argue, social fear and embarrassment at the word 'effeminate' are produced by the continuing gender (and sexuality) inequality in our society which locates power, validity and normality in the (heterosexual) male, and in turn portrays the feminine as powerless and invalid – and as inadequate, trivial, even ridiculous. Gender inequality as a social structure remains robust, in spite of the social changes precipitated by neo-liberalism. These sexist, misogynist assumptions, and the way they underpin our society's continuing traditionalism and inequality in gender relations, were vividly illustrated by an episode of the BBC's recent 'If...' series. This series featured different 'future shocks' where contemporary scenarios are taken to their possible 'natural' conclusions in a dystopian future. The episode in question was based on the 'shocking' concept of women (rather than men) controlling society. Charlie Brooker (2004) produced an entertaining and perceptive review of it. We reproduce an extract here because he identifies many issues pertinent to our discussion, particularly as he goes on to juxtapose the 'If...' episode with a programme which he suggests evokes traditional masculine preoccupations:

> ... this week's edition of the increasingly ludicrous *If*... (Wed, 9pm, BBC2) tackles the thorny problem of what might happen if women ruled the world. Well, nearly: actually, in this nightmare vision of the year 2022, men still rule parliament but the chicks have everything else sewn up. The majority of businesses are owned and run by women, the American president is a bitch, and Walkers have announced a new range of oestrogen-flavoured crisps. Men are increasingly redundant – not just in the workplace, but in the bedroom too, since scientific advances have rendered our testicles superfluous to requirement (so you might as well slam them in a car door – go on, it'll be funny) ... this is The Worm That Turned,[2] but with bigger, unintentional laughs.
>
> We men must fight back now before this nightmare comes to pass, so thank God shows like *Zero to Hero* (Sun, 4.05pm, C4) are here to show us how to make sense of masculinity in the 21st century. Essentially Scrapheap Challenge meets Batman, it's a show in which 'comic-book fans' construct ridiculous gadgets against the clock in order to complete a 'superheroic' task. This week they have to scale an eight-metre wall of metal. Contestant one decides to use magnets, while number two knocks up a wall-clinging suction device from a pair of old vacuum cleaners.
>
> (Brooker, in *The Guardian's* 'The Guide', 2004: 52)

Brooker's review illuminates the irony of the programme-makers' assumption that women dominating positions of power is shocking or 'unnatural' (in contrast to the taken-for-granted presumption that it is normal and right for men to dominate), and the hysterical scare-tactics adopted (such as linking female-domination of society to male redundancy in the bedroom and the inferred image of castration which Brooker brashly makes transparent). Again, the programme's inference is that if men do not dominate society they are rendered 'not real men' (effeminised, 'castrated').

The 'If . . .' programme, then, simultaneously highlights both society's prevailing conservativism and abhorrence of the feminine; and the fear that women are increasingly encroaching into traditionally masculine domains of public power. As we have seen this latter fear is expressed in much of the commentary around a 'crisis of masculinity', which Brooker also evokes in his parody of the show 'Zero to Hero'. However, focusing on our original argument it is suffice to say that these popular themes confirm that in spite of girls' tendency to educationally outperform boys, social commentators are far from advocating that femininity is the socially accepted model and boys should emulate feminine behaviour. But in this case, how *are* boys expected to behave? And what is the new model of masculinity that is emerging in social discourse?

The new masculinity?

As we have seen, the policy literature advocates pedagogic strategies to 'heal' 'at risk' boys and mend their self-esteem. The question then is what will these 'saved' boys look like? How will they behave? Clearly the implied assumption is that they will still retain aspects of their masculinity (as they are not to be 'like girls'), but also be hard workers and keen to get on at school. Hence in this sense they must incorporate aspects from both sides of the dichotomy presented by Francis and Archer (forthcoming) above. They should not be too obedient or conformist, but neither should they be too confrontational. They should be confident and assertive but never aggressive. This appears to be a very fine balance. It also appears to us to be founded on an idealised Western (Enlightenment) construction of the ideal learner, which remains excluding to many subjectivities, and rests on the middle-class, white boy. The key point is, though, this boy is being expected to take up traditionally feminine traits in order to guarantee his credentials. According to the social constructionist theory of gender which sees gender as necessarily relational, this appropriation of feminine traits implies a dilution of the masculine. So what is happening here? And are these tensions reflected in the wider society? A reflection on broader trends in popular culture may be illuminating.

Our initial impression was that, far from petering out, the values of the 'lad' are in the ascendancy in popular culture. Francis (1999a; 2000a) has charted the rise of 'laddism' in the mainstream media, and observed that it is unrealistic to expect boys to abandon such values while they are held up as the desirable expression of masculinity within popular culture. In Britain, the arrival of 'lad' magazines such as *Loaded* precipitated a trend throughout the existing men's magazine field, so that the staple recipe of (naked) girls, fashion, and sport would appear to have become standard (Whelehan, 2000). Front covers of these magazines have become more and more risqué, now resembling the covers of porn magazines. Moreover, these magazines have proved massively successful, with a number of new editions to the magazine stable, and supplying a huge market. Added to other examples of a proliferation of media images in which violent or misogynist performances of masculinity are celebrated (albeit 'ironic-ally'),[3] one might conclude on the surface that the hyper-masculine values of 'the lad' have become entrenched rather than waning in popular culture (Whelehan, 2000).

However, as David Gauntlett (2002) argues, there is more to the 'lads mag' than meets the eye. He argues that 'lads' mag' readers do not only buy the magazines for the 'girls and sport'; but rather these magazines embrace some previously feminine preoccupations and offer men lifestyle advice for negotiating and projecting *explicitly* socially constructed masculinity in the individualised culture. That fashion is a key staple for these magazines offers an indication as to the extent to which more traditionally feminine concerns have become institu-tionalised for men in these formats. Other features which have traditionally been the preserve of women's magazines but are now standard content in 'lads' mags' too include therapeutic and self-help articles on everything from men's health to securing heterosexual sex. Hence discourses of therapy and self-help, which rest on aspects previously ascribed feminine (reliance, support, low self-esteem, vulnerability, reflection, dependence) have seeped in and become normalised in the apparently hyper-masculine world of the men's magazine. Guantlett (2002; 2004) argues further that although 'lads' magazines do contain sexist material, much of the content in these magazines actually acknowledges the contemporary more assertive role of women within the world of work and in sexual interaction. Indeed, much of the therapeutic self-help pieces and letters pages refer to how to deal 'appropriately'/effectively with women's more active and demanding sexuality (Jackson *et al.*, 2001). Arguably Guantlett's representa-tion of the influence and impact of 'girl's power' movements and so on might be seen as idealised or over-stated; and his apparent view of men's magazines as a largely benevolent force, even educating male readers into a new, liberal masculinity appears optimistic to say the least. But his thesis that the content of lad's magazines is not so straightforwardly traditionally masculine as it might appear is a convincing one.

The intense focus on men's fashion and 'grooming' reflected in these maga-zines is mirrored by a recent burgeoning in beauty-care products specifically marketed at men (Whitehead, 2002). Whole ranges of beauty-care products are now targeted at men. Interviewed on television about this trend, marketers at Nivea revealed how they had discovered that men were increasingly 'secretly' using their female partners' products, so identified the need to establish brands which were 'for men', hence enabling men to buy them themselves without jeopardising their masculinity, and therefore opening up a lucrative new market. Discussing these trends, a colleague relayed how in a queue at Boot's chemists she had recently been behind a man who asked the shop assistant whether the shampoo he was holding was okay for him, or whether it was 'for women'? This poignantly illustrates the irony that these formally feminine preserves are accept-able only so long as they are ostensibly marked as 'appropriate for men', hence reducing the risk to a successful construction of masculinity.[4]

So, however hidden, these developments do indicate changes in contemporary constructions of masculinity. Is, then, the notion of a 'caring masculinity' actually representative? Certainly it is now more acceptable – even expected – for (particularly middle-class) men to display their 'caring side' in relation to their offspring. For example, it is now almost unheard of for men not to be present at the birth of their children. Indeed, practices to make men feel 'more involved' in the birth event have recently become relatively standardised in Britain (such as the opportunity/expectation for male partners to attend antinatal classes; and even to cut the umbilical cord following the arrival of the baby). The offer of paid paternity leave (albeit brief) is now law in Britain, as is further unpaid parental leave which includes fathers as well as mothers. (Being unpaid, this leaves the opportunity for take-up largely open to middle-class parents.) But although the extended work flexibility regarding parental leave has been declared a success due to the extent of uptake of these opportunities by working mothers, the same use has not been made by fathers. Indeed, although a great fuss is made in the popular press concerning the 'new fathers' who are more involved in their young children's care and upbringing, all the evidence indicates that it is overwhelmingly women who continue to take breaks from work in order to care for their children, and/or who are responsible for organising childcare (David, 2003).[5] Dominant discourses of parental responsibility continue to position a child's well-being as the almost exclusive responsibility of the mother.

Men have always 'cared'. We argue that what we are seeing is a reconfiguration in what is socially acceptable for men – certain behaviours previously ascribed feminine (caring for babies, physical and emotional care of the self) are now more acceptable, but only in tightly proscribed, and arguably minimal, ways. What, though, for the relationality of gender? If popular constructions of women allow (circumscribed) assertiveness and agency, and images of men incorporate (circumscribed) emotionality, does this signify the beginning of deconstruction and dissolution of constructions of gender? We argue not – we have been at pains to show throughout this book that the masculine remains elevated over the feminine, and the Othering of the feminine can only be achieved through the maintenance of gender relationality. Rather, we emphasise that we are seeing a *reconfiguration* of oppositional gender constructions, representing a key developmental moment in the history of gender. It may be that certain traits can now be incorporated into constructions of masculinity or femininity which were previously seen as inappropriate; so long as they are displayed in particular ways which are reconstructed as appropriately masculine or feminine. Or certain traits may become de-gendered, and new ones will take their place in the gender dichotomy.

However, what we feel is necessary in order to ensure that gender identity does not impact on educational achievement – and indeed on life outcomes more generally – is for an actual deconstruction of gender. Whereas notions of 'caring masculinity' suggest a *re*construction, we maintain that there will never be gender equality until we see a *de*construction, so that girls and boys are not invested in performing particular ways of learning, and maintaining different interests and practices to delineate their gender identities. Younger *et al.* (2005; Warrington *et al.*, 2006) show that it is schools which *challenge* gender cultures, and encourage boys and girls not to see aspects of learning as gendered, that boys perform their best.

Reassessing gender and achievement

So, what have we learnt in writing this book? First, that 'achievement' as represented in the debates on 'gender gap' is narrowly conceived from a credentialist model that prioritises exam success over other aspects of education. But we have established that within this domain, boys as a group are tending to underachieve in relation to girls, primarily in relation to language and literacy. Is this a concern? We reassert our initial claim that it is. It may be a modernist position which sees structural factors such as gender identity impacting on life outcomes for whole groups, and we recognise that even within this view certain groups of boys (e.g. white working-class, and/or black boys) are more at risk of underachievement than others. But it seems to us fundamentally unacceptable that boys' often substantially worse literacy and communication skills should simply be accepted and not addressed. Just as it is unacceptable that the offer of educational quality is not the same for pupils irrespective of their social class. Addressing inequalities may reflect a modernist vision, but it remains one that we subscribe to. Retaining endeavours to further equality is increasingly rather than decreasingly important, in a neo-liberalist socio-economic climate in which inequalities are widening, and yet these trends are hidden by the new-individualism which focuses on individuals rather than social groups, and locates responsibility for inequality of outcomes with individuals rather than with govern-ment or social structures. For boys, as a group, to have poorer literacy and communication skills in comparison with girls holds negative implications for all, and impacts on quality of life.

We have examined the various explanations for the 'gender gap', and the discourses which underline these. Many of these continue to blame girls and women for boys' comparative underachievement. Our analysis and evaluation of the research behind the various explanations suggests that evidence for most of these accounts is scant. That boys' constructions of masculinity tend to denigrate learning as feminine is the only one that appears heavily substantiated in the literature, although even here the extent of impact on boys' achievement tends to be assumed rather than demonstrated. However, while evidence for inherent sex differences and any impact on achievement remains negligible and embryonic, social constructionist accounts of gendered behaviour which relate to achievement are established and convincing.

In exploring constructions of gender, we have shown how boys are increas-ingly problematised in discourses around gender and achievement. We have shown how girls are not held up as a model for boys to emulate, as the feminine continues to be denigrated. On the other hand, this chapter has shown how traditional views that 'boys will be boys' are no longer deemed appropriate, as the ethos of self-responsibility and of 'standards' and credentials positions underachieving boys as lacking. Hence we are seeing a reconstruction of values around behaviours appropriate to schoolboys.

Clearly we are critical of the emphasis on credentialism in current policy trends, and of the tendency towards locating responsibility for inequalities on individuals rather than social structures. But these concerns notwithstanding, teacher readers will point out that they are under pressure to raise boys' achievement (and we have just argued the validity of concerns at boys' attainment at language and literacy). So what should be done to address the gender gap in literacy and language, and to ensure that issues around social class and ethnicity are not ignored? The following chapter charts some possible approaches.

Chapter 8

Raising achievement

What 'works in the classroom'?

Introduction

Throughout the book we have drawn attention to how the domination of the boys' underachievement agenda has given rise to recommendations for practice that have not necessarily been proven to be effective in raising achievement. Several of these recommendations are based on essentialist notions of a 'typical boy' and thus fail to take account of the differences between boys. Also, the implementation of such recommendations by schools means they would continue to reinforce conventional constructions of masculinities rather than challenging these traditional modes of 'doing boy'. A further concern created by the dominance of boys' educational needs within policy discourse is that there has been a tendency to forget about girls who underachieve, or indeed who achieve well but at a cost to their physical and mental health (see for example the discussions on middle-class, successful girls and self-harming behaviours, Chaplin (2000); Walkerdine *et al.*, (2001)). What teachers need to know is what the effective strategies for working with boys and girls are that will enable them to perform to their best.

This chapter sets out some of the approaches that have been shown to enable the breaking down of traditional gendered constructions of boys and girls as learners. Unfortunately, straightforward checklists or inventories of points to follow that will enable teachers to show precisely how they raise the achievement of the boys and girls in their class are unrealistic. Needless to say it is not so simple and getting boys and girls to recognise and engage with stereotypical gender constructions demands deep, widespread and challenging processes and practices being put into place by a school. Also, as every teacher knows, when it comes to trying out specific classroom approaches, what works one year with one class may not work with the next. However, what we are suggesting here are processes and practices for schools and teachers to build upon. Thus the chapter sets out the context for specific initiatives by focusing on what a school and staff need to do before implementing various classroom strategies. The chapter will then cover those aspects most commonly raised when talking about gender and achievement, namely single-sex teaching, mentoring and role models,

approaches to language and literacy, and, in providing a context for these, socio-cultural approaches to achievement.

To begin with though we start by considering what strategies should be avoided. Whilst not wanting to begin the chapter on a negative note, it is important to recognise there are a number of programmes or approaches that are being taken up by schools which we would argue are not helpful in challenging pupils' gendered constructions of themselves as learners.

Approaches to be discouraged

A starting point is for a school to ensure that it is not focusing exclusively on boys but on gender. Two surveys which set out to ascertain what practices were being adopted towards gender equality in the UK found that emphasis was being given to boys (Arnot *et al.*, 1998b; Sukhnandan, 1999). In one of these it was discovered that after 1995 (when boys' underachievement hit the media headlines) the percentage of strategies aimed at boys specifically increased from 14 per cent to 41 per cent (see Table 8.1).

The justifications for this swing provided by commentators writing from men's rights perspectives is that a focus on boys is needed to address the inequalities that have arisen by schools being made too 'girl friendly' (Pollack, 1998; Moir and Moir, 1999). In the UK the talks and workshop sessions led by Geoff Hannan appear to be the most widely known about in schools (Pulis 2000; Duffy, 2002). These sessions rely heavily on the apparent biological/ psychological differences between boys and girls (Hannan, 1999), for example, that boys' and girls' sense of hearing develops differently and that they have a different sense of smell. Teachers are provided with information which is supposed to enable them to provide teaching styles and approaches to classroom management which cater for gender differences. Whilst the effects of such initiatives on both teachers and pupils have yet to be rigorously researched in the UK similar programmes have been the focus of evaluation in Australia. For example, the Australian programme *Boys and Schools* (devised by Browne and Fletcher, 1995) recommends schools to organise boys into single-sex groups to discuss relationships with each other; to take on role play activities which deal with bullying and other forms of harassment; and, to devise opportunities to

Table 8.1 Changes in the targeting of equal opportunities strategies

Equal opportunities strategies targeted at	Prior to 1995	Implemented from 1997–8
Boys and girls	71%	52%
Boys only	14%	41%

Source: Information in table supplied by Sukhnandan (1999) *An Investigation into Gender Differences in Achievement: Phase 1: A Review of Recent Research and LEA Information on Provision* (NFER)

boost boys' self-esteem. Such recommendations directly draw on those strateg-ies teachers became familiar with through equal opportunities work with girls. They use the same language that was evident in equal opportunities programmes, so where girls were seen as oppressed, boys are now presented as victims. The problems created in adopting these approaches are that they ignore far more fundamental gender power differentials and promote the notion that 'boys and girls (should), respectively, be conceptualised homogeneously and in opposi-tion' (Rowan *et al.*, 2002: 18). Also, as Lingard (2003: 42) argues programmes based on these ('recuperative masculinity') principles often result in the production or recommendation of 'materials that reinforce the worst aspects of hegemonic masculinities'.

There are alternative programmes which have been adopted by some Australian schools based on pro-feminist approaches and these generate different but equally problematic concerns (see Lingard and Douglas, 1999 and Lingard, 2003 for dis-cussion). For example, these programmes aim to encourage pupils to consider how modes of masculinities are related to broader issues connected with social power (Salisbury and Jackson 1996; McClean 1997) but do so by concerning themselves first with boys' attitudes and behaviours and suggest activities which directly address their emotional and psychological experiences. (So, here there are sim-ilarities with the approaches taken by 'recuperative masculinity' projects.) Whilst an advantage of these programmes is their recognition of male power and differ-ences between men, a disadvantage is that they tend to make boys and men teachers feel bad about themselves! The propensity for pro-feminist programmes to generate a range of attitudes in boys from anger to guilt to disquiet and uncertainty is something that has been noted by a number of writers (Kenway 1995; McClean 1997; Mills 2001). Also, these programmes can result in making girls feel that schools are 'sexist against boys' (Kenway, 1995: 68). However, in the UK these pro-feminist programmes are not in evidence as the emphasis here is much more on 'what about the boys' (i.e. recuperative masculinity) tactics.

It is important then for schools to be careful not to employ strategies which focus heavily on boys, even those which claim to be ' "getting it right" for boys . . . *and* girls' (Noble and Bradford, 2000) (see Skelton, 2001a for discus-sion of these programmes). Furthermore, schools should avoid implementing 'one-off' strategies that do not pervade the whole school as bringing about changes in constructions of gendered learning identities' demands far more fundamental modifications. At the same time, we will be referring to some of those approaches which are recommended in programmes that focus on boys but, the difference is that these are suggested within a framework of policies devised by and for individual schools. We will turn now to look at what can work for schools and teachers in the classroom.

Whole school ethos

In their national study of gender and achievement, Younger and Warrington (2001) state that:

> ... schools which are successfully challenging the gender gap are those that do get boys on board; they are schools that are particularly sensitive to the sociocultural contexts of which they are a part, and their whole school ethos embodies that understanding. The aim, in the words of one headteacher, is to attempt to 'reframe the students' view of school so that academic success is valued, aspired to and seen to be attainable.
>
> (p. 12)

How do schools become 'sensitive' and develop an ethos which embraces that understanding? The key here is in whole school development where a number of activities are undertaken by staff in order to raise levels of awareness regarding the images of gender the pupils are bringing into school with them; the constructions of gender that are operating in the local community; and, the representations of masculinity and femininity that are produced by the school itself.

There are several different aspects that require attention and so it is necessary for a school to devote several sessions on working out what the 'taken-for-granted' gendered constructions are amongst staff, pupils and the local community. An introduction would be for a school to ascertain the images on masculinity and femininity that come from different aspects of pupils' lives. The following are taken from several sources (see Pickering, 1997; MacNaughton, 2000; Martino and Pallotta-Chiarolla, 2003).

Questions to consider about the school

*   What is the role of the school culture and curriculum in perpetuating or providing alternatives to the limited notions of masculinity?
*   Does the school provide professional development for staff to enable understandings about gender and how it interacts with a range of other variables such as socio-economic status, sexuality, ethnicity, geographical location and disability?

Questions for teachers to consider about their attitudes and behaviours

*   Do I expect pupils to act differently because they are boys or girls?
*   Do I have different expectations of their abilities or potential based on whether they are a boy or a girl?
*   To what extent do I differentiate between the children. Am I aware that 'girls' and 'boys' are not homogeneous groups; for example, some girls will act in assertive ways and some boys will work cooperatively?

- How do my interactions influence pupils and their understanding of what it means to be a girl or a boy?
- What aspects of my daily work practices help pupils to understand themselves and others as girls and boys?
- What are the main theories and ideas about teaching and learning that define my work with pupils? Do these take account of gender?

Questions for teachers to consider about the images of masculinity and femininity pupils are using in the school setting

- In their activities in the playground what images of masculinities and femininities are pupils acting out?
- What messages are the children getting about the way to be a 'proper' boy or girl from the materials they use in the classroom?

Questions about where these images are coming from

- What are pupils' preferred television programmes, films, music, books?
- What representations of masculinities and femininities can be found in these favourite forms of media?
- What do these tell pupils about the 'correct' ways of being a boy or a girl?
- What types of work or other roles do men and women take on in the local community?

We will now start to look at those specific strategies utilised by schools for raising achievement.

Single-sex classrooms

Teaching pupils in single-sex settings is currently one of the most widely followed practices by schools, at least according to one national survey in the UK (Sukhnandan *et al.*, 2000). As we have pointed out throughout this book, this strategy has come to the fore through the concerns over boys' underachievement rather than any considerations over the educational needs of girls. Discussions about the value of single-sex schools (as opposed to single-sex classes) for girls have occupied a central place in debates on gender and education since the 1970s with the claim being that girls did better away from the distractions and intimidations posed by boys (Jones, 1985; Mahony, 1985). (It was recognised that it tended to be middle-class girls who were most likely to attend single-sex schools, and therefore social class was an important factor in higher levels of achievement, Smithers and Robinson, 1995.) In spite of the recognised advantages

to girls the majority of co-educational schools did not embrace all boy/all girl classes with the enthusiasm we see today. It has been the focus on boys' underachievement and ways of tackling the perceived 'laddish' behaviours seen to contribute to their disaffection and lack of motivation that has led to the solution of creating 'all-boy' classes in co-educational schools.

Single-sex teaching is a strategy particularly advocated by those writing from a 'men's rights' perspective in North America (Pollack, 1998; Hoff Sommers, 2000) although not, strangely enough, by those living in the UK (Bleach, 1998b; Noble and Bradford, 2000). Martin Mills (2004: 344) writing critically on the 'men's rights' position, observes that those who subscribe to the 'boys as victims' viewpoint advocate single-sex settings as, 'boys' only classes will serve to create an environment where their "energy" can be appreciated and harnessed for their learning'. On a different note, some have argued that teaching boys and girls separately within a co-educational school is an effective marketing strategy by schools in attracting the attention of parents looking for the 'best' education for their children (Ball and Gewirtz, 1997; Mills, 2004).

So why is it that even men's rights activists in the UK, who might be assumed to be in favour of all-boys classes, maintain a degree of caution in talking about single-sex settings? One answer to this is that the findings of research into single-sex teaching offer inconclusive evidence. First, there is the argument that this form of organisation makes raising achievement a possibility because it allows teachers to tackle pupils' traditional perceptions of certain subjects (as well as encouraging boys to behave less 'laddishly' and girls to be more confident) (Suknandan et al., 2000; Warrington and Younger, 2003). However, it has been shown that teachers tend to adopt 'curriculum-as-usual' approaches and utilise the same pedagogies whether in mixed-sex or single-sex classes (Warrington and Younger, 2001; Jackson, 2002a). Thus it is perhaps not too surprising that researchers find that rather than boys concentrating more on their work when not 'distracted' by the presence of girls, they are as much, if not more diverted by an all-male peer group (Askew and Ross, 1989; Jackson, 2003).

In addition, once pupils' socio-economic status and their prior achievement are taken into account there are no significant differences in the achievement of those in single-sex classes or schools and pupils in co-educational establishments (see Marsh and Rowe, 1996; Jackson and Smith, 2002). Indeed, the evidence seems to suggest that if either sex is favoured by single-sex education in co-educational schools it is *girls*, rather than boys (Warrington and Younger, 2002; 2003). The edited collection by Kevan Bleach (1998c) highlights the conflicting 'evidence' very clearly when the chapter written by Brian Matthews ('Co-education, boys, girls and achievement') argues the superiority of co-educational classes over single-sex classes whilst Beverly Swan ('Teaching boys and girls in separate classes at Shenfield High School, Brentwood') says that, in the experience of her own school, single-sex settings are of greater value to the education of boys and girls. Of his own research investigation Bleach observes:

> The survey evidence does not resolve the arguments for or against single or mixed gender grouping arrangements. The conviction with which a particular form of organisation is used appears to be much more important.
>
> (Bleach, 1998b: 76)

Here lies the key point and one which again draws attention to the significance of a whole school approach. As we have just indicated, single-sex classes provide girls a space away from the distractions of boys and they can provide opportunities for teachers to redress stereotypical constructions of particular subjects or work with boys on violence (Kruse, 1996). However, they will only be useful within the context of an overarching school policy. To begin with it is important to recognise that it is not possible to assume that the arguments for and against single-sex classes for girls are the same as those for boys. Martin Mills (2004: 344) illustrates this in saying:

> . . . issues relating to single sex classes and schools for girls are vastly different from those currently being purveyed by the boys' lobby to justify single sex schooling for boys. The often negative effects of homo-social environments in terms of boys' perceptions and constructions of girls and women, and indeed in their treatment of each other, have been well documented (Arnot, 1984; Roulston and Mills, 2000; Martino and Meyenn, 2003) and suggest that boys' schools tend to be part of maintaining the existing gender order.

So in single-sex settings boys are more likely to exhibit and confirm demeaning attitudes towards females and 'non-macho' boys whilst in co-educational settings girls have to experience 'being hassled, and suffering put-downs' by the boys (Rennie and Parker, 1997: 264) (see also Jackson, 2002a). The opportunity then for single-sex classes for girls is seemingly quite apparent but, as has been said, it is concerns over boys' underachievement that promotes this form of organisation. The question is then what advantages are there for boys in all-boy classes?

As was said earlier, an intended aim of all-boy classes is for teachers to be able to tackle boys' traditional perceptions of subjects, such as the idea that English is a 'girls' subject. However, the research indicates that unless the teacher has a critical understanding of gender constructions him/herself then there is a danger that normalising assumptions about boys will guide the pedagogy. For example, researchers who have looked at strategies to encourage boys' literacy skills have found evidence that teachers select content and strategies informed by presumed notions of what boys like and do (see section on language and literacy). Martino and Meyenn (2002) provide examples of English teachers selecting material aimed at boys' interests (war, guns, surfing magazines) and devising 'hands on' approaches (making models, turning tasks into games) which they saw to be 'typical' of boys' approaches to learning (see also Rowan *et al.*, 2002). Furthermore, Martino and Meyenn demonstrate how teachers can hold the 'commonsense' view that seems to be a side effect of the boys' underachieve-ment lobby, that girls inhibit boys' performance in the classroom. That is where boys 'place themselves under a particular kind of self-surveillance and regula-tion, governed apparently by how they might perceive the girls' expectations of them as boys' (Martino and Meyenn, 2002: 313). Yet a large number of studies have shown how boys are less likely to be inhibited and more likely to draw on discourses of homophobia, misogyny and sexism in order to form male peer group relationships (Mac an Ghaill, 1994; Francis, 2000a; Swain, 2000; Skelton, 2001a; Martino and Pallotta-Chiarolli, 2003).

From a survey of recent research findings both in the UK and Australia it is possible to identify a number of core issues relating to single-sex class teaching:

- There continues to be no clear evidence that single-sex teaching *per se* raises achievement (Warrington and Younger, 2003), and what evidence there is appears tilted towards *girls*.
- Single-sex teaching *may* contribute to high levels of achievement but this is only likely to occur in schools were single-sex classes are embedded within a larger initiative, and where there is commitment and enthusiasm from teachers (Warrington and Younger, 2001; 2003).
- Single-sex teaching is only going to enable pupils to challenge their own social constructions of gender and thus their perceptions of curriculum, learning and so forth if undertaken by teachers who are able to deconstruct and critique their own gendered assumptions about boys and girls and who are sensitive to how these affect their chosen pedagogy (Martino and Meyenn, 2002).

On a final note, at the time of writing national newspapers were beginning to report the findings of the DfES funded national study on gender and achieve-ment. The researchers involved in this project have published the preliminary findings of their investigations as the study progressed and which we have used throughout this book to inform and support our own discussions (see Warrington and Younger, 2001, 2002; 2003; Younger *et al.*, 2005). The researchers have been quite adamant in saying repeatedly that for any school strategy on gender and achievement to work then it must be part of a whole-school scheme which is based on socio-cultural approaches. That is, teachers have got to recognise and tackle their own understandings of how gender is constructed in schooling and then to help pupils work to deconstruct their stereotypical gendered notions. Which is why they argue (based on their evaluation of strategies) that taking one-off ideas, like mentoring or single-sex classes is, if not exactly useless, then certainly not helpful. As we have shown in this section the researchers on the DfES project have quite clearly expressed the view that single-sex classes are *only* effective in those schools with a whole-school approach to gender and not in those establishments which had adopted it on an *ad hoc* basis. The researchers must then be surprised to see government ministers reporting that the findings of this project had produced 'startling' information that schools which had introduced a micro form of single-sex organisation had 'boosted performance' (David Miliband reported in *The Times*, 17 November 2004). Minister for Education David Miliband goes onto say that schools (should) consider introducing this form of classroom arrangement 'to encourage the sexes to help each other without being distracted by their friends'. It would seem that ministers are keen to promote simplistic and easily implemented ideas at the expense of addressing the far more deep seated, complex and difficult to tackle issues of gender construction which the project has uncovered and recommends that schools take on board.

Mentoring

A survey of UK local education authorities' provision of equal opportunities strategies indicated that mentoring and role-modelling were in the top three most popular strategies employed by primary and secondary schools (Sukhnandan, 1999). There is plenty of support for the idea of mentor programmes for a range of socially excluded groups (and as we have said in Chapter 3, boys are currently constructed as such in UK educational policy). We are told that Black mentor programmes are 'known to assist in increasing self-esteem and raising pupils' expectations of themselves' (Wright *et al.*, 2000: 130). However, others have objected to these on the basis that they distract attention away from institutionalised racism and 'oversimplify and over-essentialise black male student identities and experiences in school' (Raphael Reed, 1998: 63; Sewell, 1997). Mentoring has the backing of the UK government who include it as one of the strategies in its statutory guidance on dealing with disaffected and excluded pupils (Osler and Vincent, 2003). Certainly in her report on girls and school exclusion, Audrey Osler and her colleagues write that this form of support is 'welcomed by children and has proved effective in improving communication and in dealing with difficulties at an early stage' (Osler *et al.*, 2002: 77). But here again there are some who view the use of mentoring amongst socially exclude youth with more caution. Helen Colley (2003) in a trenchant critique of mentoring for social inclusion argues by offering a number of case studies of mentees and their mentors that the process is a 'risky' business. She shows how, whilst for some the experience may be perceived as successful although not in the simplistic 'experienced mentor re-engages disaffected mentee' way policy approaches assume. For two mentees in her study, the experience was one where the 'mentee suffer(ed) repeated failure and confirmed exclusion from her academic aspirations, but the mentor also lost confidence in herself, experiencing guilt, stress and fear' (Colley, 2003: 537). Colley argues this to be the fault of a reliance on narrow measures of prescribed outcomes which are determined by policy-makers, failure in which generates 'a climate of blame'.

With regard to discussions with teachers on mentoring as a means of addressing boys' underachievement then some problems have been detected. In research by Sukhnandan *et al.* (2000) teachers' perceptions of the drawbacks of mentoring were identified; that is, that sessions were often not regular enough to really help pupils and that staff were not allocated sufficient time to undertake these effectively; where staff were not given a chance to decide who they mentored or pupils an opportunity to decide who they would like to be their mentor; where staff received no training; where problems occurred because participation was only available to some groups of students and was voluntary. One study of cross-age tutoring in a rural primary school and an urban secondary school aimed at improving the social and academic (in particular, language work) skills of pupils, it was found that 'there was no clear pattern of improvement in the language skills of either group of tutees but both felt more positively about reading' (Morrison *et al.*, 2000: 187).

The message here regarding the implementation of mentoring strategies is the same as those echoed in the above discussion on single-sex classrooms; that is, to incorporate these into a whole-school approach. The findings of Younger *et al.* (2005) (and Warrington *et al.*, 2006) suggest that mentoring does have the potential to help pupils achieve but only when there is a system in place in the school. That is, schools have to ensure that time is allocated, protected and given high status in which the mentoring can take place; where there is a tutorial system that is evidently focused on addressing academic issues, and where staff and students are data literate (Younger *et al.*, 2005; Warrington *et al.*, 2006). So once again it is clear that a whole-school framework towards achievement, which takes into account (social and cultural) differences between pupils and is fully recognised, engaged with and supported by the staff, is the only way in which mentoring will be effective.

It was said at the beginning of this section that mentoring *and* role modelling were amongst the most popular approaches deployed by schools to raise achieve-ment. If mentoring has been seen to be effective when used within a clearly established framework there is no such evidence to support the use of role-models. Whilst the UK government appears to be firmly behind the idea that increasing the number of male teachers will influence boys' achievement, this is a wish list item rather than one that is supported by research. Now, whilst a clear case can be made for providing pupils with a teaching staff that is more representative of society at large, this is not the same as assuming that more men will automatically provide boys with alternative, i.e. 'non-laddish', images of masculinity. Indeed our earlier research has indicated that men teachers often emphasise traditional forms of masculinity in order to demonstrate they are 'properly masculine' (Francis and Skelton, 2001). The key reasons are that men teachers (more especially those in primary schools) may also be concerned to construct a masculinity which will be respected by their male pupils and anxious not to bring their (heterosexual) masculinity into question, as men working with young children are frequently considered 'suspicious' (King, 2000; Sargent, 2001; Skelton, 2003). In addition, many boys do not want to identify with their male teachers and, in some cases, they can be marginalised by them

(Connolly 1995; Skelton 2001a). One recent study even shows that, not only could the researchers find no evidence in their quantitative analysis of school results that higher numbers of male teachers increased primary schoolboy attainment, but that poorer discipline was more likely to be found in schools with greater concentrations of male teachers (Thornton and Brichenco, 2002). We are not arguing here that additional male teachers or an increase in a male presence in the school cannot make a positive difference to pupils as indeed it may be that matching teachers and children by gender and ethnicity could be helpful in bringing about a situation of greater justice and equity in schools. For example, in the case of ethnic minority children, there are tangible benefits in having teachers who share the similar critical life experiences including those relating to racism. And also, a more representative teaching profession and teaching staff who are actively aware of how gender is constructed and played out in school sites by adults as well as children may also contribute to breaking down racial and gender stereotypes. Of course, as is implied here, it is the awareness of gender that is significant rather than the gender of a teacher her/ himself. So, what we can say is that by simply providing more images of men, be that as male primary teachers who teach reading, or finding out what the top ten book recommendations are of players in the local football team, will not alter boys' fundamental notions of themselves as learners in the school environment.

Language and literacy

Earlier in the book we showed that the one area of the curriculum where there is a significant gap between boys and girls (and that this is an international phenomenon) is in terms of language and literacy (see Chapter 4). As a consequence both 'sides' of the boys' underachievement debate have offered strategies and solutions for tackling boys' literacy skills (that is 'recuperative masculinity' advocates versus the 'pro-feminist' lobby). Several of the recommended tactics are common to both: for example, utilising a variety of approaches to literacy. Rather than emphasis on the technical aspects of reading and writing more stress is placed on literacy in its broadest sense. Thus pupils are provided with opportunities to develop text skills using, for example, notice boards, computers, games, as well as reading materials spanning comics, newspapers, information journals, hobby magazines and material relating to popular culture (Millard, 1997; Noble and Bradford, 2000; Marsh, 2003 Ofsted, 2003b). Also, the use of drama as a means of stimulating and enabling pupils' (and in particular, boys') interest in literacy has also been widely recommended (Bleach, 1998c; Younger et al., 2005; Warrington et al., 2006).

Jackie Marsh (2000) carried out research in an infant classroom looking at how 'superheroes' could be used to stimulate interest in literacy but, also, to counteract conventional stereotypes of gender and gendered learning whereby girls do not like 'superhero' stories and boys avoid literacy tasks at all times.

First, as she points out, the male versions of superheroes, such as *Superman* and *Batman* are traditionally very 'masculine' in that they are strong, aggressive and anti-social, while female superheroes are reduced to a childlike status by their names (*Batgirl* and *Supergirl*). Second, Marsh argues that girls are interested in superhero stories but, what puts them off are the contexts in which the stories are presented which tend to be in male environments and male storylines so that females rarely have a central role to play. To overcome these kind of difficulties she describes how a 'Batcave' was set up in a corner of the classroom with a view to stimulating children's literacy skills:

> The cave contained two desks, a computer, writing materials (notepads, pens, pencils, lined and unlined paper, two blank books labelled 'Batman's Diary' and 'Batwoman's Diary') and reading materials (maps, comics, messages, instructions). There was a dressing-up rack which contained home-made tabards, commercially produced Batman outfits, a cloak and a hat.
>
> (Marsh, 2000: 212)

The teacher spent time talking to the children about what kinds of things the Batcave could provide which was important as with guidance on how to use literacy-related materials in role play areas, young children will increase the number of literacy-related events. So, the children were given books and videos on Batman and discussed them as a class. In the following ten days Jackie Marsh recorded girls engaging in 371 literacy activities and boys in 357, a relatively low level of significance of difference. Perhaps not surprisingly boys and girls did engage with literacy quite differently. For girls greater use was made of their Bat diaries (than the boys), whilst the boys were more likely to write messages (and girls to write letters).

What is significant about Marsh's research is that the teacher set out to disrupt conventional gender discourses as well as stimulate the literacy skills of both boys and girls. This is a crucial aspect of how strategies for developing language and literacy are presented and delivered to boys. And, it is on this that the 'recuperative masculinity' supporters differ from 'pro-feminist' advocates in their understandings of how strategies, such as using a range of texts and in various ways, and greater use of computers, should be deployed.

Just to reiterate the points made earlier in this chapter, for recuperative masculinity supporters a range of texts that respond to 'boys' tastes and inter-ests' such as 'horror, science-fiction, X-files analogues and fantasy' should be provided (Frater, 1998: 75). The argument here is based on the notion that boys have a 'need for adventure and excitement' so 'a boy can become enthralled with a library book on sharks or karate, a project on the Roman Legions or football and the media . . .' (Neall, 2002: 140). Biddulph cites a co-educational secondary school where the boys' results showed a significant increase when single-sex English teaching was introduced and 'the classes started to take on a distinctly boys' or girls' flavour' (1997: 137). Others note boys' supposed dislike of conventional books (and libraries) and suggest ways in which they can be encouraged to get involved with these:

> Giving boys responsibility within the library, of explaining its functions and organisation to younger boys, showing how the library can help them in their interests, are all useful ways of raising its profile and attractiveness. This can be further enhanced if the library enjoys a wider role as a resource or information centre. Boys are attracted to ICT and the library can be made synonymous with excitement and fun, which is not the image it presently enjoys in most boys' minds.
>
> (Noble and Bradford, 2000: 109)

Thus, what we have here, are examples of how stereotypical images of boys are being drawn on and reinforced in the suggested approaches. As Pickering (1997) found, it was in schools where reading was constructed as *not* gendered that boys read most – in these schools over half the boys thought that men and women read the same types of books (rather than 'gender-appropriate' books). Hence they did not see it as a controversial activity in terms of their gender constructions, and read as broadly and avidly as girls. This does not mean that teachers should not make use of texts that are associated with 'boys' interests' or fail to develop many boys' fascination for ICT. Rather, as pro-feminist advocates recommend, opportunities can be taken to use these with boys and girls as a means of encouraging critical and transformative literacy skills.

In their book *Boys, Literacies and Schooling* (2002) Leonie Rowan and her colleagues set out to deconstruct essentialist accounts of boys, masculinity and literacy which, they argue, abound in educational literature. They strenuously emphasise the need for teachers to have a working knowledge of how gendered attitudes, expectations, and behaviours inform interactions with boys and girls and then how to set about tackling these. To illustrate their points they take what is the core element of the literacy work they were exploring: computer games. Using Nintendo as the analogy, they say that this programme creates three 'moments'. In the first 'moment' the game is purchased and played with according to the instructions as provided by the manufacturer. This is the stage akin to teachers 'knowing' or being told that 'all boys' like adventure, sport and fantasy books so ensure boys are given access to these in order to raise their achievements in English. To paraphrase Rowan *et al.* (2002) this is 'what you see is what you might get'; that is, give boys computer programmes on sport because they like them and what you generate is boys who like computer programmes on sport. A second 'moment' is what they see as an 'extension pack' whereby individuals get more out of the game by adding new components or using the game more creatively. This is getting below the surface features of the game. For teachers, this is getting boys and girls to question stereotypes they are offered (by the media, manufacturers, schools even!). Here they begin to recognise that things are not as they appear on the surface but are more problematic and challenging than first appears. A third 'moment' is what Rowan *et al.* (2002) refer to as 'the new game'. They say that 'in this moment the game as a whole is taken as something to be explained rather than negotiated, or as something to be critiqued rather than mastered, or a something to be transformed rather than completed' (Rowan *et al.*, 2002: 201). What this looks like in practice is discussed in the final section.

Socio-cultural approaches to raising achievement

What we have returned to over and again in each of these sections is that schools and teachers require a knowledge and understanding of how gendered identities are constructed by themselves, pupils and the school site itself in order to challenge perceptions of gendered learning identities. The evidence to support the argument that the only way to influence pupils' gendered learning identities is through actively deconstructing traditional stereotypes is provided in numerous studies (MacNaughton, 2000; Francis, 2000a; McLellan, 2002; Davies, 2003; Martino and Pallotta-Chiarolli, 2003; Younger *et al.*, 2005; Warrington *et al.*, forthcoming). In particular, the large-scale DfES-funded study of strategies for 'raising boys' achievement' conducted by Warrington and Younger and their colleagues has shown conclusively that it is in schools where gender constructions are less accentuated that boys tend to produce higher attainment. And that it is strategies which work to reduce constructions of gender difference which are most effective in facilitating their achievement (Warrington and Younger, 2002; Warrington *et al.*, forthcoming). Starting with the questions raised in the introduction to this chapter teachers need to develop ways of getting their pupils to reflect and critique 'taken-for-granted' but gendered assumptions of classroom/media texts, ways of being organised, managed and assessed, engaging with learning, and so forth. Three examples, taken from books already referred to, provide illustrative, practical applications of socio-cultural approaches.

The first example is concerned with tackling violent behaviours amongst boys in schools (Mills, 2001). Here Martin Mills reiterates that each school context is different and, indeed, that the situation in a school changes over a period of time, hence the need to keep updating knowledge and understanding of the pupils and staff. He suggests a number of activities to help develop an awareness of the particular issues around violence in a school, the majority of which should be the subject of discussion with pupils:

- Find out from staff and pupils who are the 'most popular' boys in the school. What is it that makes them popular? How do these boys solve conflicts? If there are differences between those who are labelled 'most popular' what attributes are assigned to them?

- What are the attitudes towards sport in the school? Which sports are most valued within the school? Who plays these sports? In what ways is violence within a sport regarded and dealt with?
- What curriculum subjects are most valued within the school? How are boys and girls who choose non-traditional subjects treated by their classmates and others? Do any of these students experience harassment because of the choices they make?
- What are boys' attitudes towards girls in the school? How do these attitudes differ among boys? What do boys think about gender equity, sexual harassment policies and so on? How do girls in the school feel they are treated by boys?
- How is difference recognised and valued within the school? How prevalent within the school are negative attitudes towards gays and lesbians? Which boys most often attract homophobic insults? Does the school have an effective anti-racism policy? Does it have an effective sexual harassment policy?

(Selected points drawn from Mills, 2001: 50–1)

A second example is taken from the Rowan *et al.* (2002) book on literacy in which the teachers they worked with in one school designed a series of lessons for boys in a single-sex class based on the following principles. It needs to be noted that a separate set of objectives was designed for a mixed-sex group which highlights the importance of devising relevant approaches for specific groups. The following set of objectives for the all-boy group was based around boys' engagement with computer programs and therefore specifically for the ICT sessions:

- Map the boys' existing skills relating to Nintendo games and computer word processing.
- Discuss with the boys their development of those skills, and how they were different from the experiences of other boys and from some girls.
- Have the boys conduct online research relating to computer game groups, including those designed explicitly for girls.
- Provide boys with an opportunity to become experts in a new Nintendo game, and to develop 'cheat sheets' for that game.
- Identify these skills as literacies and highlight their connection to other 'real world' literacies.
- Ensure that the boys reflect critically upon the characters in the game – and identify the gendered roles each performed (or did not perform; in this case the boys became experts in a game where the central agent was a woman).
- Encourage critical reading of all texts used.
- Allow the boys to reflect upon the pedagogies they used in teaching their new skills to others.

At the same time the teacher had a set of objectives for herself which included:

- Negotiate the objectives of each lesson with the boys.
- Provide consistent positive feedback to the boys relating to their development of new skills.
- Critique/problematise 'macho' behaviour and celebrate alternative displays of behaviour.
- Encourage the boys to reflect upon the learning process (in oral and written reflections).
- Incorporate a wide range of text types.

(Selected points drawn from Rowan *et al.*, 2002: 116–17)

The third and final example is again deconstructing gender identities through literacy but with very young children. Some years ago one of us (Christine) read of a research project by Bronwyn Davies (1989) in which she told a number of feminist fairytales to young children to ascertain how they were 'reading' these texts. These feminist fairytales were, to those of us teaching in primary schools, a welcome antidote to the classic 'Disney'-type versions of Cinderella, Sleeping Beauty, Rapunzel and so on who were always beautiful, white, expensively and elegantly dressed, passive and grateful to get the prince at the end of the book. Teachers would read feminist fairytales to children aged from 5–7, such as *Prince Cinders, Princess Smartypants* and *The Wrestling Princess* anticipating that they would recognise and appreciate the much stronger female characters and 'softer' male temperaments represented in these tales. However, Bronwyn Davies' research indicated that this was far from the case with the very young children in particular being quite bewildered by what they were presented with. Several years later Christine had the opportunity to replicate her research with a group of 6–7-year-olds and discovered very similar findings. It is worth providing an example at length in order to illustrate that, as teachers, we cannot simply expect children to 'receive the message'. Rather we have to actively intervene to deconstruct stereotypes.

The book chosen to read to a mixed-sex group of 6-year-old children was *The Paperbag Princess* (Munsch and Martchenko, 1980). Briefly the story tells of Princess Elizabeth who, at the beginning, is engaged to Prince Ronald. Both characters are dressed in conventional 'regal' clothes with Prince Ronald sporting a gold medallion around his neck and carrying a tennis racquet. A dragon descends and takes off Prince Ronald by the seat of the prince's trousers. On the way the dragon sets fire to everything in his path which results in Princess Elizabeth having her clothes burnt off and the only thing she can find to wear is a paper bag. Undeterred she sets off to rescue Prince Ronald. She eventually finds him imprisoned in the dragon's castle. Elizabeth tricks the dragon into showing how clever he is by getting him to fly around the world twice and breathing out enough fire to destroy hundreds of forests. At the end of his endeavours the dragon is exhausted and promptly falls asleep which allows Elizabeth the chance to free Ronald from his prison in the castle. Rather than being grateful to Elizabeth for saving him Ronald tells her off for being dirty and ragged. Elizabeth responds by telling Ronald that although he is very pretty and his clothes are very neat he is a 'toad' and she skips off into the sunset over the caption informing the children that 'They didn't get married after all'. Both boys and girls in the group Christine read this story to ranked Prince Ronald as the 'bravest and best' person in the story, followed by the dragon with Elizabeth rated nowhere. When the children were asked why Ronald was the 'bravest and best' a number of reasons were given based on the illustrations:

- Ronald was a gold medal winner at Wimbledon (conclusion drawn from his holding a tennis racquet and wearing a medallion).
- He didn't cry when the dragon carried him off/he 'let' the dragon carry him off to protect Elizabeth.
- Ronald 'hid' from the dragon in the castle (the accompanying illustration to the text in the book showed Ronald looking out of a window in the dragon's castle).

The reasons for the dragon's popularity were more understandable given that he could fly around the world and breathe out fire. Elizabeth, however, was seen as naughty because she wore a paper bag, she was dirty, and she did not look beautiful. The children did not see that Elizabeth rejected Ronald at the end of the story rather that Ronald had decided he did not want to marry her because she was dirty and had no proper clothes. In keeping with the broad tenor of Davies's (1989) argument, the children were not able to 'see' an alternative version of the princess because she did not fit into their existing knowledge framework of how princesses look and behave; or with gendered discourses around 'good' child behaviour (e.g. girls should not get/be dirty, see Davies, 1989). Davies talks about the importance of 'category maintenance' work for young children whereby, because gender is still a fluid category for them up until the age of about 5–6, they work hard to fit the images they come across into their existing conceptualisations. It is only as they become more confident with gender boundaries can they start to understand and appreciate possible 'deviations'. So the children who were read the story of *The Paperbag Princess* could not 'see' an alternative image of a princess in a story – because she was not beautiful, passive and elegantly dressed she was a 'deviant' and therefore had to be rejected. This does not mean that young children should not be read feminist fairytales or not provided with images that are different from those they are most likely to encounter – quite the reverse. However, it takes active involvement on the part of the teacher to ensure that children are able to 'deconstruct' conventional stereotypes. Here, for instance, Christine could have proceeded to provide a range of illustrations of princesses in traditional fairytales, modern renditions of tales, feminist fairytales, stories from different cultures and in factual books. This compilation of illustrations would be accompanied by questions which encouraged the children to recognise different but acceptable versions of 'princess characters' in stories, for example:

- Are all princesses young and beautiful?
- Do all princesses wear long dresses?
- Can princesses do real jobs?

Other research has shown how successful such strategies in literacy lessons are for opening up discussions on gender with children, which enable them to think critically about their own gendered behaviour and that of others in the social worlds around them (e.g. Davies, 1997; 2003; Wing, 1997; Yeoman, 1999). These opportunities have been found to be relished by most children, although some boys can find them challenging (Davies, 2003; Reay 2003). All these researchers agree that it is crucial that the teacher carefully monitors class discussions in order to ensure that hegemonic power relations are not abused and/or re-asserted. Francis (2000a) suggests that such approaches may be developed in the secondary classroom, given her respondents' interest and enthusiasm for discussion of gender issues.

Final words

What we have shown in this book is that discussions around 'gender and achievement' are complicated and far more complex than one is led to assume by policy-makers and media headlines. There is a gender gap in literacy with boys underperforming in relation to girls, which deserves attention. But in other areas the gap is not significant and certainly not deserving of the attention it receives in comparison with the lesser attention given to larger gaps around social class and 'race'. At the same time, there are problems with education and schooling which are gender related but these are more than simply 'boys' behaviours and attitudes'. We have also seen how the labelling of boys as socially excluded through being 'problem boys' or ' "at risk" boys' is generating strategies that place the responsibility for rectifying this on emotional and psychic 'healing' rather than acknowledging these might be a consequence (or self-fulfilling prophecy) generated as a result of more fundamental structural inequities.

   We want to finish with a few words about the current conception of 'achievement'. We hope to have charted how the current panic about 'boys' underachievement', and the preoccupations with 'excellence', 'standards' and the construction of educational achievement as educational credentials, are driven by movements in socio-economic policy reflecting the neo-liberal, new-individualist turn. We have shown how the emerging discourses on gender and achievement carry the therapeutic but also demonising tendencies of these movements, which foreground competition, success, self-responsibility and notions of 'free choice', with their hidden dualisms of failure, losing, and dependence. There are many girls and boys of all social classes and ethnicities who experience psychic and emotional problems because of the obsessive pressures of assessment and getting into the 'right' schools (Chaplin, 2000; Walkerdine *et al.*,

2000; Lucey and Reay, 2002a). As Walkerdine *et al.*, (2001) and Lucey and Reay (2002a; 2002b) have shown, while the government pronouncements about eradication of failure sound superficially positive, the government's benchmark 'success' can never exist as a concept without 'failure' with which to juxtapose it. Not only are current policy drives forcing particular groups of pupils (and parents) to internalise this failure, but the obsession with credentials leads even many 'achieving' pupils to believe their performance is 'never good enough'. Without wishing to diminish some of the issues around gender and educational credentials analysed in this book, we end with a plea for a return to a broader notion of educational achievement, which recognises diverse successes as well as the continuing gender issues in pupils' experience of education and learning.

Appendix I

Table A1.1 Achievements at Key Stage 1 level 2 and above in 2003, by ethnicity and gender

Key Stage 1	Reading					
	Eligible pupils			% Achieving		
	Boys	Girls	Total	Boys	Girls	Total
White	238,818	226,788	465,606	81	89	85
White British	230,864	219,468	450,332	81	89	85
Irish	1,168	996	2,164	80	88	84
Traveller of Irish Heritage	187	183	370	21	36	28
Gypsy/Roma	355	356	711	37	47	42
Any other White background	6,244	5,785	12,029	76	84	80
Mixed	9,299	8,863	18,162	82	89	85
White and Black Caribbean	3,238	3,209	6,447	78	88	83
White and Black African	859	857	1,716	83	88	86
White and Asian	1,893	1,748	3,641	86	91	88
Any other mixed background	3,309	3,049	6,358	82	90	85
Asian	20,244	19,377	39,621	77	84	80
Indian	6,253	5,906	12,159	85	91	88
Pakistani	8,525	8,186	16,711	72	81	76
Bangladeshi	3,528	3,506	7,034	71	78	75
Any other Asian background	1,938	1,779	3,717	80	85	82
Black	10,870	10,416	21,286	74	83	78
Black Caribbean	4,072	4,003	8,075	74	84	79
Black African	5,616	5,282	10,898	74	81	77
Any other Black background	1,182	1,131	2,313	75	84	79
Chinese	852	907	1,759	86	93	90
Any other ethnic group	2,545	2,364	4,909	71	77	74
Unclassified[1]	9,998	9,358	19,356	72	81	76
All pupils	292,626	278,073	570,699	80	88	84

Table A1.1 cont.

Key Stage 1	Writing					
	Eligible pupils			% Achieving		
	Boys	Girls	Total	Boys	Girls	Total
White	238,823	226,793	465,616	77	87	82
White British	230,869	219,473	450,342	77	88	82
Irish	1,168	996	2,164	77	85	81
Traveller of Irish Heritage	187	183	370	20	37	28
Gypsy/Roma	355	356	711	33	43	38
Any other White background	6,244	5,785	12,029	72	83	78
Mixed	9,299	8,863	18,162	77	87	82
White and Black Caribbean	3,238	3,209	6,447	73	86	79
White and Black African	859	857	1,716	80	86	83
White and Asian	1,893	1,748	3,641	82	89	85
Any other mixed background	3,309	3,049	6,358	78	87	82
Asian	20,244	19,377	39,621	73	82	78
Indian	6,253	5,906	12,159	82	89	86
Pakistani	8,525	8,186	16,711	67	79	73
Bangladeshi	3,528	3,506	7,034	69	78	73
Any other Asian background	1,938	1,779	3,717	77	83	80
Black	10,870	10,416	21,286	68	80	74
Black Caribbean	4,072	4,003	8,075	67	81	74
Black African	5,616	5,282	10,898	68	78	73
Any other Black background	1,182	1,131	2,313	69	81	75
Chinese	852	907	1,759	84	93	88
Any other ethnic group	2,545	2,364	4,909	66	76	71
Unclassified[1]	9,998	9,358	19,356	67	80	73
All pupils	292,631	278,078	570,709	76	86	81

Source: http://www.dfes.gov.uk/rsgateway/DB/SFR/s000448

Note:
1 Includes information refused or not obtained

Table A1.2 Achievement at Key Stage 2 level 4 and above in 2003 by ethnicity and gender

| Key Stage 2 | English | | | | | |
| | Eligible pupils | | | % Achieving | | |
	Boys	Girls	Total	Boys	Girls	Total
White	261,398	249,529	510,927	70	81	76
White British	254,306	242,494	496,800	70	81	76
Irish	1,150	1,154	2,304	77	87	82
Traveller of Irish Heritage	163	179	342	17	29	23
Gypsy/Roma	270	299	569	22	37	30
Any other White background	5,509	5,403	10,912	70	79	74
Mixed	8,256	8,157	16,413	72	82	77
White and Black Caribbean	3,038	3,105	6,143	67	79	73
White and Black African	678	694	1,372	73	81	77
White and Asian	1,613	1,531	3,144	77	86	81
Any other mixed background	2,927	2,827	5,754	74	84	79
Asian	19,141	18,379	37,520	64	75	69
Indian	6,538	6,298	12,836	76	83	79
Pakistani	7,900	7,594	15,494	55	67	61
Bangladeshi	2,926	2,829	5,755	62	75	68
Any other Asian background	1,777	1,658	3,435	70	77	73
Black	10,143	9,996	20,139	61	74	68
Black Caribbean	4,406	4,339	8,745	61	75	68
Black African	4,630	4,583	9,213	61	73	67
Any other Black background	1,107	1,074	2,181	65	76	71
Chinese	901	895	1,796	77	87	82
Any other ethnic group	2,360	2,102	4,462	59	68	63
Unclassified[1]	12,393	10,891	23,284	63	76	69
All pupils	314,592	299,949	614,541	69	80	75

Table A1.2 cont.

Key Stage 2	Mathematics					
	Eligible pupils			% Achieving		
	Boys	Girls	Total	Boys	Girls	Total
White	261,425	249,527	510,952	74	72	73
White British	254,333	242,493	496,826	74	73	73
Irish	1,150	1,154	2,304	78	79	78
Traveller of Irish Heritage	164	179	343	20	17	19
Gypsy/Roma	270	298	568	27	28	27
Any other White background	5,508	5,403	10,911	73	71	72
Mixed	8,261	8,158	16,419	73	72	72
White and Black Caribbean	3,040	3,107	6,147	68	66	67
White and Black African	679	694	1,373	72	72	72
White and Asian	1,614	1,532	3,146	79	77	78
Any other mixed background	2,928	2,825	5,753	75	75	75
Asian	19,196	18,412	37,608	68	65	67
Indian	6,542	6,300	12,842	79	75	77
Pakistani	7,903	7,598	15,501	60	56	58
Bangladeshi	2,973	2,856	5,829	64	62	63
Any other Asian background	1,778	1,658	3,436	75	72	74
Black	10,145	9,997	20,142	60	61	60
Black Caribbean	4,406	4,340	8,746	57	60	59
Black African	4,632	4,583	9,215	62	62	62
Any other Black background	1,107	1,074	2,181	62	62	62
Chinese	901	896	1,797	88	89	88
Any other ethnic group	2,361	2,102	4,463	68	66	67
Unclassified[1]	12,400	10,889	23,289	66	66	66
All pupils	314,689	299,981	614,670	72	71	72

Table A1.2 cont.

Key Stage 2	Science					
	Eligible pupils			% Achieving		
	Boys	Girls	Total	Boys	Girls	Total
White	261,445	249,552	510,997	87	88	87
White British	254,353	242,517	496,870	87	88	88
Irish	1,150	1,154	2,304	88	91	90
Traveller of Irish Heritage	164	179	343	34	38	36
Gypsy/Roma	270	299	569	46	50	48
Any other White background	5,508	5,403	10,911	84	84	84
Mixed	8,261	8,160	16,421	86	88	87
White and Black Caribbean	3,041	3,107	6,148	85	86	85
White and Black African	679	694	1,373	84	86	85
White and Asian	1,613	1,532	3,145	89	90	89
Any other mixed background	2,928	2,827	5,755	87	89	88
Asian	19,197	18,412	37,609	79	79	79
Indian	6,541	6,300	12,841	87	87	87
Pakistani	7,904	7,598	15,502	72	72	72
Bangladeshi	2,974	2,856	5,830	76	77	77
Any other Asian background	1,778	1,658	3,436	82	81	82
Black	10,145	9,997	20,142	76	79	77
Black Caribbean	4,406	4,339	8,745	76	80	78
Black African	4,632	4,584	9,216	75	76	75
Any other Black background	1,107	1,074	2,181	78	81	79
Chinese	901	896	1,797	88	92	90
Any other ethnic group	2,362	2,102	4,464	74	76	75
Unclassified[1]	12,401	10,891	23,292	82	83	83
All pupils	314,712	300,010	614,722	86	87	86

Source: http://www.dfes.gov.uk/rsgateway/DB/SFR/s000448/

Note:
1 Includes information refused or not obtained

Table A1.3 Achievement at Key Stage 3 level 5 and above in 2003 by ethnicity and gender

| Key Stage 3 | English | | | | | |
| | Eligible pupils | | | % Achieving | | |
	Boys	Girls	Total	Boys	Girls	Total
White	249,631	241,450	491,081	63	77	70
White British	242,557	234,459	477,016	63	77	70
Irish	1,165	1,225	2,390	70	80	75
Traveller of Irish Heritage	118	118	236	45	53	49
Gypsy/Roma	128	152	280	22	42	33
Any other White background	5,663	5,496	11,159	59	73	66
Mixed	5,814	6,123	11,937	62	76	69
White and Black Caribbean	2,112	2,285	4,397	53	70	62
White and Black African	467	525	992	63	74	69
White and Asian	1,129	1,124	2,253	73	83	78
Any other mixed background	2,106	2,189	4,295	64	78	71
Asian	17,888	16,735	34,623	59	73	66
Indian	6,659	6,210	12,869	71	84	77
Pakistani	6,974	6,346	13,320	50	65	57
Bangladeshi	2,581	2,664	5,245	50	65	58
Any other Asian background	1,674	1,515	3,189	64	76	70
Black	9,524	9,835	19,359	47	65	56
Black Caribbean	4,272	4,497	8,769	46	66	56
Black African	3,941	4,069	8,010	49	63	56
Any other Black background	1,311	1,269	2,580	48	69	58
Chinese	1,067	1,023	2,090	74	86	80
Any other ethnic group	2,318	2,114	4,432	53	65	59
Unclassified[1]	16,811	14,865	31,676	56	71	63
All pupils	303,053	292,145	595,198	62	76	69

Table A1.3 cont.

| Key Stage 3 | Mathematics | | | | | |
| | Eligible pupils | | | % Achieving | | |
	Boys	Girls	Total	Boys	Girls	Total
White	*249,251*	*241,022*	*490,273*	*71*	*73*	*72*
White British	242,193	234,067	476,260	71	73	72
Irish	1,161	1,211	2,372	76	75	75
Traveller of Irish Heritage	118	118	236	49	48	49
Gypsy/Roma	127	150	277	28	41	35
Any other White background	5,652	5,476	11,128	69	71	70
Mixed	*5,811*	*6,095*	*11,906*	*67*	*71*	*69*
White and Black Caribbean	2,109	2,276	4,385	60	65	62
White and Black African	467	523	990	64	72	68
White and Asian	1,129	1,116	2,245	77	80	78
Any other mixed background	2,106	2,180	4,286	69	73	71
Asian	*17,865*	*16,697*	*34,562*	*65*	*66*	*66*
Indian	6,649	6,194	12,843	77	80	79
Pakistani	6,962	6,332	13,294	55	54	55
Bangladeshi	2,580	2,660	5,240	56	57	57
Any other Asian background	1,674	1,511	3,185	74	75	75
Black	*9,491*	*9,802*	*19,293*	*51*	*57*	*54*
Black Caribbean	4,256	4,479	8,735	49	56	53
Black African	3,928	4,057	7,985	53	57	55
Any other Black background	1,307	1,266	2,573	52	58	55
Chinese	*1,060*	*1,021*	*2,081*	*89*	*90*	*90*
Any other ethnic group	*2,311*	*2,106*	*4,417*	*64*	*65*	*64*
Unclassified[1]	*16,841*	*14,890*	*31,731*	*66*	*68*	*67*
All pupils	*302,630*	*291,633*	*594,263*	*70*	*72*	*71*

Table A1.3 cont.

Key Stage 3	Science					
	Eligible pupils			% Achieving		
	Boys	Girls	Total	Boys	Girls	Total
White	249,731	241,285	491,016	70	70	70
White British	242,663	234,300	476,963	70	70	70
Irish	1,164	1,225	2,389	74	73	73
Traveller of Irish Heritage	117	118	235	45	45	45
Gypsy/Roma	128	151	279	34	37	35
Any other White background	5,659	5,491	11,150	65	66	65
Mixed	5,819	6,121	11,940	65	68	67
White and Black Caribbean	2,116	2,283	4,399	58	62	60
White and Black African	467	524	991	67	69	68
White and Asian	1,128	1,127	2,255	75	76	76
Any other mixed background	2,108	2,187	4,295	67	70	68
Asian	17,888	16,730	34,618	58	59	59
Indian	6,656	6,205	12,861	71	74	72
Pakistani	6,976	6,347	13,323	47	47	47
Bangladeshi	2,580	2,662	5,242	48	49	48
Any other Asian background	1,676	1,516	3,192	68	70	69
Black	9,527	9,832	19,359	48	53	51
Black Caribbean	4,280	4,494	8,774	47	54	51
Black African	3,940	4,069	8,009	48	51	50
Any other Black background	1,307	1,269	2,576	50	57	54
Chinese	1,065	1,023	2,088	81	83	82
Any other ethnic group	2,321	2,116	4,437	57	58	58
Unclassified[1]	16,840	14,910	31,750	64	65	65
All pupils	303,191	292,017	595,208	68	68	68

Source: http://www.dfes.gov.uk/rsgateway/DB/SFR/s000448/

Note:
1 Includes information refused or not obtained

Table A1.4 Achievements at GCSE/GNVQ in 2003 by ethnicity and gender

GCSE/GNVQ	5 or more A*–C					
	Number of 15-year-olds			% Achieving		
	Boys	Girls	Total	Boys	Girls	Total
White	239,854	232,149	472,003	46.2	56.7	51.3
White British	233,151	225,855	459,006	46.1	56.6	51.3
Irish	1,093	1,111	2,204	58.4	61.8	60.1
Traveller of Irish Heritage	97	64	161	43.3	39.1	41.6
Gypsy/Roma	90	138	228	24.4	22.5	23.2
Any other White background	5,423	4,981	10,404	46.3	58.2	52.0
Mixed	4,869	5,320	10,189	42.7	55.4	49.3
White and Black Caribbean	1,778	1,959	3,737	32.3	46.8	39.9
White and Black African	390	410	800	39.5	55.1	47.5
White and Asian	878	915	1,793	60.6	68.6	64.7
Any other mixed background	1,823	2,036	3,859	44.9	57.7	51.6
Asian	18,620	17,391	36,011	47.1	59.0	52.8
Indian	7,151	6,899	14,050	60.3	70.3	65.2
Pakistani	7,162	6,329	13,491	35.7	48.1	41.5
Bangladeshi	2,741	2,689	5,430	38.5	52.6	45.5
Any other Asian background	1,566	1,474	3,040	53.8	64.6	59.0
Black	9,208	9,737	18,945	29.1	43.1	36.3
Black Caribbean	4,159	4,403	8,562	25.1	40.3	32.9
Black African	3,790	4,145	7,935	34.1	46.8	40.7
Any other Black background	1,259	1,189	2,448	27.2	40.3	33.6
Chinese	1,082	967	2,049	70.9	79.2	74.8
Any other ethnic group	2,330	1,948	4,278	41.3	51.2	45.8
Unclassified[1]	17,439	15,170	32,609	43.1	52.2	47.4
All pupils	293,402	282,682	576,084	45.5	56.1	50.7

Table A1.4 cont.

GCSE/GNVQ	No passes					
	Number of 15-year-olds			% Achieving		
	Boys	Girls	Total	Boys	Girls	Total
White	239,854	232,149	472,003	6.3	4.3	5.3
White British	233,151	225,855	459,006	6.2	4.2	5.3
Irish	1,093	1,111	2,204	4.9	3.7	4.3
Traveller of Irish Heritage	97	64	161	17.5	17.2	17.4
Gypsy/Roma	90	138	228	21.1	21.7	21.5
Any other White background	5,423	4,981	10,404	9.7	6.3	8.1
Mixed	4,869	5,320	10,189	7.6	5.1	6.3
White and Black Caribbean	1,778	1,959	3,737	7.6	5.6	6.6
White and Black African	390	410	800	9.5	7.3	8.4
White and Asian	878	915	1,793	4.1	3.6	3.8
Any other mixed background	1,823	2,036	3,859	8.9	4.9	6.8
Asian	18,620	17,391	36,011	4.5	3.1	3.8
Indian	7,151	6,899	14,050	2.7	1.9	2.3
Pakistani	7,162	6,329	13,491	5.7	3.6	4.7
Bangladeshi	2,741	2,689	5,430	5.4	3.6	4.5
Any other Asian background	1,566	1,474	3,040	5.9	6.0	6.0
Black	9,208	9,737	18,945	8.4	6.0	7.1
Black Caribbean	4,159	4,403	8,562	8.4	4.3	6.3
Black African	3,790	4,145	7,935	8.1	7.8	8.0
Any other Black background	1,259	1,189	2,448	8.9	6.0	7.5
Chinese	1,082	967	2,049	4.7	3.9	4.3
Any other ethnic group	2,330	1,948	4,278	11.5	8.6	10.2
Unclassified[1]	17,439	15,170	32,609	8.6	6.6	7.7
All pupils	293,402	282,682	576,084	6.5	4.4	5.5

Source: http://www.dfes.gov.uk/rsgateway/DB/SFR/s000448/

Note:
[1] Includes information refused or not obtained

Appendix 2

Table A2.1 Achievements at Key Stage 2 level 4 and above in 2003 by FSM and gender

Key Stage 2	English					
	Eligible pupils			% Achieving		
	Boys	Girls	Total	Boys	Girls	Total
Non FSM	258,656	247,213	505,869	74	84	79
FSM	54,507	51,547	106,054	48	61	54
Unclassified	1,429	1,189	2,618	49	63	55
All pupils	314,592	299,949	614,541	69	80	75

Key Stage 2	Mathematics					
	Eligible pupils			% Achieving		
	Boys	Girls	Total	Boys	Girls	Total
Non FSM	258,687	247,215	505,902	77	76	76
FSM	54,565	51,574	106,139	54	52	53
Unclassified	1,437	1,192	2,629	52	54	53
All pupils	314,689	299,981	614,670	72	71	72

Key Stage 2	Science					
	Eligible pupils			% Achieving		
	Boys	Girls	Total	Boys	Girls	Total
Non FSM	258,709	247,245	505,954	89	90	89
FSM	54,569	51,576	106,145	71	72	72
Unclassified	1,434	1,189	2,623	63	68	65
All pupils	314,712	300,010	614,722	86	87	86

Source: http://www.dfes.gov.uk/rsgateway/DB/SFR/s000448/

Table A2.2 Achievements at GCSE/GNVQ in 2003 by FSM and gender

5 or more A*–C

GCSE/GNVQ	Number of 15-year-olds			% Achieving		
	Boys	Girls	Total	Boys	Girls	Total
Non FSM	251,134	242,202	493,336	49.9	60.8	55.2
FSM	41,096	40,182	81,278	20.4	28.5	24.4
Unclassified	1,172	298	1,470	0.2	0.0	0.1
All pupils	293,402	282,682	576,084	45.5	56.1	50.7

No passes

GCSE/GNVQ	Number of 15-year-olds			% Achieving		
	Boys	Girls	Total	Boys	Girls	Total
Non FSM	251,134	242,202	493,336	4.8	3.4	4.1
FSM	41,096	40,182	81,278	14.3	10.1	12.2
Unclassified	1,172	298	1,470	93.2	93.6	93.3
All pupils	293,402	282,682	576,084	6.5	4.4	5.5

Source: http://www.dfes.gov.uk/rsgateway/DB/SFR/s000448/

Appendix 3

Table A3.1 GCE A level examination results of 17-year-old[1] students in all schools and colleges by subject, gender and grade in 2002–3

FINAL FIGURES

| 17-year-olds[1] | Males | | | | | | | | |
| | Grade obtained | | | | | | | | |
	A	B	C	D	E	U	Other grades	A–E (%)	Total entries
Biological sciences	2,990	2,943	3,073	2,746	2,225	1,063	14	92.8	15,054
Chemistry	3,698	3,150	2,519	1,938	1,351	567	16	95.6	13,239
Physics	4,867	3,754	3,393	3,020	2,208	1,001	10	94.5	18,253
Other science	560	471	544	451	350	134	*	94.6	2,511
Mathematics	10,347	5,425	4,465	3,372	2,333	1,235	61	95.2	27,238
Psychology	916	1,489	1,841	1,817	1,244	583	19	92.4	7,909
Computer studies	875	1,165	1,472	1,433	1,092	497	14	92.2	6,548
ICT	517	1,312	2,249	2,520	1,952	760	40	91.4	9,350
Design and technology	1,156	1,747	2,241	2,110	1,257	375	13	95.6	8,899
Home economics	*	8	6	16	12	*	0	91.5	47
Business studies	2,109	3,981	4,777	3,830	1,814	370	26	97.7	16,907
Geography	3,058	4,016	3,882	2,954	1,495	314	13	97.9	15,732
History	3,756	4,123	4,081	2,952	1,319	283	19	98.2	16,533
Economics	2,634	2,194	1,720	1,116	517	132	10	98.3	8,323
Social studies	2,440	3,018	2,931	2,336	1,391	513	64	95.5	12,693
Physical education	866	1,847	2,621	2,677	1,846	480	17	95.2	10,354
Vocational studies	124	188	237	242	236	93	*	91.3	1,125
Art and design	2,063	1,959	2,118	1,731	959	376	26	95.6	9,232
English	4,510	5,403	6,288	4,566	1,885	313	58	98.4	23,023
Communication studies	278	645	663	389	136	49	*	97.6	2,164
Media/film/TV studies	675	1,552	2,231	1,775	645	138	14	97.8	7,030
French	1,229	966	721	465	262	69	*	98.0	3,717
German	577	445	368	290	157	35	7	97.8	1,879
Spanish	455	356	237	140	75	12	*	99.0	1,276
Other modern languages	412	239	125	51	31	13	15	96.8	886
Classical studies	702	521	404	287	95	23	*	98.8	2,033
Music	684	722	818	660	363	116	11	96.2	3,374
Religious studies	730	742	662	379	196	56	*	97.8	2,769
General studies	3,017	4,220	5,646	5,792	4,481	2,065	140	91.3	25,361
Total	56,246	58,604	62,334	52,055	31,929	11,670	628	95.5	273,466

Table A3.1 cont.

| 17-year-olds[1] | **Females** | | | | | | | | |
| | Grade obtained | | | | | | | | |
	A	B	C	D	E	U	Other grades	A–E (%)	Total entries
Biological sciences	5,760	5,375	4,966	4,082	2,952	1,158	27	95.1	24,320
Chemistry	4,444	3,611	2,670	1,843	1,140	379	15	97.2	14,102
Physics	1,682	1,231	951	692	481	163	*	96.8	5,202
Other science	212	215	233	222	145	40	*	96.2	1,068
Mathematics	6,388	3,544	2,481	1,804	952	454	29	96.9	15,652
Psychology	5,370	6,460	6,261	4,702	2,590	787	60	96.8	26,230
Computer studies	98	166	175	188	143	62	*	92.3	834
ICT	394	948	1,254	1,319	852	268	10	94.5	5,045
Design and technology	1,029	1,453	1,488	1,063	474	107	0	98.1	5,614
Home economics	88	119	123	110	61	14	0	97.3	515
Business studies	1,853	2,939	3,247	2,429	1,132	243	11	97.9	11,854
Geography	3,823	3,652	3,131	1,957	820	169	7	98.7	13,559
History	4,353	4,672	4,008	2,916	1,219	276	8	98.4	17,452
Economics	1,212	889	663	389	179	44	*	98.6	3,379
Social studies	5,219	6,002	5,559	3,805	2,008	598	59	97.2	23,250
Physical education	1,346	1,628	1,737	1,344	721	193	9	97.1	6,978
Vocational studies	77	119	128	158	131	76	0	89.0	689
Art and design	6,499	5,294	4,873	3,062	1,360	401	52	97.9	21,541
English	10,873	14,605	15,706	10,799	3,587	483	65	99.0	56,118
Communication studies	631	1,343	1,461	721	200	34	*	99.1	4,394
Media/film/TV studies	1,455	2,776	3,202	2,060	655	90	7	99.1	10,245
French	2,402	2,123	1,658	1,125	562	151	8	98.0	8,029
German	916	901	747	599	294	87	7	97.4	3,551
Spanish	887	747	565	366	177	46	*	98.2	2,791
Other modern languages	677	321	201	76	30	15	15	97.8	1,335
Classical studies	969	844	617	297	93	12	*	99.5	2,833
Music	798	837	909	645	314	75	*	97.8	3,580
Religious studies	1,588	1,971	1,643	1,034	369	116	*	98.2	6,724
General studies	3,791	5,283	6,702	6,430	4,625	1,833	101	93.3	28,765
Total	74,839	80,068	77,362	56,239	28,266	8,374	511	97.3	325,659

[1] Age at the start of the 2002–3 academic year i.e. 31 August 2002.

* = figures 5 or less.

Source: DfES, 2004

Appendix 4

Table A4.1 HE qualifications obtained in the UK by mode of study, domicile, gender and subject area 2001–2

	Total HE qualifications obtained	First degrees						Higher degrees		
		Total first degrees	First class	Upper second	Lower second	Third class/pass	Unclassified	Total higher degrees	Doctorate	Other higher degrees
1 Total full-time	380,915	244,120	23,860	111,605	78,040	15,770	14,850	61,605	10,660	50,945
2 UK domiciled	310,840	216,230	20,880	101,385	68,410	12,620	12,930	28,030	6,460	21,570
3 Female	177,285	120,915	11,175	61,500	36,525	5,025	6,695	13,305	2,855	10,450
4 Male	133,555	95,310	9,705	39,885	31,885	7,600	6,235	14,725	3,605	11,120
5 Overseas domiciled	70,075	27,895	2,985	10,220	9,630	3,145	1,915	33,575	4,200	29,375
6 Female	33,690	13,560	1,360	5,465	4,715	1,170	840	15,515	1,525	13,985
7 Male	36,385	14,335	1,620	4,750	4,910	1,975	1,075	18,060	2,670	15,390

Source: HESA (www.hesa.ac.uk/holisdocs/pubinfo/student/quals0102.htm)

Note:
In this table 0, 1, 2 are rounded to 0. All other numbers are rounded up or down to the nearest 5.

Table A4.2 All HE students by level of study, subject of study(#8), domicile and gender 2002–3

	Total HE students	FT UGs	FT PGs	PT UGs	PT PGs	United Kingdom			Other EU			Non-EU		
						Total	Female	Male	Total	Female	Male	Total	Female	Male
Computer science	134,035	85,535	14,400	24,130	9,970	113,305	28,860	84,450	5,010	1,015	3,995	15,715	4,155	11,560
Computer science	102,580	64,905	10,310	19,990	7,370	87,175	21,330	65,845	4,055	780	3,275	11,345	2,840	8,505
Information systems	24,130	15,885	3,155	3,040	2,045	20,030	6,335	13,700	710	190	520	3,385	1,125	2,265
Software engineering	5,790	3,870	755	645	525	4,755	625	4,125	175	20	155	865	160	705
Artificial intelligence	805	685	85	10	30	675	220	455	55	25	30	75	20	55
Others in computing sciences	730	195	100	440	0	665	345	320	20	0	20	45	15	30
Engineering and technology	131,575	76,855	20,050	18,185	16,490	95,735	13,690	82,045	12,435	1,865	10,570	23,410	4,260	19,145
Broadly-based programmes within engineering and technology	155	95	20	35	5	120	20	100	15	0	10	20	5	15
General engineering	18,990	8,540	3,025	4,445	2,980	13,890	1,825	12,065	1,835	275	1,560	3,270	555	2,715
Civil engineering	16,325	8,915	2,610	2,385	2,410	11,165	1,740	9,420	2,390	525	1,865	2,770	510	2,260
Mechanical engineering	21,070	13,685	2,255	3,010	2,125	16,325	1,335	14,990	1,720	130	1,590	3,025	290	2,735
Aerospace engineering	6,690	5,100	565	370	650	5,410	585	4,825	640	70	570	635	80	560
Naval architecture	670	425	75	105	65	450	25	425	135	10	125	85	15	75
Electronic and electrical engineering	37,440	23,635	5,955	4,390	3,465	25,370	2,490	22,880	3,500	310	3,190	8,570	1,440	7,125
Production and manufacturing engineering	9,885	4,905	1,495	2,245	1,240	7,825	1,040	6,785	625	100	530	1,430	235	1,195
Chemical, process and energy engineering	5,585	3,175	1,375	150	885	3,590	915	2,675	425	150	270	1,570	540	1,030
Others in engineering	965	355	235	195	180	690	95	595	135	25	110	145	25	120
Minerals technology	350	165	100	10	75	215	35	180	35	10	25	100	15	85
Metallurgy	650	110	390	0	155	385	140	240	70	25	50	195	70	125
Ceramics and glasses	165	65	20	50	35	150	75	75	0	0	0	15	5	5
Polymers and textiles	2,995	2,275	370	190	160	2,415	1,905	510	115	80	40	465	195	265

Materials technology not otherwise specified	2,990	1,590	710	195	500	2,190	640	1,550	245	70	175	555	180	375
Maritime technology	1,595	1,085	215	150	140	1,025	130	895	255	20	235	310	20	290
Industrial biotechnology	135	125	10	0	0	70	20	50	15	5	10	50	35	15
Others in technology	4,925	2,620	625	255	1,425	4,445	665	3,780	275	60	215	205	45	160
Architecture, building and planning	45,830	21,600	5,095	11,510	7,625	38,790	10,965	27,825	2,635	1,180	1,455	4,405	1,505	2,895
Broadly-based programmes within architecture, building and planning	0	0	0	0	0	0	0	0	0	0	0	0	0	0
Architecture	15,685	9,590	2,500	1,390	2,205	12,130	3,735	8,390	1,660	825	830	1,900	765	1,135
Building	17,590	7,125	790	7,405	2,270	15,595	2,030	13,565	465	110	360	1,530	320	1,210
Landscape design	2,180	1,160	310	545	165	1,935	955	980	115	65	50	130	75	55
Planning (urban, rural and regional)	9,760	3,575	1,355	1,955	2,875	8,655	4,105	4,550	350	175	180	755	325	430
Others in architecture, building and planning	615	155	140	210	110	480	140	335	45	10	35	95	25	70
Social studies	168,920	94,310	18,430	36,950	19,230	145,745	92,440	53,305	8,085	4,115	3,975	15,090	7,590	7,500
Broadly-based programmes within social studies	425	240	15	150	15	405	230	170	15	5	5	10	10	0
Economics	29,140	21,885	4,250	925	2,075	19,105	6,050	13,060	3,370	1,250	2,120	6,660	3,055	3,610
Politics	24,130	15,925	4,550	1,325	2,335	18,785	7,910	10,875	1,965	1,015	950	3,385	1,605	1,780
Sociology	34,480	23,515	1,910	6,105	2,950	32,375	23,385	8,990	865	565	295	1,245	765	475
Social policy	9,630	4,430	1,405	960	2,835	8,345	5,940	2,405	270	165	105	1,010	530	485
Social work	43,365	12,930	2,975	21,490	5,975	42,670	34,050	8,620	350	285	65	350	235	115
Anthropology	5,290	3,355	930	420	585	4,200	2,960	1,240	450	335	120	635	420	215
Human and social geography	13,535	9,555	1,165	2,100	715	12,435	6,905	5,530	340	205	135	760	375	390
Others in social studies	8,920	2,475	1,230	3,470	1,745	7,425	5,005	2,420	465	285	180	1,030	595	435
Law	77,680	44,435	13,340	9,430	10,475	62,860	38,145	24,715	4,000	2,105	1,895	10,825	5,415	5,405
Broadly-based programmes within law	2,070	1,740	145	110	75	1,815	1,120	690	65	40	25	195	90	105
Law by area	24,510	14,275	4,260	3,030	2,945	17,235	10,570	6,665	1,930	1,020	905	5,345	2,685	2,665
Law by topic	48,990	27,350	8,525	6,030	7,085	42,195	25,425	16,770	1,925	985	935	4,870	2,455	2,415
Others in law	2,115	1,070	410	260	375	1,620	1,030	590	85	55	30	410	185	225

Table A4.2 cont.

	Total HE students	FT UGs	FT PGs	PT UGs	PT PGs	United Kingdom			Other EU			Non-EU		
						Total	Female	Male	Total	Female	Male	Total	Female	Male
Business and administrative studies	284,550	148,160	34,675	41,950	59,760	221,965	114,775	107,190	16,540	7,285	9,255	46,040	22,065	23,975
Broadly-based programmes within business and administrative studies	490	265	65	90	70	400	195	205	20	5	15	70	30	40
Business studies	136,385	69,990	15,550	20,870	29,970	105,905	51,280	54,625	9,205	3,930	5,275	21,275	9,275	12,000
Management studies	55,770	28,655	6,160	6,195	14,765	44,710	22,665	22,040	2,600	1,115	1,485	8,465	3,985	4,480
Finance	14,995	6,425	4,405	2,135	2,030	8,645	3,445	5,205	1,200	350	850	5,150	2,345	2,805
Accounting	27,020	17,810	1,660	6,570	980	21,670	10,185	11,485	555	210	345	4,795	2,690	2,110
Marketing	22,695	13,625	3,755	2,465	2,850	17,470	10,130	7,340	1,560	870	690	3,665	2,090	1,575
Human resource management	16,450	3,185	2,015	2,775	8,475	14,640	11,150	3,490	520	310	210	1,290	845	445
Office skills	515	390	5	60	55	470	305	170	15	5	5	30	20	10
Tourism, transport and travel	8,365	6,710	855	420	380	6,655	4,845	1,815	660	435	225	1,050	695	355
Others in business and administrative studies	1,860	1,105	200	370	185	1,400	575	825	205	50	160	255	95	155
Mass communications and documentation	42,175	30,135	4,615	3,095	4,330	36,840	22,225	14,615	2,170	1,450	720	3,165	2,150	1,015
Broadly-based programmes within mass communications and documentation	15	10	0	0	0	10	5	5	0	0	0	5	0	0
Information services	5,395	1,350	1,030	565	2,450	4,555	3,015	1,540	340	255	85	500	315	185
Publicity studies	4,975	3,550	630	280	520	4,095	3,005	1,090	320	225	100	560	415	140
Media studies	22,600	19,000	1,470	1,265	860	20,205	11,235	8,970	1,130	720	410	1,265	860	405
Publishing	2,140	1,145	155	765	75	1,995	1,280	710	45	35	10	100	65	35
Journalism	5,995	4,185	1,220	210	380	5,020	2,970	2,050	315	205	115	660	440	220
Others in mass communications and documentation	1,055	895	110	10	45	960	710	250	20	15	5	75	45	30

Languages	130,225	77,735	8,625	36,050	7,805	108,960	75,070	33,890	7,515	5,250	2,265	13,745	8,290	5,455
Broadly-based programmes within languages	150	140	0	10	0	110	85	30	20	15	5	15	10	5
Linguistics	4,965	2,460	1,135	345	1,030	3,310	2,450	860	525	410	115	1,130	730	400
Comparative literary studies	3,530	975	360	1,845	355	3,160	2,285	875	170	140	30	200	140	55
English studies	54,875	39,025	3,260	9,545	3,040	45,880	33,470	12,405	1,715	1,175	535	7,280	4,260	3,020
Ancient language studies	160	100	15	25	25	140	85	55	10	5	5	10	5	5
Celtic studies	3,310	820	85	2,195	215	2,990	1,840	1,150	200	130	70	120	75	45
Latin studies	335	85	45	150	60	290	180	110	20	15	10	25	10	15
Classical Greek studies	300	25	35	230	15	260	170	90	25	20	5	15	10	5
Classical studies	3,305	2,430	280	335	265	3,045	1,885	1,155	165	110	55	100	50	45
Others in linguistics, classics and related subjects	2,035	365	790	550	330	1,290	955	330	365	300	65	385	285	100
French studies	13,175	7,940	225	4,730	275	12,065	8,230	3,835	575	415	160	540	380	160
German studies	5,235	3,210	155	1,680	190	4,660	2,960	1,700	325	210	115	250	160	90
Italian studies	3,745	1,630	80	1,945	90	3,365	2,350	1,015	260	180	80	120	90	30
Spanish studies	8,135	4,320	105	3,510	200	7,310	4,935	2,380	540	375	165	285	205	85
Portuguese studies	530	290	10	215	10	490	305	185	25	15	10	10	5	5
Scandinavian studies	605	140	10	450	5	575	275	300	20	20	5	10	10	0
Russian and East European studies	1,830	850	190	680	110	1,590	885	700	115	70	50	125	80	45
Others in European languages, literature and related subjects	12,900	5,835	670	5,650	745	9,010	6,060	2,950	1,900	1,300	600	1,995	1,190	805
Chinese studies	915	395	115	370	35	725	345	380	80	50	30	105	75	35
Japanese studies	1,425	545	110	630	140	1,025	480	545	75	40	35	325	195	130
South Asian studies	475	260	105	20	90	345	190	150	40	25	20	90	60	30
Other Asian studies	60	15	35	0	10	35	10	20	5	0	5	25	10	15
African studies	245	125	35	35	50	190	120	75	25	20	5	30	15	20
Modern Middle Eastern studies	1,840	565	325	760	190	1,425	810	615	100	65	35	315	115	205
American studies	4,575	3,960	260	105	250	4,360	2,730	1,630	95	65	30	120	60	55
Australasian studies	40	10	20	0	10	25	10	15	5	5	0	10	5	5
Others in Eastern, Asiatic, African, American and Australasian languages, literature and related subjects	1,515	1,220	175	40	80	1,295	965	330	105	80	30	115	55	55

Table A4.2 cont.

	Total HE students	FT UGs	FT PGs	PT UGs	PT PGs	United Kingdom			Other EU			Non-EU		
						Total	Female	Male	Total	Female	Male	Total	Female	Male
Historical and philosophical studies	87,630	46,935	6,755	23,725	10,215	80,890	45,890	35,000	2,555	1,425	1,125	4,185	1,955	2,230
Broadly-based programmes within historical and philosophical studies	680	215	5	460	0	670	480	190	5	5	0	5	0	5
History by period	37,000	24,860	2,105	7,095	2,935	35,125	18,985	16,145	815	435	380	1,060	565	490
History by area	1,500	620	310	395	180	1,265	640	620	80	35	40	160	75	85
History by topic	12,245	5,195	1,340	4,260	1,450	11,020	7,595	3,425	475	355	120	745	505	240
Archaeology	7,900	2,975	775	3,370	780	7,330	4,370	2,960	260	185	80	305	200	105
Philosophy	10,770	7,020	910	1,360	1,480	9,685	4,265	5,420	490	200	295	595	235	360
Theology and religious studies	14,645	4,965	1,220	5,275	3,185	13,010	7,635	5,380	370	175	195	1,260	335	925
Others in historical and philosophical studies	2,890	1,085	85	1,515	205	2,785	1,920	860	50	35	15	55	35	20
Creative arts and design	132,675	104,620	8,105	14,010	5,935	118,665	70,845	47,820	5,955	3,725	2,225	8,055	5,335	2,720
Broadly-based programmes within creative arts and design	235	205	0	20	5	230	140	90	5	0	0	5	5	0
Fine art	18,620	12,900	1,200	3,430	1,090	16,970	11,315	5,655	715	510	200	940	655	285
Design studies	53,615	47,345	2,480	2,495	1,295	47,005	26,905	20,100	2,535	1,610	925	4,080	2,790	1,290
Music	19,685	12,800	2,180	3,195	1,510	17,210	8,250	8,960	1,120	520	600	1,350	760	590
Drama	17,175	14,465	950	1,145	615	15,870	11,275	4,590	640	480	160	665	455	210
Dance	1,850	1,540	80	110	115	1,635	1,345	290	135	105	25	80	70	10
Cinematics and photography	10,230	8,360	570	905	390	9,265	4,110	5,155	515	290	225	450	265	185
Crafts	1,210	900	5	300	10	1,130	910	225	25	20	5	50	30	20
Imaginative writing	2,745	775	250	1,405	315	2,645	1,790	860	35	20	15	65	40	20
Others in creative arts and design	7,310	5,325	390	1,005	590	6,705	4,810	1,890	235	170	70	370	260	110

Education	169,800	35,020	29,895	43,570	61,315	158,280	116,185	42,095	3,335	2,410	925	8,185	4,985	3,205
Broadly-based programmes within education	105	15	15	0	75	90	65	25	5	5	0	10	10	0
Training teachers	77,460	21,585	26,310	12,485	17,080	74,440	54,890	19,550	1,360	1,080	280	1,660	930	730
Research and study skills in education	5,545	290	145	3,910	1,200	5,145	3,200	1,940	90	40	50	310	170	140
Academic studies in education	62,835	8,380	2,580	17,720	34,150	56,750	43,345	13,400	1,390	975	415	4,695	2,920	1,780
Others in education	23,855	4,745	845	9,455	8,810	21,860	14,685	7,175	490	315	175	1,510	955	555
Combined	212,785	9,700	85	186,280	16,720	208,445	120,740	87,705	1,170	705	465	3,165	1,920	1,250
Total – All subject areas	2,175,115	1,111,310	206,755	566,305	290,745	1,899,850	1,101,055	798,790	90,580	44,245	46,335	184,685	85,175	99,510
Supplementary subject information(1)														
Psychology	50,780	35,795	4,635	3,735	6,615	46,860	37,195	9,665	2,335	1,825	505	1,585	1,215	370
Geography and environmental sciences	35,365	25,185	3,815	3,255	3,115	32,120	15,855	16,260	1,200	635	565	2,050	925	1,125
Economics and politics	53,270	37,810	8,800	2,255	4,410	37,890	13,960	23,930	5,335	2,265	3,070	10,045	4,660	5,390
English	54,875	39,025	3,260	9,545	3,040	45,880	33,470	12,405	1,715	1,175	535	7,280	4,260	3,020

Source: *Students in Higher Education Institutions 2002/3* (http://www.hesa.ac.uk/holisdocs/pubinfo/student/subject0203.htm

Notes:

In this table 0, 1, 2 are rounded up or down to 0. All other numbers are rounded up or down to the nearest 5.

\# see relevant footnote in Notes to tables (authors' comment: see original source).

1 Numbers reported under 'Supplementary subject information' are within and not additional to the overall total, but are disaggregated from it on a different pattern from the 19 subject areas.

Notes

1 Introduction

1 See press release: wyswyg://15/http://www.dest.gov.... ters/nelson/nov02/n250_271102.htm
2 See, for example, head of Ofsted David Bell's speech to the Fawcett Society, 2004.
3 Walkerdine (1988) and Lee (1980) are notable exceptions here.
4 We have argued that because strategies such as separate 'boys' reading boxes' actually exacerbate, rather than challenge, gender difference, they will inevitably make only a superficial impact (if any) on boys' reading, and meanwhile will further entrench the attitudes that put boys off reading in the first place (Francis, 2000a; Skelton, 2001a). Even the Ofsted report *Yes he Can* (2003a) demonstrates that it is in schools where *all* pupils are expected to engage with a *wide variety* of texts that boys do well at reading.
5 Although this has not always historically been the case. For example, in the Cockcroft Report (HMSO, 1982) on the education of 15–18-year-olds, the term middle-class was interchanged with 'more able' and working-class interchanged with 'less able'.
6 For discussion of contemporary responses to work by eugenicists such as Eysenck and Brand, see *The Times Higher*, 26 April 1996.
7 Hopkins (2004) 'Achieving maximum quality with maximum equity – government's agenda and expectations', speech at the QMW seminar 'Delivering effective action on boys' achievement', London, Royal Overseas League, 17 March 2004.

2 Perspectives on gender and achievement

1 By which we mean, socially and culturally produced patterns of language, which constitute power by producing objects and subjects in particular ways. As Francis (1999) elucidates, a housewife, for example, could be positioned as fulfilling her natural role through traditionalist discourses of gender essentialism, or could be produced as a victim of oppression in liberal feminist discourse.
2 Many men who share and support feminist ideas refer to themselves as 'pro-feminists', and their work has made an important contribution, particularly in the areas of masculinity and gender relations.
3 A large body of contemporary research, including findings from our own work, demonstrates that the gendered nature of classroom interaction, and the reflection of masculine values in curriculum and educational preoccupations, shows more continuity than change. See Chapter 6 of this book, or our introductory chapter to *Girls and Boys in the Primary Classroom* (2003) for elaboration.
4 The title of a much-discussed television documentary drawing on evolutionary psychology perspectives on gender difference, for Britain's Channel 4.

5 See, for example, the contents of the L. Ellis and L. Ebertz (eds) (1998) collection *Males, Females and Behaviour*, which includes chapters such as 'Effects of perinatal and puberal steroid imprinting on sexual behaviour of adult rats'; 'The involvement of neonatal 5HT receptor-mediated effects on sexual dimorphism of adult behaviour in the rat'; and 'Developmental significance of the postnatal testosterone "surge" in male primates'.

6 The conception of 'typologies' of masculinity inherent in this approach has been criticised by some (e.g. MacInnes, 1998; Francis, 2000a; Whitehead, 2002). Others have questioned the notion of 'subjugated' masculinities (Francis, 2000a), and indeed the very notion of masculinity as multiple, arguing that such conceptions revert to a basic essentialism (Cealey-Harrison and Hood Williams, 2000a) – as MacInnes (1998: 63) surmises, 'it is difficult to avoid the conclusion that all they [different "masculinities"] have in common is possession of a penis'.

3 The construction of gender and achievement in education policy

1 Identification of the extent (if any) to which girls perform better in single-sex schools is complicated by the fact that in the UK a higher proportion of single-sex schools select pupils on the basis of ability than is the case in mixed-sex schools; hence skewing results (Elwood and Gipps, 1996; Dennison and Coleman, 2000).

2 As we have observed elsewhere, the assumptions that men and women teachers (a) teach differently according to gender, and (b) that children identify more with/are inspired by teachers of their own gender, are completely untested (Carrington and Skelton, 2003). Indeed, work by Lahelma (2000) suggests that pupils do not see teacher gender as impacting on their teaching and/or relationships with pupils. We are currently engaged in a project that explores these issues further (ESRC Project Grant Award No. R000239585).

3 It should be noted that equal opportunities strategies in schools in the 1980s were actually small-scale and localised given the resistance of the then government towards the inclusion of education in the Sex Discrimination Act (see Arnot, 1987).

4 Evaluating 'boys' underachievement'

1 Preliminary figures on the gender gap for 2004 indicate that this has narrowed to 8.4 points (*The Times*, 17 November 2004: 30).

5 Explaining gender differences in achievement

1 On one occasion when being interviewed on BBC radio's Women's Hour, heavily pregnant with my first child, British TV personality Esther Rantzen rubbished my views on air and said that I would soon find out that gender is innate once my baby was born!

2 Valerie Walkerdine (1983) argued that the child-centred approach adopted by primary schools was highly gendered. Her position was that the emphasis in child-centred philosophy on 'developing the needs of the individual' might seem to be non-gendered but the characteristics used to describe children such as inventive, creative and enquiring were actually those associated with masculinity. Equally the teacher within child-centred philosophy does not actively teach but provides a 'facilitating environment'; that is one where the teacher is passive and nurturant (feminine characteristics) in order to produce active learners (who are male).

3 Indeed, studies show that pupils themselves are increasingly aware of these discourses around gender and achievement (Francis, 1999a; Younger *et al.*, 1999).

6 What has happened to the girls?

1 We qualify this with the word 'relatively' because the most powerful and senior work positions continue to be overwhelmingly dominated by men (Rees, 1999).

2 See Osler and Vincent (2003) for discussion of girls who disengage fully from education.

3 This has been shown to vary according to ethnicity, however. For example, British-Chinese girls are more likely than white girls to enjoy maths and other traditionally masculine subjects (Francis and Archer, 2005).

4 Illustrating again how the statistics are 'read' in a variety of ways.

5 But excluding subjects aligned to medicine, such as physiotherapy, etc.

7 The future for boys and girls?

1 It is intriguing to reflect that concepts being applied to boys in this discourse of the 'at risk boy', such as passivity, fearful, low self-esteem, etc. are stereotypically feminine, and as such the discourse positions boys as unmasculine. This is an interesting contradiction to the dominant construction of the boy (masculine) as representing what is normal, right and healthy in relation to a (derided) feminine Other (Walkerdine, 1990).

2 *The Worm That Turned* is a famous extended sketch by British comedians 'The Two Ronnies' (Ronnie Barker and Ronnie Corbett), projecting concerns about 'Women's libbers' to their 'natural conclusions', i.e. a scenario where women (dressed in dominatrix garb) rule the world, and men are ruthlessly oppressed.

3 Examples include the American television series 'The Sopranos' and 'Nip and Tuck'.

4 Of course, as our colleague Louise Archer has pointed out, this construction of grooming and concern with appearance as an aspect of masculinity is not novel, as historic constructions have incorporated 'the peacock'/'the fop'. But the re-emergence of such preoccupations with appearance is a contemporary development.

5 Becky Francis' partner, who recently gave up his job to take a turn at home with the young children, finds that his decision is very rarely congratulated or affirmed by others, particularly men, who tend to meet his decision with puzzlement or even pity.

References

Abrams, R. (2004) *Why Love Matters*, London: Routledge.

Adler, A. and Adler, P. (1998) *Peer Power: Peer Adolescent Culture and Identity*, New Brunswick: Rutgers University Press.

Adler, S., Laney, J. and Packer, M. (1993) *Managing Women*, Buckingham: Open University Press.

Ailwood, J. and Lingard, B. (2001) The endgame for national girls' schooling policies in Australia? *Australian Journal of Education*, 45: 9–22.

Ainley, P. (1994) *Degrees of Difference: Higher Education in the 1990s*, London: Lawrence and Wishart.

Ainley, P. (1998) Towards a learning or a certified society? Contradictions in the New Labour modernisation of lifelong learning, *Journal of Education Policy*, 13: 559–73.

Ali, S. (2003) To be a girl: culture and class in schools, *Gender and Education*, 15: 269–83.

Al-Khalifa, E. (1989) Management by halves: women teachers and school management, in H. De Lyon and F. Migniuolo (eds) *Women Teachers*, Buckingham: Open University Press.

American Association of University Women (1992) *How Schools Short-change Girls*, Washington, DC: AAUW.

Archer, J. and Lloyd, B. (1982) *Sex and Gender*, London: Pelican.

Archer, L. (2003) *Race, Masculinity and Schooling*, Buckingham: Open University Press.

Archer, L. and Francis, B. (2005) They never go off the rails like other groups: teachers' constructions of British-Chinese pupils' gender identities and approaches to learning, *British Journal of Sociology of Education*, 26 (2).

Archer, L., Hutchings, M. and Ross, A. (2003) *Higher Education and Social Class*, London: Routledge.

Archer, L. and Yamashita, H. (2003) Theorising inner-city masculinities: 'race', class, gender and education, *Gender and Education*, 15: 115–31.

Arnot, M. (1987) Political lip-service or radical reform? Central government responses to sex equality as a policy issue, in M. Arnot and G. Weiner (eds) *Gender and the Politics of Schooling*, London: Unwin Hyman.

Arnot, M. and Weiner, G. (eds) (1987) *Gender and the Politics of Schooling*, London: Unwin Hyman.

Arnot, M., Gray, J., James, M. and Rudduck, J. (1998a) *A Review of Recent Research on Gender and Educational Performance*, London: Ofsted Research Series, The Stationery Office.

Arnot, M., Millen, D. and Maton, K. (1998b) *Current Innovative Practice in Schools in the United Kingdom*, Final Report, Cambridge: University of Cambridge for the Council of Europe.

Arnot, M., David, M. and Weiner, G. (1999) *Closing the Gender Gap*, Cambridge: Polity Press.

Ashley, M. (2001) 'Caring for the Boys: Lessons From Attachment Theory'. Symposium at British Educational Research Association Annual Conference, Leeds, 14 September.

Ashley, M. (2003) *Women Teaching Boys*, Stoke-on-Trent: Trentham Books.

Askew, S. and Ross, C. (1989) *Boys Don't Cry: Boys and Sexism in Education*, Milton Keynes: Open University Press.

Aspinwall, K. and Drummond, M.J. (1989) Socialized into primary teaching, in H. De Lyon and F. Migniuolo (eds) *Women Teachers*, Milton Keynes: Open University Press.

Assiter, A. (1996) *Enlightened Women*, London: Routledge.

Balbus (1987) Disciplining women: Michel Foucault and the power of feminist discourse, in S. Benhabib and D. Cornell (eds) *Feminism as Critique*, Cambridge: Polity Press.

Ball, S. (1999) Labour, learning and the economy: a 'policy sociology' perspective, *Cambridge Journal of Education*, 29: 195–206.

Ball, S. and Gewirtz, S. (1997) Girls in the education market: choice, competition and complexity, *Gender and Education*, 9: 207–22.

Ball, S.J., Maguire, M. and Macrae, S. (2000) *Choices, Transitions and Pathways: New Youth, New Economies in the Global City*, London: Falmer Press.

Barber, M. (1994) *Young People and their Attitudes to School*, Keele: Keele University.

Baron-Cohen, S. (2004) *The Essential Difference*, London: Penguin.

Bauman, Z. (2001) *Community: Seeking Safety in an Insecure World*, Cambridge: Polity Press.

Bauman, Z. (2005) *Work, Consumerism and the New Poor*, 2nd edn, Maidenhead: Open University Press/McGraw-Hill.

Beauviour, S. de (1960) *The Second Sex*, London: First Four Square Edition.

Beck, U. (1992) *The Risk Society*, London: Sage.

Beck, U. (1998) 'The cosmopolitan manifesto', *New Statesman*, 20 March.

Beck, U. and Beck-Gernsheim, E. (2002) *Individualisation*, London: Sage.

Belenky, M., Clinchy, B.M., Goldberger, N.R. and Tarule, J.M. (1986) *Women's Ways of Knowing*, New York: Basic Books.

Belotti, E. (1975) *Little Girls*, London: Writers and Readers.

Benett, Y. and Carter, D. (1981) *Side-tracked? A Look at the Careers Advice Given to Fifth-Form Girls*, Manchester: EOC.

Benjamin, S. (2003) Gender and special educational needs, in C. Skelton and B. Francis (eds) *Boys and Girls in the Primary Classroom*, Buckingham: Open University Press.

Bennett, C. (1996) 'The boys with the wrong stuff', *The Independent*, 5 November 1998, p. 17.

Berger, P. and Luckmann, T. (1966) *The Social Construction of Reality*, New York: Doubleday and Co.

Biddulph, S. (1997) *Raising Boys*, London: Thorsons.

Birkhead, T. (2001) *Promiscuity: An Evolutionary History of Desire*, Cambridge, MA: Harvard University Press.

Black, P. and Wiliam, D. (1998) Assessment and classroom learning, *Assessment in Education: Principles and Practice*, 5: 7–73.

Blair, T. (2002) Prime Minister's keynote speech to e-Summit, 19 November (www.pm.gov.uk/output/Page 1734.asp).

Blatchford, P., Creeser, R. and Mooney, A. (1990) Playground games and playtime: the children's view, *Educational Research*, 32: 163–74.

Bleach, K. (1998a) Why the likely lads lag behind, in K. Bleach (ed.) *Raising Boys' Achievement in Schools*, Stoke-on-Trent: Trentham Books.

Bleach, K. (1998b) What difference does it make? in K. Bleach (ed.) *Raising Boys' Achievement in Schools*, Stoke-on-Trent: Trentham Books.

Bleach, K. (ed.) (1998c) *Raising Boys' Achievement in Schools*, Stoke-on-Trent: Trentham Books.

Bly, R. (1990) *Iron John*, New York: Addison-Wesley.

Broadfoot, P. (1996) *Education, Assessment and Society*, Buckingham: Open University Press.

Brooker, C. (2004) 'Charlie Brooker's screen burn', *The Guardian*: 'The Guide', 27 March 2004.

Browne, N. (2004) *Gender Equity in the Early Years*, Maidenhead: Open University Press/ McGraw-Hill.

Browne, R. and Fletcher, R. (eds) (1995) *Boys in Schools*, Sydney: Finch.

Buckingham, J. (2002) Getting it right some of the time: an appraisal of the Report on the Inquiry into the Education of Boys, *Issue Analysis*, No. 27, 14 November 2002 (www.cis.org.au/IssueAnalysis/ia27/IA27.htm).

Burman, E. (2005) Childhood neo-liberalism and the feminisation of education, *Gender and Education*, 17.

Buss, D. (1994) *Evolution of Desire: Strategies for Human Mating*, New York: Basic Books.

Butler, J. (1990) *Gender Trouble*, New York: Routledge.

Buttrose, I. (2000) Turning boys into sissies, *The Australian Women's Weekly*, September, p. 78.

Byers, S. (1998) Co-ordinated action to tackle boys' underachievement. Speech presented to the 11th International Congress for School Effectiveness and Improvement, University of Manchester Institute of Science and Technology, 5 January.

Byrne, E. (1978) *Women in Education*, London: Tavistock.

Cairns, J. and Inglis, B. (1989) A content analysis of ten popular history textbooks for primary schools with particular emphasis on the role of women, *Educational Review*, 41 (3): 221–6.

Cameron, C., Moss, P. and Owen, C. (1999) *Men in the Nursery*, London: Paul Chapman.

Carrington, B. and Skelton, C. (2003) Re-thinking 'role models': equal opportunities in teacher recruitment in England and Wales, *Journal of Education Policy*, 18 (3): 253–65.

Cealey Harrison, W. and Hood-Willams, J. (2001) *Beyond Sex and Gender*, London: Sage.

Chaplin, R. (2000) Beyond exam results? Differences in the social and psychological perceptions of young males and females at school, *Educational Studies*, 26: 177–90.

Christian, H. (1994) *The Making of Anti-sexist Men*, London: Routledge.

Clarke, C. (2004) Speech for National Science Week event at No. 11 Downing Street, 16 March (www.hm-treasury.gov.uk/newsroom_and_speeches/press/2004/press_26_04.cfm).

Clarricoates, K. (1980) The importance of being Ernest . . . Emma . . . Tom . . . Jane. The perception and categorisation of gender conformity and gender deviation in primary schools, in R. Deem (ed.) *Schooling for Women's Work*, London: Routledge and Kegan Paul.

Cockcroft Report (1982) *Mathematics Counts*, London: HMSO.

Coffield, F., Moseley, D., Hall, E. and Ecclestone, K. (2004) *Should We be Using Learning Styles? What Research has to Say to Practice*, London: Learning and Skills Research Centre.

Cohen, M. (1993) 'A geneology of conversation: gender subjectivation and learning French in England', unpublished PhD, London: Institute of Education.

Cohen, M. (1998) 'A habit of healthy idleness': boys' underachievement in historical perspective, in D. Epstein, J. Elwood, V. Hey and J. Maw (eds) *Failing Boys?* Buckingham: Open University Press.

Colley, H. (2003) Engagement mentoring for 'disaffected' youth: a new model of mentoring for social inclusion, *British Educational Research Journal*, 29: 521–42.

Connell, R. (1987) *Gender and Power*, Cambridge: Polity.

Connell, R. (1989) Cool guys, swots and wimps: the interplay of masculinity and education, *Oxford Review of Education*, 15: 291–303.

Connell, R. (1994) Psychoanalysis on masculinity, in H. Brod and M. Kaufman (eds) *Theorising Masculinities*, Thousand Oaks, CA: Sage.

Connell, R. (1995) *Masculinities*, Cambridge: Polity.

Connolly, P. (1995) Boys will be boys?: Racism, sexuality, and the construction of masculine identities amongst infant boys, in M. Blair and J. Holland (eds) *Equality and Difference: Debates and Issues in Feminist Research and Pedagogy*, Clevedon: Multilingual Matters.

Connolly, P. (1998) *Racism, Gender Identities and Young Children*, London: Routledge.

Connolly, P. (2003) Gendered and gendering spaces: playgrounds in the early years, in C. Skelton and B. Francis (eds) *Boys and Girls in the Primary Classroom*, Buckingham: Open University Press.

Connolly, P. (2004) *Boys and Schooling in the Early Years*, London: RoutledgeFalmer.

Connolly, P. (2005) 'Just how many measures of gender differences in educational achievement do we really need?' paper at the GEA Conference 'Gender, Power and Difference', University of Cardiff, 29–31 March 2005.

Cruddas, L. and Haddock, L. (2003) *Girls' Voices*, Stoke-on-Trent: Trentham.

David, M. (2003) *Personal And Political*, Stoke-on-Trent: Trentham.

Davies, B. (1989) *Frogs and Snails and Feminist Tales*, Sydney: Allen and Unwin.

Davies, B. (1993) *Shards of Glass*, Sydney, Allen and Unwin.

Davies, B. (1997) Constructing and deconstructing masculinities through critcal literacy, *Gender and Education*, 9: 9–30.

Davies, B. (2003) Death to critique and dissent? The policies and practices of new managerialism and of 'evidence-based practice', *Gender and Education*, 15: 91–103.

Davison, A. and Edwards, C. (1998) A different style of learning, in K. Bleach (ed.) *Raising Boys' Achievement in Schools*, Stoke-on-Trent: Trentham Books.

Dawkins, R. (1976) *The Selfish Gene*, Oxford: Oxford University Press.

Delamont, S. (1999) Gender and the discourse of derision, *Research Papers in Education*, 14: 3–21.

Denison, C. and Coleman, J. (2000) Young people and gender: a review of research, London: Women's Unit, Cabinet Office.

Department for Education and Employment (1998) *The Learning Age*, Green Paper, London: DfEE.

Department for Education and Skills (2002) *Student Achievement in England*, London: HMSO. (The report of a survey carried out by the Social Survey Division of the Office for National Statistics, and commissioned by the Department for Education and Skills as part of the OECD Programme for International Student Assessment (PISA 2000).)

Department for Education and Skills (2003) *Using the National Healthy School Standard to Raise Boys' Achievement*, Wetherby: Health Development Agency.

Department for Education and Skills (2004a) API data, http//www.dfes.gov.uk/trends/upload/xls/4_6t.xls

Department for Education and Skills (2004b) standards.dfes.gov.uk/gender and achievement/understanding/analysis/

Department for Education and Skills (2004c) National Statistics, First Release SFR 01/2004 (14 January 2004).

Department of Trade and Industry (1998) Competitiveness White Paper: Building the Knowledge Driven Economy (www.dti.gov.uk/comp/competitive/ec_ch2.htm).

Department of Trade and Industry (2004) (www.set4women.gov.uk).

Deschenes, S., Cuban, L. and Tyack, D. (2001) Mismatch: historical perspectives on schools and students who don't fit them, *The Teachers College Record*, 103: 525–47.

Duffy, M. (2003) Achievement gap, *TES Friday, Times Educational Supplement*, 15 November 2003, pp. 15–18.

Du Gay, P. (1996) *Consumption and Identity at Work*, London: Sage.

Ecclestone, K. (2002) *Learning Autonomy in Post-16 Education: the Politics and Practice of Formative Assessment*, London: RoutledgeFalmer.

Ecclestone, K. (2004a) Learning or therapy? The demoralisation of education, *British Journal of Educational Studies*, 52: 112–37.

Ecclestone, K. (2004b) From Freire to fear: the rise of therapeutic pedagogy in post-16 education, in J. Satterthwaite and E. Atkinson (eds) *The Disciplining of Education: New Languages of Power and Resistance*, Stoke-on-Trent: Trentham.

Ecclestone, K. (2005) Legitimising the diminished self: the implications of therapeutic education for democracy (forthcoming).

Ellis, L. and Ebertz, L. (1998) *Males, Females and Behaviour: Toward Biological Understanding*, Westport, CT: Greenwood Publishing.

Elwood, J. and Gipps, C. (1998) Review of recent research on the achievement of girls in single-sex schools, unpublished Report for the AMGS.

Elwood, J. and Murphy, P. (2000) Gender and performance at 14: tests, tiers and achievement, paper presented at International Association for Educational Assessment, Jerusalem, Israel, 14–19 May.

Emmerich, W., Goldman, S., Kirsh, B., and Sharabany, R. (1977) Evidence for a transitional phase in the development of 'gender constancy', *Child Development*, 48: 930–6.

Epstein, D. (1997) Boyz' own stories: masculinities and sexualities in schools, *Gender and Education*, 9: 105–15.

Epstein, D. (1998) Real boys don't work: 'underachievement', masculinities and the harassment of 'sissies', in D. Epstein, J. Elwood, V. Hey and J. Maw (eds) *Failing Boys?* Buckingham: Open University Press.

Epstein, D., Elwood, J., Hey, V. and Maw, J. (1998) Schoolboy frictions: feminism and 'failing boys', in D. Epstein, J. Elwood, V. Hey and J. Maw (eds) *Failing Boys?* Buckingham: Open University Press.

Equal Opportunities Commission (1984) *Do you provide Equal Educational Opportunities?*, Manchester: EOC.

Equal Opportunities Commission (2003) *Facts About Men and Women*, Manchester: EOC.

Equal Opportunities Commission (2004) *Plugging Britain's Skills Gap: Challenging Gender Segregation in Training and Work*, Manchester: EOC and ESF.

Ermisch, J. and Francesconi, M. (2001) *The Effect of Parents' Employment on Children's Lives*, Oxford: Family Policy Studies Centre.

Fairclough, N. (2000) *New Labour, New Language?*, London: Routledge.

Faludi, S. (1999) *Stiffed: The Betrayal of the American Male*, New York: Morrow.

Feingold, A. (1992) Sex differences in variability in intellectual abilities: a new look at an old controversy, *Review of Educational Research*, 61: 61–84.

Fluty, D. (1997) Single parenting in relation to adolescents' achievement scores, Research Center for Families and Children, *Newsletter*, 6, 2. (www.uky.edu/HES/rcfc/vol6no2/page4.html)

Foster, V., Kimmel, M. and Skelton, C. (2001) Setting the scene, in W. Martino and B. Meyenn (eds) *Teaching Boys: Issues of Masculinity in Schools*, Buckingham: Open University Press.

Foucault, M. (1977) *Discipline and Punish: The Birth of the Prison*, London: Tavistock Publications.

Francis, B. (1996) Doctor/nurse, teacher/caretaker: children's gendered choice of adult occupation in interviews and role plays, *British Journal of Education and Work*, 9: 47–58.

Francis, B. (1998) *Power Plays*, Stoke-on-Trent: Trentham.

Francis, B. (1999a) An investigation of the discourses children draw on in their constructions of gender, *Journal of Applied Social Psychology*, 29: 300–16.

Francis, B. (1999b) Modernist reductionism or post-structuralist relativism: can we move on? An evaluation of the arguments in relation to feminist educational research, *Gender and Education*, 11: 381–93.

Francis, B. (1999c) Lads, lasses and (New) Labour: 14–16-year-old student responses to the 'laddish behaviour and boys' underachievement' debate, *British Journal of Sociology of Education*, 20: 357–73.

Francis, B. (2000a) *Boys, Girls and Achievement*, London: RoutledgeFalmer.

Francis, B. (2000b) The gendered subject: students' subject preferences and discussions of gender and subject ability, *Oxford Review of Education*, 26: 35–47.

Francis, B. (2001) Relativism, realism and feminism: an analysis of some theoretical tensions in research on gender identity, *Journal of Gender Studies*, 11: 39–53.

Francis, B. (2002) Is the future really female? The impact and implications of gender for 14–16-year-olds' career choices, *Journal of Education and Work*, 15: 75–87.

Francis, B. and Archer, L. (2005) British-Chinese pupils' constructions of gender and learning, *Oxford Review of Education*, 31 (3).

Francis, B. and Archer, L. (forthcoming) Negotiating the dichotomy of boffin and triad: British-Chinese pupils' constructions of 'laddism', *The Sociological Review*.

Francis, B., Hutchings, M. and Archer, L. (2002) *The Learning Preferences and Perceptions of Education Among Pupils at Girls' Schools*, Report for the AMGS.

Francis, B., Hutchings, M. and Read, B. (2004) *Science in Girls' Schools: Factors that contribute to Girls' Engagement and Attainment*, London: IPSE.

Francis, B., Read, B., Melling, L. and Robson, J. (2003) University lecturers' perceptions of gender and undergraduate writing, *British Journal of Sociology of Education*, 24: 357–73.

Francis, B., Robson, J. and Read, B. (2001) An analysis of undergraduate writing styles in the context of gender and achievement, *Studies in Higher Education*, 26: 313–26.

Francis, B. and Skelton, C. (2001) Men teachers' constructions of masculinity in the classroom, *Sex Education*, 1: 9–21.

Frank, B., Kehler, M., Lovell, T. and Davison, K. (2003) A tangle of trouble: boys, masculinity and schooling – future directions, Special issue: Boys, schooling and masculinities, *Educational Review*, 55: 119–33.

Fraser, N. (1995) From redistribution to recognition? Dilemmas of justice in a post-socialist age, *New Left Review*, 212: 68–93.

Frater, G. (1998) Boys and literacy, in K. Bleach (ed.) *Raising Boys' Achievement in Schools*, Stoke-on-Trent: Trentham.

Frosh, S., Phoenix, A. and Pattman, R. (2001) *Young Masculinities*, Basingstoke: Palgrave.

Fryer, R. (1997) *Learning for the Twenty-First Century*, London: National Advisory Group for Continuing Education and Lifelong Learning.

Fuller, M. (1980) Black Girls in a London Comprehensive School, in R. Deem (ed.) *Schooling for Women's Work*, London: Routledge and Kegan Paul.

Furedi, F. (2004) *Where Have All the Intellectuals Gone? Confronting 21st Century Philistinism*, London: Continuum Press.

Furlong, A. and Cartmel, F. (1997) *Young People and Social Change*, Buckingham: Open University Press.

Gaskell, J. (1992) *Gender Matters from School to Work*, Buckingham: Open University Press.

Gauntlett, D. (2002) *Media, Gender and Identity*, London: Routledge.

Gauntlett, D. (2004) The bad thing about men's magazines: Amy Jankowitcz and David Guantlett in conversation, (http://theoryhead.com/gender/discuss.htm).

Geake, J.G. and Cooper, P.W. (2003) Implications of cognitive neuroscience for education, *Westminster Studies in Education*, 26 (10): 7–20.

Gerhardt, S. (2004) *Why Love Matters: How Affection Shapes a Baby's Brain*, London: Routledge.

Giddens, A. (1998) *The Third Way*, Cambridge: Polity.

Gillborn, D. and Mirza, H. (2000) *Educational Inequality: Mapping Race, Class and Gender*, London: HMI.

Gilligan, C. (1982) *In a Different Voice*, Cambridge, MA: Harvard University Press.

Gipps, C. and Murphy, P. (1994) *A Fair Test?*, Buckingham: Open University Press.

Gorard, S. (2000) One of us cannot be wrong: the paradox of achievement gaps, *British Journal of Sociology of Education*, 21 (3): 391–400.

Gorard, S., Rees, G. and Salisbury, J. (1999) Reappraising the apparent underachievement of boys at school, *Gender and Education*, 11 (4): 441–59.

Grabrucker, M. (1988) *There's a Good Girl*, London: The Women's Press.

Gray, J. (1992) *Men are from Mars, Women are from Venus*, London: Thorsons.

Gregory, R. (1969) *A Shorter Textbook of Human Development*, Maidenhead: McGraw-Hill.

Griffin, C. (1998) 'Representations of youth and the "boys' underachievement" debate: just the same old stories?', paper presented at 'Gendering the Millennium' Conference, University of Dundee, 11–13 November 1998.

Gurian, M. (1996) *The Wonder of Boys: What Parents, Mentors and Educators Can Do to Raise Boys into Exceptional Men*, New York: Tarcher/Putnam.

Gurian, M. (1998) *A Fine Young Man*, New York: Tarcher/Putnam.

Gurian, M. (2002) *Boys and Girls Learn Differently!* San Francisco: Jossey Bass.

Halpern, D. (1992) *Sex Differences in Cognitive Abilities*, New Jersey: Lawrence Erlbaum.

Hannan, G. (1999) *Improving Boys' Performance*, London: Folens.

Harding, S. (1991) *Whose Science? Whose Knowledge?* Buckingham: Open University Press.

Harlen, W. (2004) Assessment and learning research synthesis group, *EPPI Review*.

Harlen, W., Gipps, C., Broadfoot, P. and Nuttall, D. (1992) Assessment and the improvement of education, *The Curriculum Journal*, 3: 215–30.

Hartsock, N. (1990) Foucault on power: a theory for women, in L. Nicholson (ed.) *Feminism/Postmodernism*, London: Routledge.

Hayes, D. and Lingard, B. (2003) Introduction: rearticulating gender agendas in schooling: an Australian perspective, *International Journal of Inclusive Education*, 7 (1): 1–6.

Haywood, C. and Mac an Ghaill, M. (1996) Schooling masculinities, in M. Mac an Ghaill (ed.) *Understanding Masculinities*, Buckingham: Open University Press.

Haywood, C. and Mac an Ghaill, M. (2001) The significance of teaching English boys: exploring social change, modern schooling and the making of masculinities, in W. Martino and B. Meyenn (eds) *What About the Boys?* Buckingham: Open University Press.

Haywood, C. and Mac an Ghaill, M. (2003) *Men and Masculinities*, Buckingham: Open University Press.

Head, J. (1996) Gender identity and cognitive style, in P. Murphy and C. Gipps (eds) *Equity in the Classroom*, London: Falmer.

Head, J. (1999) *Understanding the Boys*, London: Falmer.

Henwood, F. (1996) WISE Choices? Understanding occupational decision making in a climate of equal opportunities for women in science and technology, *Gender and Education*, 8 (2): 199–214.

Herbert, C. (1989) Talking of silence: the sexual harassment of schoolgirls, London: Falmer.

Hey, V. (1997) *The Company She Keeps: An Ethnography of Girls' Friendships*, Buckingham: Open University Press.

Hey, V. (2003) Joining the club? Academia and working class femininities, *Gender and Education*, 15 (3): 319–35.

Hey, V., Leonard, D., Daniels, H. and Smith, M. (1998) Boys' underachievement, special needs practices and questions of equity, in D. Epstein, J. Elwood, V. Hey and J. Maw (eds) *Failing Boys?* Buckingham: Open University Press.

Higher Education Statistics Agency (2004) Qualifications obtained by and examination results of higher education students at higher education institutions in the United Kingdom for the academic year 2002/03. National Statistics First Release HESA SFR 70, 14 January 2004.

Higher Education Statistics Agency (2005) Qualifications obtained by students on higher education courses at higher education institutions in the United Kingdom by level of course, gender and subject area 1998/99 to 2002/3(1), (http://www.hesa.ac.uk/press/sfr70/sfr70.htm).

Hill, D. (2000) Back to the stone age, *The Observer Review*, 27 February 2000, p. 1.

Hoff Sommers, C. (2000) *The War Against Boys (How Misguided Feminism is Harming Our Young Men)*, New York: Simon and Schuster.

Hogget, P. (2003) A service to the public: the containment of ethical and moral conflicts by public bureaucracies, paper given at the Defending Bureaucracies Workshop, St Hugh's College, Oxford, March.

Hood-Williams, J. (1998) Stories for sexual difference, *British Journal of Sociology of Education*, 18: 81–99.

Hopkins, D. (2004) Speech to the QMW Seminar, *Raising the Achievement of Boys*, Overseas House, London, 17 March 2004.

Howe, C. (1997) *Gender and Classroom Interaction: A Research Review*, Edinburgh: SCRE.

House of Representatives Standing Committee on Education and Training (2002) *Boys: Getting it Right. Report into the Inquiry of Education of Boys*, Canberra: Commonwealth of Australia.

Hutchings, M. (2001) Towards a representative teaching profession: gender, paper presented at the University of North London, 11 December.

Jackson, C. (2002a) Can single-sex classes in co-educational schools enhance the learning experiences of girls and/or boys? An exploration of pupils' perceptions, *British Educational Research Journal*, 28: 37–48.

Jackson, C. (2002b) 'Laddishness' as a self-worth protection strategy, *Gender and Education*, 14: 37–51.

Jackson, C. (2003) Motives for 'laddishness' at school; fear of failure and fear of the 'feminine', *British Educational Research Journal*, 24 (4): 583–98.

Jackson, C. and Smith, I.D. (2002) Poles apart? An exploration of single-sex and mixed-sex educational environments in Australia and England, *Educational Studies*, 25: 410–22.

Jackson, P., Stevenson, N. and Brooks, K. (2001) *Making Sense of Men's Magazines*, Cambridge: Polity Press.

Jones, A. (1997) Teaching post-structuralist feminist theory in education: student resistances, *Gender and Education*, 9: 261–69.

Jones, C. (1985) Sexual tyranny: male violence in a mixed secondary school, in G. Weiner (ed.) *Just a Bunch of Girls*, Milton Keynes: Open University Press.

Jones, L.G. and Jones, L.P. (1989) Context, confidence and the able girl, *Educational Research*, 31: 189–94.

Jordan, E. (1995) Fighting boys and fantasy play: the construction of masculinity in the early years of school, *Gender and Education*, 7: 69–86.

Kanter, R.M. (1993) *Men and Women of the Corporation*, 2nd edn, New York: Basic Books.

Kehily, M. and Nayak, A. (1997) 'Lads and laughter': humour and the production of heterosexual hierarchies, *Gender and Education*, 9: 69–87.

Kelly, A. (1988) 'The customer is always right'. . . girls' and boys' reactions to science lessons, *School Science Review*, 69: 662–75.

Kelly, A. (1989) 'When I grow up I want to be . . .': a longitudinal study of career preferences, *British Journal of Guidance and Counselling*, 22: 179–200.

Kenway, J. (1995) Masculinities in schools: under siege, on the defensive and under reconstruction, *Discourse*, 16: 59–79.

Kenway, J. and Fitzclarence, L. (1997) Masculinity, violence and schooling: challenging 'poisonous pedagogies', *Gender and Education*, 9: 117–33.

Kessler, S. and McKenna, W. (1978) *Gender: An Ethnomethodological Approach*, Chicago: University of Chicago Press.

Kimball, M. (1989) A new perspective on women's math achievement, *Psychological Bulletin*, 105: 198–214.

Kimura, D. (1992) Sex differences in the brain, *Scientific American*, September, 119.

King, J. (2000) The problem(s) of men in early years education, in N. Lesko (ed.) *Masculinities at School*, London: Sage.

Klein, M. (1952) *Developments in Psychoanalysis*, London: Hogarth Press.

Kohlberg, L. (1966) A cognitive developmental analysis of children's sex-role concepts and attitudes, in E. Maccoby (ed.) *The Development of Sex Differences*, Stanford, CA: Stanford University Press.

Kruse, A.M. (1996) Single-sex settings: pedagogies for girls and boys in Danish schools, in P. Murphy and C. Gipps (eds) *Equity in the Classroom*, London: Falmer Press with UNESCO.

Labour Party (1996) *Boys will be Boys?* (Consultation Paper).

Lacan, J. (1977) *Ecrits: A Selection*, London: Tavistock.

Lahelma, E. (2000) Lack of male teachers: A problem for students or teachers? *Pedagogy, Culture and Society*, 8: 173–85.

Lavigeur, J. (1980) Co-education and the tradition of separate needs, in D. Spender and E. Sarah (eds) *Learning to Lose*, London: The Women's Press.

Lee, A. (1980) Together we learn to read and write, in D. Spender and E. Sarah (eds) *Learning to Lose*, London, The Women's Press.

Lees, S. (1992) *Sugar and Spice*, London: Penguin.

Leigh, A. (2003) The rise and fall of the Third Way, *A Journal of Contemporary Analysis*, 75, 2, March/April (http://www.onlineopinion.com.au/view.asp?article=398).

Leonard, D. (1996) The debate around co-education, in S. Kemal, D. Leonard, M. Pringle and S. Sadeque (eds) *Targeting Underachievement: Boys or Girls?* London: Institute of Education/CREG.

Lewin, Tamar (1998) How boys lost out to girl power, *New York Times*, 12 December, section 4, p. 1.

Lewis, P. (2000) An enquiry into male wastage from primary ITE courses at a university college and success indicators for retention, paper presented to Recruitment and Retention of Teachers Seminar Conference at the University of North London, 19 January.

Library and Information Commission (2000) Libraries: The Essence of Inclusion. (http://www.lic.gov.uk/publications/policyreports/inclusion.html).

Lightbody, P. (1997) A respectable job: factors which influence young Asian's choice of career, *British Journal of Guidance and Counselling*, 17: 179–200.

Lightbody, P. and Durndell, A. (1996) Gendered career choice: is sex-stereotyping the cause or the consequence? *Educational Studies*, 22: 133–46.

Lightfoot, Liz (1998) Boys left behind by modern teaching, *Daily Telegraph*, 15 August 1998.

Lingard, B. (2003) Where to in gender policy in education after recuperative masculinity politics? *International Journal of Inclusive Education*, 7: 33–56.

Lingard, B. and Douglas, P. (1999) *Men Engaging Feminisms*, Buckingham: Open University Press.

Lingard, D., Martino, W., Mills, M. and Bahr, M. (2002) Addressing the educational needs of boys, report to Department of Education, Science and Training, Canberra: DEST.

Lloyd, B. and Duveen, G. (1992) *Gender Identities and Education*, London: Harvester Wheatsheaf.

Lucey, H. (2001) Social class, gender and schooling, in B. Francis and C. Skelton (eds) *Investigating Gender*, Buckingham: Open University Press.

Lucey, H. (2004) Differentiated citizenship: psychic defence, social division and the construction of local secondary school markets, in The Open University Faculty of Social Science Course Materials, DD305 Personal Lives and Social Policy, Milton Keynes: The Open University.

Lucey, H. and Reay, D. (2000a) Excitement and anxiety in the move to secondary school, *Oxford Review of Education*, 26: 191–205.

Lucey, H. and Reay, D. (2002b) A market in waste: psychic and structural dimensions of school-choice policy in the UK and children's narratives on 'demonised' schools, *Discourse*, 23: 23–40.

Lucey, H. and Reay, D. (2002c) Carrying the beacon of excellence: social class differentiation and anxiety at a time of transition, *Journal of Education Policy*, 17: 321–36.

Lucey, H., Brown, M., Denvir, H., Askew, M. and Rhodes, V. (2003) Girls and boys in the primary maths classroom, in C. Skelton and B. Francis (eds) *Boys and Girls in the Primary Classroom*, Maidenhead: McGraw-Hill.

Maby, T. (2004) How to turn boys on to studying, *Independent Education and Careers, The Independent*, 21 October, pp. 4–5.

Mac an Ghaill, M. (1994) *The Making of Men*, Buckingham: Open University Press.

Mac an Ghaill, M. (1999) 'New' cultures of training: emerging male (hetero)sexual identities, *British Educational Research Journal*, 25: 419–25.

MacInnes, J. (1998) *The End of Masculinity*, Buckingham: Open University Press.

MacNaughton, G. (2000) *Rethinking Gender in Early Childhood Education*, London: Paul Chapman.

Mahony, P. (1985) *Schools for the Boys? Co-education Reassessed*, London: Hutchinson.

Mahony, P. (1997) The under-achievement of boys in the UK: old tunes for new fiddles? *Social Alternatives*, 16: 267–83.

Mahony, P. (1998) Girls will be girls and boys will be first, in D. Epstein, J. Elwood, V. Hey and J. Maw (eds) *Failing Boys?* Buckingham: Open University Press.

Mahony, P. (2003) Recapturing imaginations and the gender agenda: reflections on a progressive challenge from an English perspective, *International Journal of Inclusive Education*, 7: 75–81.

Mahony, P. and Smedley, S. (1998) New times old panics: the underachievement of boys, *Change: Transformation in Education*, 1: 41–50.

Mahony, P. and Hextall, I. (2000) *Reconstructing Teaching*, London: RoutledgeFalmer.

Mansell, W. (2004) Teachers mark down bad boys, *Times Educational Supplement*, 26 March, p. 3.

Marsh, J. (2000) 'But I want to fly too!': girls and superhero play in the infant classroom, *Gender and Education*, 12: 209–20.

Marsh, J. (2003) Literacy, gender and popular culture, in C. Skelton and B. Francis (eds) *Boys and Girls in the Primary Classroom*, Maidenhead: McGraw-Hill/Open University Press.

Marsh, H. and Rowe, K. (1996) The effects of single-sex and mixed-sex mathematics classes within a coeducational school: a reanalysis and comment, *Australian Journal of Education*, 40: 147–62.

Martin, M. (1997) Emotional and cognitive effects of examination proximity in female and male students, *Oxford Review of Education*, 23: 479–86.

Martino, W. (1999) 'Cool boys', 'party animals', 'squids' and 'poofters': interrogating the dynamics and politics of adolescent masculinities in schools, *British Journal of Sociology of Education*, 20: 240–63.

Martino, W. (2000) Policing masculinities: investigating the role of homophobia and heteronormativity in the lives of adolescent schoolboys, *Journal of Men's Studies*, 8: 213–36.

Martino, W. and Meyenn, B. (2001) *What About the Boys?* Buckingham: Open University Press.

Martino, W. and Meyenn, B. (2002) 'War, guns and cool, tough things': interrogating single-sex classes as a strategy for engaging boys in English, *Cambridge Journal of Education*, 32: 303–24.

Martino, W. and Berrill, D. (2003) Boys, schooling and masculinities: interrogating the 'right' way to educate boys, *Educational Review*, 55: 99–117.

Martino, W. and Pallotta-Chiarolli, M. (2001) *Boys' Stuff: Boys Talking About What Matters*, Sydney: Allen and Unwin.

Martino, W. and Pallotta-Chiarolli, M. (2003) *So What's a Boy?* Buckingham: Open University Press.

Maynard, T. (2002) *Boys and Literacy: Exploring the Issues*, London: RoutledgeFalmer.

McKie, J. (1999) 'Girl power' in *The Observer Magazine*, 20 June 1999. http://observer.guardian.co.uk/life/story/0,,288790,00.html

McClean, C. (1997) Engaging with boys' experiences of masculinity: implications for gender reform in schools, in J. Kenway (ed.) Point and counterpoint: boys' education in the context of gender reform, *Curriculum Perspectives*, 17: 57–78.

McLellan, R. (2002) Socio-cultural approaches to raising boys' achievement at secondary school, paper presented at BERA Annual Conference, Exeter University, 12–14 September.

McNay, L. (2000) *Gender and Agency*, Cambridge: Polity.

McRobbie, A. (2000) *Feminism and Youth Culture*, London: Routledge.

Mead, G. (1934) *Mind, Self and Society*, Chicago: Chicago University Press.

Miedzian, M. (1992) *Boys Will Be Boys*. London: Virago.

Millard, E. (1997) *Differently Literate*. London: Falmer.

Miller, L. and Budd, J. (1999) The development of occupational sex-role stereotypes, occupational preferences and academic subject preferences of children ages 8, 12 and 16, *Educational Psychology*, 19: 17–35.

Miller, L., Neathey, F., Pollard, E. and Hill, D. (2004) *Occupational Segregation, Gender Gaps and Skill Gaps*, Manchester: EOC and ESF.

Mills, M. (2001) *Challenging Violence in Schools*, Buckingham: Open University Press.

Mills, M. (2003) Shaping the boys' agenda: the backlash blockbusters, *International Journal of Inclusive Education*, 7: 57–73.

Mills, M. (2004) The media, marketing, and single sex schooling, *Journal of Education Policy*, 19: 343–60.

Milne, A., Myers, D., Rosenthal, A. and Ginsburg, A. (1986) Single parents, working mothers, and the educational achievement of school children, *Sociology of Education*, 59: 125–39.

Mirza, H. (1992) *Young, Female and Black*, London: Routledge.

Mitchell, J. and Rose, J. (1982) *Feminine Sexuality, Jacques Lacan and the École Freudienne*, London: Macmillan.

Moir, A. and Moir, B. (1999) *Why Men Don't Iron*, London: Harper Collins.

Monaghan, E. and Glickman, S. (1992) Hormones and aggressive behaviour, in J. Brecker, S. Breedlove and D. Crews (eds) *Behavioural Endocrinology*, Cambridge, MA: MIT Press.

Morrison, I., Everton, T., Rudduck, J., Cannie, J. and Strommen, L. (2000) Pupils helping other pupils with their learning: cross-age tutoring in a primary and secondary school, *Mentoring and Tutoring*, 8 (3): 187–200.

Mortimore, P. and Whitty, G. (1997) *Can School Improvement Overcome the Effects of Disadvantage?* London: Institute of Education.

Mouffe, C. (1996) *Deconstruction and Pragmatism*, London: Routledge.

Mulkey, L., Crain, R. and Harrington, A.J. (1992) One-parent households and achievement: economic and behavioral explanations of a small effect, *Sociology of Education*, 65: 8–65.

Muncsh, R.N. and Martchenko, M. (1993) *The Paperbag Princess*, London: Scholastic.

Murphy, P. (1989) Gender and assessment in science, in P. Murphy and B. Moon (eds) *Developments in Learning and Assessment*, London: Hodder and Stoughton.

National Center For Education Statistics (2001) *Educational Achievement and Black-White Inequality*, Statistical Analysis Report July 2001.

Neall, L. (2002) *Bringing Out The Best in Boys*, Gloucester: Hawthorn Press.

Nelson, S., Clark, R. and Acs, G. (2001) Beyond the two-parent family: How teenagers fare in cohabitating couple and blended families, *New Federalism: National Survey of America's Families*, Series B (No. B-31).

Neumark, V. (1997) Daddy's boys, *Times Educational Supplement*, 11 July 1997, 12–13.

Noble, C. (1998) Helping boys do better in their primary schools, in K. Bleach (ed.) *Raising Boys' Achievement in Schools*, Stoke-on-Trent: Trentham.

Noble, C. and Bradford, W. (2000) *Getting it Right for Boys . . . and Girls*, London: Routledge.

Nolan, J. (1998) *The Therapeutic State: Justifying Government at Century's End*, New York: New York University Press.

Northen, S. (2004) Why men aren't from Mars, *Times Educational Supplement*, 3 September, p. 19.

Oakley, A. (1972) *Sex, Gender and Society*, London: Temple Smith.

O'Boyle, M.W. (2000) Neuroscientific research findings and their potential application to gifted educational practice, *Australasian Journal of Gifted Education*, 9: 6–10.

O'Brien, M. (2003) Girls and transition to secondary-level schooling in Ireland: 'moving on' and 'moving out', *Gender and Education*, 15, 249–67.

O'Connor, M. (1999) *Education Review*, 14, May/June National Union of Teachers.

The Observer (1998) Leader comment, 5 January 1998, 12.

OECD (1996) *Lifelong Learning for All*, Paris: OECD Publications.

OECD PISA 2000 (2003) *Literacy Skills for the World of Tomorrow*, Paris: OECD.

Ofsted (1993) *Boys and English*, London: HMSO.

Ofsted (2003a) *Yes He Can – Schools Where Boys Write Well*, London: Ofsted Publications.

Ofsted (2003b) *Boys' Achievement in Secondary Schools*, London: Ofsted Publications.

Osler, A., Street, C., Lall, M. and Vincent, K. (2002) *Not a Problem? Girls and School Exclusion*, London: National Children's Bureau and Joseph Rowntree Foundation.

Osler, A. and Vincent, K. (2003) *Girls and Exclusion: Rethinking the Agenda*, London: RoutledgeFalmer.

Ozga, J. (ed.) (1990) *Women in Educational Management*, Buckingham: Open University Press.

Paechter, C. (1998) *Educating the Other*, London: Falmer.

Paechter, C. (2000) *Changing School Subjects: Power, Gender and Curriculum*, Buckingham: Open University Press.

Pang, M. (1999) The employment situation of young Chinese adults in the British labour market, *Personnel Review*, 28: 41–57.

Parsons, T. (1956) The American family: its relations to personality and to the social structure, in T. Parsons and R. Bales (eds) *Family: Socialisation and Interaction Process*, London: Routledge and Kegan Paul.

Partington, G. (1976) *Women Teachers in the 20th Century*, Windsor: NFER.

Phoenix, A. (2001) Racialisation and gendering the (re)production of educational inequalities, in B. Francis and S. Skelton (eds) *Investigating Gender: Contemporary Perspectives in Education*, Buckingham: Open University Press.

Pickering, J. (1997) *Raising Boys' Achievement*, Stafford: Network Educational Press.

Pirie, M. (2001) How exams are fixed in favour of girls, *The Spectator*, January, pp. 12–14.

Plummer, G. (2000) *Failing Working-Class Girls*, Stoke-on-Trent: Trentham.

Pollack, W. (1998) *Real Boys*, New York: Owl Books.

Powney, J. and Weiner, G. (1991) *Outside of the Norm: Equity and Management in Educational Institutions*, European Commission-funded report, London: South Bank University.

Pulis, M.V. (2000) Boys' under-performance in an inner-city multi-ethnic environment, paper presented to the Third European Conference: Network on Intercultural and Multicultural Education in Europe (Haugesund, Norway), 19–22 May.

Purvis, J. (1991) *A History of Women's Education in England*, Buckingham: Open University Press.

Qualifications and Curriculum Authority (1998) *Can do Better: Raising Boys' Achievement in English*, London: QCA.

Raphael Reed, L. (1998) 'Zero tolerance': gender performance and school failure, in D. Epstein, J. Elwood, V. Hey and J. Maw (eds) *Failing Boys? Issues in Gender and Achievement*, Buckingham: Open University Press.

Reay, D. (1990) Working with boys, *Gender and Education*, 2: 269–81.

Reay, D. (1998) *Class Work*, London: UCL Press.

Reay, D. (2001a) The paradox of contemporary femininities in education: combining fluidity with fixity, in B. Francis and C. Skelton (eds) *Investigating Gender*, Buckingham: Open University Press.

Reay, D. (2001b) 'Spice girls', 'nice girls', 'girlies' and 'tomboys': gender discourses, girls' cultures and femininities in the primary classroom, *Gender and Education*, 13: 153–66.

Reay, D. (2002) 'Shaun's story': troubling discourses of white working-class masculinities, *Gender and Education*, 14: 221–33.

Reay, D. (2003) Troubling, troubled and troublesome? Working with boys in the primary classroom, in C. Skelton and B. Francis (eds) *Boys and Girls in the Primary Classroom*, Buckingham: Open University Press.

Reay, D. and Ball, S. (1998) Making their minds up: family dynamics of school choice, *British Educational Research Journal*, 24, 431–48.

Reay, D., Davies, J., David, M. and Ball, S. (2001) Choices of degree or degrees of choice? Class, 'race' and the higher education choice process, *Sociology*, 35: 855–74.

Reay, D. and Lucey, H. (2003) The limits of choice: children and inner-city schooling, *Sociology*, 37: 121–43.

Redwood, F. (1994) Now let's give boys a boost, *Daily Telegraph*, 7 December, p. 23.

Rees, T. (1999) *Mainstreaming Equality in the European Union*, London: Routledge.

Regan, C. (1998) Boys' underachievement? Not the real question, *Socialist Teacher*, 6: 20–1.

Rennie, L. and Parker, L. (1997) Students' and teachers' perceptions of single sex and mixed-sex mathematics classes, *Mathematics Education Research Journal*, 9: 257–73.

Renold, E. (2000) 'Coming out': gender, (hetero)sexuality and the primary school, *Gender and Education*, 12: 309–25.

Renold, E. (2003) 'Presumed innocence': (hetero)sexual, homophobic and heterosexist harassment amongst children in the primary school, *Childhood*, 9: 415–33.

Riddell, S. (1989) Pupils, resistance and gender codes, *Gender and Education*, 1 (2) 183–96.

Riddell, S. (1992) *Polities and the Gender of the Curriculum*, London: Routledge.

Rogers, L. (2000) *Sexing the Brain*, London: Weidenfeld and Nicolson.

Rolfe, H. (1999) *Gender Equality and Career Service*, Manchester: Equal Opportunities Commission.

Rose, H. and Rose, S. (2001) Introduction, in H. Rose and S. Rose (eds) *Alas Poor Darwin: Arguments Against Evolutionary Psychology*, London: Vintage.

Rose, N. (1989) Individualising psychology, in J. Shotter and K. Gergen (eds) *Texts of Identity*, London: Sage.

Rose, N. (1999) *Powers of Freedom*, Cambridge: Cambridge University Press.

Rose, S. (2001) Escaping evolutionary psychology, in H. Rose and S. Rose (eds) *Alas Poor Darwin: Arguments Against Evolutionary Psychology*, London: Vintage.

Rosenfield, M. (1998) Reexamining the plight of young males, *Washington Post*, 26 March 1998, p. A1.

Rowan, L., Knobel, M., Bigum, C. and Lankshear, C. (2002) *Boys, Literacies and Schooling*, Buckingham: Open University Press.

Ryder, J. (1998) Peer counselling at the Boswells School, Chelmsford, in K. Bleach (ed.) *Raising Boys' Achievement in Schools*, Stoke-on-Trent: Trentham Books.

Salisbury, J. and Jackson, D. (1996) *Challenging Macho Values*, London: Falmer.

Sammons, P. (1995) Gender, ethnic and socio-economic differences in attainment and progress: a longitudinal analysis of student achievement over 9 years, *British Educational Research Journal*, 21 (4): 465–85.

Sampson, E. (1989) The deconstruction of the self, in J. Shotter and K. Gergen (eds) *Texts of Identity*, London: Sage.

Sargent, P. (2001) *Real Men or Real Teachers?* Merriman, Tennessee: Men's Studies Press.

Sayers, J. (1984) Psychology and gender divisions, in S. Acker, J. Megarry, S. Nisbet and E. Hoyle (eds) *World Yearbook of Education 1984: Women and Education*, London: Kogan Page.

Seidler, V. (1989) *Rediscovering Masculinity*, London: Routledge.

Sewell, T. (1997) *Black Masculinities and Schooling*, Stoke-on-Trent: Trentham.

Sewell, T. (1998) Loose cannons: exploding the myth of the 'black macho' lad, in D. Epstein, J. Elwood, V. Hey and J. Maw (eds) *Failing Boys?* Buckingham: Open University Press.

Sharpe, S. (1976) *Just Like a Girl*. Harmondsworth: Penguin.

Sharpe, S. (1994) *Just Like a Girl*, 2nd edn, Harmondsworth: Penguin.

Siraj-Blatchford, I. (ed.) (1993) *'Race', Gender and the Education of Teachers*, Buckingham: Open University Press.

Skelton, C. (1997) Primary boys and hegemonic masculinities, *British Journal of Sociology of Education*, 18: 349–69.

Skelton, C. (2000a) Being 'one of the lads': infant boys, masculinities and schooling, in G. Walford and C. Hudson (eds) *Genders and Sexualities in Educational Ethnography*, New York: JAI Press.

Skelton, C. (2000b) 'A passion for football': dominant masculinities and primary schooling, *Sport, Education and Society*, 5 (1): 5–18.

Skelton, C. (2001a) *Schooling the Boys*, Buckingham: Open University Press.

Skelton, C. (2001b) Typical boys? Theorising masculinity in educational settings, in B. Francis and C. Skelton (eds) *Investigating Gender*, Buckingham: Open University Press.

Skelton, C. (2002) Constructing dominant masculinity and negotiating the 'male gaze', *International Journal of Inclusive Education*, 6 (1): 17–31.

Skelton, C. (2003) Male primary teachers and perceptions of masculinity, *Educational Review*, 55: 195–209.

Skelton, C. (2005) The 'self-interested' woman academic: a consideration of Beck's model of the 'individualised individual', *British Journal of Sociology of Education*, 26 (1): 3–14.

Skelton, C. and Francis, B. (2003) Introduction: boys and girls in the primary classroom, in C. Skelton and B. Francis (eds) *Boys and Girls in the Primary Classroom*, Buckingham: Open University Press.

Slavin, R. (1994) *Educational Psychology: Theory and Practice*, 4th edn, Boston: Allyn and Bacon.

Smith, E. (2003) Understanding underachievement: an investigation into the differential attainment of secondary school pupils, *British Journal of Sociology of Education*, 24: 575–87.

Smith, J. (1998) *Different for Girls*, London: Chatto and Windus.

Smith, J. (1999) We need more males in primary teacher education! Or do we? paper presented to the Australian Association for Research in Education Conference, Melbourne, 30 November.

Smithers, A. and Robinson, P. (1995) *Co-educational and Single-sex Schooling*, Manchester: CEER, University of Manchester.

Sokal, A. and Bricmont, J. (1998) *Intellectual Impostures*, London: Profile Books.

Somners, E. and Lawrence, S. (1992) Women's ways of talking in teacher-directed and student-directed peer response groups, *Linguistics and Education*, 4: 1–36.

Soper, K. (1990) *Troubled Pleasures*, London: Verso.

Spender, D. (1982) *Invisible Women*, London: Writers and Readers.

Squires, J. (1990) Introduction, in J. Squires (ed.) *Principled Positions: Postmodernism and the Rediscovery of Value*, London: Routledge.

Stafford, P., Heaver, C., Ashworth, K., Bates, C., Walker, R., McKay, S. and Trickey, H. (1999) *Work and Young Men*, York: York Publishing Services.

Stanworth, M. (1981) *Gender and Schooling*, London: Hutchinson.

Steedman, C. (1982) *The Tidy House*, London: Virago.

Stevens, P. (ed.) (1999) *Between Mothers and Sons*, New York: Scribners.

Stones, R. (1983) *Pour Out the Cocoa Janet*, York: Longman.

Sukhnandan, L. (1999) *An Investigation into Gender Differences in Achievement: Phase 1: A Review of Recent Research and LEA Information on Provision*, Slough: National Foundation for Educational Research.

Sukhnandan, L., Lee, B. and Kelleher, S. (2000) *An Investigation into Gender Differences in Achievement, Phase 2: School and Classroom Strategies*, Slough: National Foundation for Educational Research.

Swain, J. (2000) 'The money's good, the fame's good, the girls are good': the role of playground football in the construction of young boys' masculinity in a junior school, *British Journal of Sociology of Education*, 21: 95–109.

Swan (1998) Teaching boys and girls in separate classes at Shenfield High School, Brentford, in K. Bleach (ed.) *Raising Boys' Achievement in Schools*, Stoke-on-Trent: Trentham Books.

Sydney Morning Herald (1997) 'Nobody loves us, everybody hates us . . . Why today's teenage boys have become pariahs', 22 November.

Teacher Training Agency (TTA) (1998) *National Standards for Headteachers*, London: TTA.

Terry, B. and Terry, L. (1998) A multi-layered approach to raising boys' (and girls') achievement, in K. Bleach (ed.) *Raising Boys' Achievement in Schools*, Stoke-on-Trent: Trentham Books.

The Times (2004) The seat of learning is to be boy, boy, girl, girl. Unless it is boy, girl, boy, girl, boy, 17 November 2004: 3.

Thomas, K. (1990) *Gender and Subject in Higher Education*, Buckingham: Open University Press.

Thompson, B. (2001) A thankless task? Women managers in initial teacher training, paper presented at British Educational Research Association Conference, University of Leeds, 13–15 September.

Thorne, B. (1993) *Gender Play: Girls and Boys in School*, Buckingham: Open University Press.

Thornton, M. and Brichenco, P. (2002) Staff gender balance in primary schools, paper presented at the British Educational Research Association Annual Conference, University of Exeter, 12–14 September.

Times Educational Supplement (1995a) Lapped by girls, 14 July 1995.

Times Educational Supplement (1995b) Stop giving boys wrong messages, 20 October 1995.

Times Educational Supplement (2004a) TES correspondents' report on efforts to close the gender gap in teaching and learning, 19 March 2004: 20.

Times Educational Supplement (2004b) Teachers mark down bad boys, 26 March 2004.

Times Educational Supplement (2004c) Naughty boys will fail if we trust teachers, 28 May 2004.

Times Educational Supplement (2004d) Keep the bad boys busy, 30 July 2004.

Tinklin, T. (2003) Gender differences and high attainment, *British Educational Research Journal*, 29: 307–25.

Twain, M. (1924) *Autobiography*, Vol. 1, New York: Harper and Brothers.

Van de Gaer (2004) The 'laddish' culture and the effect of school related attitudes of pupils, classrooms, teachers and schools' public on the gender gap in language achievement, paper presented at the American Educational Research Association Conference, San Diego, 12–16 April.

Vuorikoski, M. (2004) Private correspondence with authors, 13 July.

Walden, R. and Walkerdine, V. (1985) *Girls and Mathematics*, London: Institute of Education, Bedford Way Papers.

Walford, G. (1980) Sex bias in physics textbooks, *School Science Review*, 1: 224–5.

Walker, J. (1988) *Louts and Legends*, Sydney: Allen and Unwin.

Walkerdine, V. (1983) It's only natural: rethinking child-centred pedagogy, in A.M. Wolpe and J. Donald (eds) *Is There Anyone Here From Education?* London: Pluto.

Walkerdine, V. (1988) *The Mastery of Reason*, London: Routledge.

Walkerdine, V. (1990) *Schoolgirl Fictions*, London: Verso.

Walkerdine, V. (2003) Reclassifying upward mobility: femininity and the neoliberal subject, *Gender and Education*, 15: 237–47.

Walkerdine, V. and the Girls and Mathematics Unit (1989) *Counting Girls Out*, London: Virago.

Walkerdine, V. and Lucey, H. (1989) *Democracy in the Kitchen*, London: Virago.

Walkerdine, V., Lucey, H. and Melody, J. (2001) *Growing Up Girl*, London: Macmillan.

Warrington, M. and Younger, M. (2000) The other side of the gender gap, *Gender and Education*, 12: 493–507.

Warrington, M. and Younger, M. (2001) Single-sex classes and equal opportunities for girls and boys: perspectives through time from a mixed comprehensive school in England, *Oxford Review of Education*, 27: 339–56.

Warrington, M. and Younger, M. (2002) Speech at the 'Raising boys' achievement conference', Homerton College Cambridge, 11 July 2002.

Warrington, M. and Younger, M. (2003) 'We decided to give it a twirl': single-sex teaching in English comprehensive schools, *Gender and Education*, 15: 339–50.

Warrington, M., Younger, M. and Williams, J. (2000) Student attitudes, image and the gender gap, *British Educational Research Journal*, 26: 393–407.

Warrington, M., Younger, M. and Bearne, E. (forthcoming) *Raising Boys' Achievement in Primary Schools: Towards a Holistic Approach*, Maidenhead: Open University Press/ McGraw-Hill.

Weaver-Hightower, M. (2003) Crossing the divide: bridging the disjunctures between theoretically oriented and practice-oriented literature about masculinity and boys at school, *Gender and Education*, 15: 407–23.

Weiler, K. (1993) Feminism and the struggle for a democratic education: a view from the United States, in M. Arnot and K. Weiler (eds) *Feminism and Social Justice in Education*, London: Falmer Press.

West, Peter (2002) Submission to: inquiry into the education of boys (http:// menshealth.uws.edu.au/documents/InquiryBoysEd.html) (accessed 30 November 2004).

Whelehan, I. (2000) *OverLoaded*, London: The Women's Press.

White, A. (1989) *Poles Apart? The Experience of Gender*, London: J.M. Dent and Sons.

Whitehead, J. (1996) Sex stereotypes, gender identity and subject choice at A-level, *Educational Research*, 38: 147–60.

Whitehead, J. (1998) Masculinity, motivation and academic success: a paradox, presented at 'Gendering the Millennium Conference', University of Dundee, September 1998.

Whitehead, S. (2002) *Men and Masculinities*, Cambridge: Polity.

Wikeley, F. and Stables, A. (1999) Changes in school students' approaches to subject option choices: a study of pupils in the West of England in 1984 and 1996, *Educational Research*, 41: 287–99.

Wilkinson, S. (1995) *No Turning Back: Generations and the Gender Quake*, London: Demos.

Wilkinson, S. and Mulgan, G. (1995) *Freedom's Children: Work, Relationships and Politics for 18–34-Year-Olds in Britain Today*, London: Demos.

Willis, P. (1977) *Learning to Labour*, Aldershot: Saxon House.

Wing, A. (1997) How can children be taught to read differently? Bill's New Frock and the hidden curriculum, *Gender and Education*, 9: 491–504.

Wright, C., Weekes, D. and McGlaughlin, A. (2000) *'Race', Class and Gender in Exclusion from School*, London: Falmer.

Wyn, J., Acker, S. and Richards, E. (2000) Making a difference: women in management in Australian and Canadian faculties of education, *Gender and Education*, 12: 435–47.

Yates, L. (1997) Gender equity and the boys debate: what sort of challenge is it?, *British Journal of Sociology of Education*, 18 (3): 337–47.

Yeoman, E. (1999) 'How does it get into my imagination?' Elementary school children's inter-textual knowledge and gendered storylines, *Gender and Education*, 11: 427–40.

Younger, M. and Warrington, M. (2001) Raising boys' achievement: interim report (www.standards.dfes.gov.uk/genderandachievement/goodpractice/) (accessed 26 October 2004).

Younger, M., Warrington, M. and Williams, J. (1999) The gender gap and classroom interactions: reality or rhetoric? *British Journal of Sociology of Education*, 20: 325–41.

Younger, M., Warrington, M. and McLellan, R. (2005) *Raising Boys' Achievements in Secondary Schools: Issues, Dilemmas and Opportunities*, Maidenhead: Open University Press/McGraw-Hill.

Index